THE
SECRET WAR
FOR THE
OCEAN DEPTHS

THE
SECRET WAR
FOR THE
OCEAN DEPTHS

Soviet-American Rivalry
for Mastery of the Seas

Thomas S. Burns

Rawson Associates Publishers, Inc.
New York

Library of Congress Cataloging in Publication Data
Burns, Thomas S
  The secret war for the ocean depths.

  Bibliography: p.
  Includes index.
  1. United States. Navy. 2. United States—
Military policy. 3. Russia (1923–   U.S.S.R.).
Voenno-Morskoi Flot. 4. Russia—Military policy.
5. Sea-power. 6. Submarine warfare. I. Title.
VA50.B85   1978   359'.03'0973   76–53716
ISBN 0–89256–018–5

Designed by Gene Siegel
First Edition

This book is dedicated to the officers and men
of the United States submarine *Thresher*.

Weapons change but man who uses them changes not at all. To win battles you do not beat weapons—you beat the soul of man, of the enemy man.

——General George S. Patton, U.S.A.

Contents

Acknowledgments

No book that attempts to present a broad perspective on any subject relating to warfare can be prepared by the writer alone. At every stage of the work he will require the cooperation and assistance of many others—historians, librarians, researchers, military personnel, and civil servants who are willing to provide information, advice and counsel. Particularly in the study of a changing military science, intelligent assessments of its progress and direction can only be made with the help of many experts. And so I am grateful for the assistance of all those who have worked with me in this project, the many Navy and Air Force officers who so generously contributed in areas of their particular expertise. Many research librarians were involved from military libraries, the Library of Congress, the libraries of Southwestern College, MIT, UCLA, UCSD, USC, and Harvard. I was also fortunate to have the assistance of a number of military contractors involved in submarine warfare, particularly the General Electric Company, Simplex Corporation, and ITT.

Excellent information was supplied by foreign military commands and weapons contractors, particularly in France and the United Kingdom. Unfortunately, there was no way to achieve any degree of cooperation from the Russians, a situation which distorts the picture, not so much in conclusions of fact as in the conclusions related to the philosophy and intent of the USSR.

Finally, a word of thanks to those who read and commented on the work in progress and gave advice and guidance. They sometimes agreed and at other times disagreed with my conclusions, but in every case diligently checked and confirmed the facts. And for assisting me through a long maze of research studies, technical reports, and documentation I owe much to Mary Elizabeth Burns.

Introduction

The Cold War between the United States and the Soviet Union has taken place on many fronts over the past thirty years, in political and military confrontations that have become interwoven—and these conflicts have culminated in the position of the two superpowers today. A phase of this broad spectrum of conflict is the struggle for the domination of the hydrospace of the world—the Wet Cold War—a war-within-a-war that may well be the most significant theater of all. As the global confrontation progresses, the antagonists are introducing the same technical innovations and revolutions in strategy and tactics that characterize the progression of the general conflict but with an uncharacteristic degree of caution. When they confront one another on the oceans in the warfare taking place over, on, and under the seas, it is with the realization that naval warfare has radically changed since the introduction of atomic propulsion and ballistic and cruise nuclear-tipped missiles. It is a new plateau: a weapons revolution coupled with the opening of a new frontier that must be explored in parallel with the implementation of these weapons—a situation unique in the history of warfare.

In pursuing the Cold War since 1945, the policies of expansionism have won territories and conquered peoples for the Soviet Union, but they have been counterproductive economically and have opened to question the advantages of the ideological victories claimed. The United States policy of containment has also been demanding in terms of both economic and political stress.

On the other hand, the conquest of hydrospace would bring one or both of the superpowers enormous economic gains, secure military installations, and potential food and mineral wealth far beyond anything they could anticipate from any continental conquest or the settlement of the Cold War along the present national borders.

The seas are the logical meeting place for direct confrontation between the two antagonists. Their land armies cannot contest each other directly anywhere in the world without precipitating a nuclear holocaust; the conquest of space by either superpower is too remote to be of military significance before the twenty-first century. It is along the shorelines of the oceans of the world that Russia and the United States have their most extended borders, and they are gradually recognizing that a concentration of manpower and funding for technology and exploration and engineering will yield the most profitable return when they are invested in the new modes of sea power. Thus both nations are establishing their prime military priorities of the Cold War as the ocean theaters, and thus defining the battlefield for the greatest and perhaps final conflict.

The Wet Cold War, as we shall call it for brevity, is too broad and extensive to be dealt with in any single study; at best, we can present a mosaic of the significant, heroic, and perhaps indicative activities taking place in the oceans around the world. It is easier to characterize the struggle than to describe it in any detail: this war involves a burgeoning technology, the development of new classes of weapons, the tactics of submarine warfare and antisubmarine warfare, and a new breed of military leader who dominates not only the strategies but also the massive weapons development programs. A study of the Wet Cold War must emphasize these programs that have resulted in the fleets of nuclear-propelled submarines, the development of the submarine-launched ballistic missile, the long-range sonar surveillance networks, and the worldwide coordinated research dedicated to solving the problems of operating armies and navies under the seas.

The Cold War between the United States and the Soviet Union

is probably too close now to be seen in perspective, and in the most technically sophisticated theater of this war—the war at sea— it is even more difficult to explain or attempt to rationalize the politics and strategies involved. However, even with a confused and limited perspective, it is valuable to study the revolutionary developments of the war at sea, since it is a phenomenon without precedent in the history of international conflict. By concentrating on the broad aspects of the weapons systems employed; by tracing the movement of Soviet and United States oceanic strategies; the emergence of the submarine as the ultimate naval weapon; the response of the navies of the world in terms of antisubmarine war- fare weapons; the evolution of the submarine-launched ballistic missile, and the introduction of the submarine-launched cruise missile; the beginning of large scientific efforts in ocean study and engineering to make way for military adventures—through such an analysis we may be able to measure the assets and liabilities of the two superpowers in the fight to control the oceans of the world. This study was prepared after researching the plans, pro- grams, strategies, and tactics of the Allies and Soviet bloc includ- ing the nuclear propulsion program directed by Admiral Rickover, the Fleet Ballistic Missile program directed by Admiral Raborn, the intelligence activities of the *Glomar Explorer*, the covert in- stallation of the CAESAR system to monitor the oceans, the Soviet naval builders, and many others. This study reviewed the military budgets as they affect the aspirations of the superpowers; the strategic arms limitations agreements and what restrictions they impose on the military establishments; the leaders like Rickover, Raborn, Khrushchev, and Gorshkov who have, by the force of their personalities, shaped the military postures of the United States and Soviet Union, and the other nations poised to make a sea- power bid. To understand the Wet Cold War it is necessary not only to examine it related to the overall East-West struggle, but also to rise above the details of weapons and national programs and the byplay of leadership and the movement of the technologies and to view these events as a first step in man's effort to enter the hydrospace of the planet, an effort comparable to the first explorations of each continent. Now it is an exploration based on military necessity. In the past, such explorations were the first phases of discovery, before the settlement and development of the frontier began.

The world may look forward to a time when the condition of the irreducible East-West dilemma has passed, when there is no longer an absolute predicament forcing Russia and the United States to face each other as deadly antagonists. And at that future time, if both nations can cooperate, they will finally come to accept the economic and technical mandate from the peoples of the world to develop the wealth of three-quarters of the surface of the earth.

THE
SECRET WAR
FOR THE
OCEAN DEPTHS

1 The Development of America's Oceanic Strategy

But sea power has never led to despotism. The nations that have enjoyed sea power even for a brief period—Athens, Scandinavia, the Netherlands, England, the United States—are those that have preserved freedom for themselves and have given it to others. Of the despotism to which unrestrained military power leads we have plenty of examples from Alexander to Mao.

—SAMUEL ELIOT MORISON

Perhaps the most difficult economic problem the United States and Soviet Union face is the commitment to prepare for a broad-based war. The two countries are pledged to maintain a spectrum of weapons against many types of military adventures, diplomatic offensives, and political eventualities. It is this complex balance of forces and the consequent requirement to promote and fund so many different technologies that has pushed the two nations toward arming the oceans of the world. Not only does the hydrospace loom as the ultimate battleground of World War III —it is also the area where the investment in new weapons is most justified in terms of the cost of technology, the relative invulnerability of the weapons, and the useful life of the systems. Thus the submarine has become supreme in ocean warfare while

3

the manned bomber is being replaced by missiles, robots, and satellites. The ICBM fixed sites on land suffer a creeping vulnerability as the payloads and accuracy of the missiles targeted at them improve and the multiple and steerable and targetable reentry vehicles carrying hydrogen warheads proliferate. Meanwhile, the subsea military missile sites and sea-based antimissile platforms become more secure locations for ICBM and ABM weapons dispersal.

Currently there are three military strategic forces: the submarine, the manned bomber, and the intercontinental missile. All three forces are maintained so that a breakthrough in any one weapons system which might give one or the other superpower an advantage would be nullified by the effectiveness of the other two systems. This is necessary in order that an effective deterrent exist—the cornerstone of the present U.S.-U.S.S.R. policy of détente. There must be a minimum overall deterrent capability; each nation must feel a security against a war-winning first strike by the other in order that some degree of political balance be maintained.

Now we are coming to the first major threat to this policy: the prospect that the United States may achieve such an underseas supremacy that the balance-of-forces equation may be seriously disturbed. The United States may well be the first nation to master some of the deeper mysteries of sea physics that have heretofore limited subsea weapons development. American scientists are close to improving the long-range detection of sound in the ocean; their new systems will easily detect submarines at very great ranges. The United States Navy has advanced steadily toward the goal of complete mastery of the hydrospace and is now planning to build a fleet of submarine dreadnaughts that will survive any combination of ASW (antisubmarine) weapons. This Trident-class submarine may be effective even in a sea medium monitored and subject to high noise levels close to 100 percent (insonification) and peppered with homing atomic weapons.

The covert struggle for control of the world hydrospace has become of paramount interest to the two superpowers; it is over, on, and particularly under the oceans of the world that the struggle for political and military domination will eventually be decided. At present, the United States has gained two major advantages over the Soviet Union in sea warfare potential: first because the Soviets do not have a sufficient number of bases and friendly ports around the world, and second because the Soviets lack surveillance sonar. They do not have the facilities necessary to establish a long-range sonar detection system powerful enough to monitor the important ocean areas of the world. These handicaps are not publicized by either of the superpowers, but they have influenced national policy in both countries for over a decade. The Russians have attempted to extend their large sonar capability, just as they have labored to build up their advanced bases. Still, for the fore-seeable future, both will remain far inferior to the facilities of the United States. The Soviets face up to this deficiency by adopting a defiant philosophy, but their weakness at sea is reflected in all their political programs.

Before the Cold War extended to Southeast Asia, the United States had a number of strategic policy choices. They ranged from isolationism—the traditional American defensive strategy—to act-ing as the world's policeman. There were strong proponents for each of these extreme positions and, of course, supporters for many intermediate positions. However, the long, costly involvement in Vietnam has probably limited United States future strategy to what is achievable, cost acceptable, and tailored to the options now available as it faces a new role in world affairs. Based on a changing geopolitical situation, United States leaders are now aware of the limitations, dangers, and costs of international involvement in even limited wars. Yet, on the other hand, they are also aware of the impossibility of returning to isolationism. While they may prefer a strategy based on traditional isolationism, which may be advantageous economically, technologically, geographically, and politically, they are forced to deal with the aspirations and goals of the other nations of the world, and particularly the other super-power and major adversary, the Soviet Union. Thus the American strategy is, of necessity, framed on compromise—a blend of iso-lationism and involvement.

After World War II, in that confused time of probing by both East and West, there were arguments put forward that a world government was possible—that although the League of Nations had failed, the United Nations could succeed. As these hopes faded, gradually they were replaced by the proposal that the United States should establish world order by fiat, if necessary, and by its ability to employ direct power and influence to control vital areas of the world. Such a benevolent rule, it was assumed, would be in the best interest of all nations and would create a balance in world conditions. But as the years of the Cold War progressed, it became obvious that this policy was not practical either—since by errors of commission and omission the United States soon became as overextended as Imperial Rome or the British Empire. The national leadership gradually realized that America's attempt at control would be increasingly resisted by Russia, China, and other nations—until it became obvious that only a world war could effect this policy of policing. Consequently, Washington decided that the costs of such a policy were too high for the American people to accept; although Americans might support a policy of global intervention, they would not support a policy which might lead to a world war even if it appeared to be in the interest of achieving long-term peace and security.

Thus the policy of the United States has come to be what may be termed a modified oceanic strategy, heavily influenced by cautious and expedient internationalism. American military forces are committed in limited foreign conflicts in order to maintain a balance of power—but only when such a balance of power is obvious, necessary, and consistent with national goals. There will be other military actions that have balance-of-power implications, but they will be pursued in a very different manner from that of the Vietnam conflict. There have been opportunities for African and Middle East interventions recently, but the American people have resisted all attempts at involvement. However, we have a continuing interest in the Israel-Arab dispute, and a confrontation could result in military action if the United States defense interests were threatened. The Arab oil supply is vital to the United States economy, and we would probably risk even a large-scale, drawn-out conflict to preserve it.

There are areas of national interest large enough to draw America into war again, but it is unlikely that we will be drawn into another Asian conflict unless and until our policies are realistic enough to use nuclear weapons and advanced technology in pursuing such a war. The United States will not accept another man-for-man confrontation like Korea and Vietnam—and this means that the next intervention will be a substantially upgraded type of warfare, with all the attendant risks of wider involvement when more sophisticated weaponry is employed. Our basic interests have not changed since the end of World War II, and we are not likely to go through another period of national divisiveness—the world conflict has progressed too far to afford the indulgence of a disloyal and dissenting minority. America is approaching that condition of instability that her enemies should most fear: a military-industrial complex growing increasingly superior in technology and weaponry while the national leadership, by its indecision and lack of policy, gradually loses the ability to maintain an international status quo.

For the United States, the Wet Cold War has become a sea-based struggle which requires control of the oceans of the world—a control achieved by dominating the surface, air, and subsurface. This strategy involves not only operational air power, ship power, missile power, and submarine power, but also rapid advancements in ocean engineering, oceanography, and the related military sciences. America is increasing and modernizing its navy and expanding naval bases both at home and abroad and continuing the fortification of the ocean depths. Subsurface fleets of submarines, major surveillance networks, atomic energy implantments, and sea-bed-mounted weapons systems of all types will be needed. Surface and subsurface fleets will have to be independent of close and continuous logistics support for long periods of time. Advanced subsurface weaponry will arm its submarine superforce to combat surface forces in future battles for the control of the seas. Antisubmarine warfare measures will win control of the ocean's depths and reduce the impact of the enemy's submarine fleets. Control of the seas requires all of these programs and more —and the United States Navy has been charged with maintaining this control at any cost as the keystone of the developing oceanic strategy.

The oceanic strategy is not a defensive strategy; control of the seas allows optimum mobility and flexibility. As new designs of hovercraft, hydrofoil, nuclear propulsion, surface-effect ships, robots, and cruise missiles are put into service, the United States Navy will become ever more powerful and independent of shore-based logistics and air support. It will create a strategy built around sea- and subsea-based weapons and control of most of the world land mass adjoining the seas. Such a force will more than prove a match for any land-based power since this super sea power will control two-thirds of the earth's surface.

Both Russia and the United States are putting a much higher percentage of their missiles over, on, and under the sea, with particular emphasis on the submarine-launched, ballistic-missile (SLBM) firing submarines. From a covert point of view, the advantage of submarine sea-control systems is obvious—perhaps too obvious, since the submarine's deterrent advantage is slowly being lost to long-range sonar systems. But the race is close, and neither the submarine or antisubmarine warfare forces has taken an undisputed position of tactical superiority at this time.

Some proponents of the oceanic strategy agree on tactics but still argue about long-range strategy. All sides agree that sea power is vital to an oceanic-control philosophy. The United States must have a navy not only preeminent in the world, but also clearly superior to any force that could be ranged against it; a navy that will not allow any power to challenge it. But at that point the strategic unanimity ceases. One group favors a balanced navy which includes aircraft carriers, cruisers, missile ships, submarines, antisubmarine warfare vessels, and all of the special craft, logistics, and supply ships necessary to support these fleets. Another group holds that the navy should emphasize sea-based launching platforms for both strategic and tactical missiles. A surface fleet of modest proportion should be maintained, but the greatest emphasis should be placed on the submarine and underseas weapons. This group contends that such a submarine weapons superiority would be the winning edge in any all-out nuclear confrontation between Russia and the United States, since it would dominate the surface and subsurface of the oceans of the world with tactical nuclear weapons in a very short time.

Regardless of how the oceanic strategy is defined, both groups agree that U.S. forces must support the allied forces around the world and provide a deterrent for any Soviet aggressive action. But they support different methods of achieving these goals: one prefers the balanced fleet built around the carrier task force as the navy's superweapon; the other, the subsea weapons as represented by the Trident fleet and the CAESAR sonar surveillance system. Nevertheless, both agree that oceanic strategy will permit the United States military a choice of the time, place, and method of either small-scale intervention or grand-scale attack in any future conflicts. And so long as the confrontation with Russia in the Cold War involves a global strategy, then the superpower that controls the ocean is clearly the superior one. It is simply not possible to achieve the same power with land armies on a global basis, or even air power short of general thermonuclear warfare.

Both Korea and Vietnam were sufficiently forceful examples of how hobbling the United States military establishment crippled fighting efficiency. The lesson was not lost on our political leaders. Presumably, in future wars, the United States will use the military power at her disposal—whatever is necessary to win. Such effective methods as naval blockades, mining, and tactical atomic weaponry will be employed in sufficient force to win. And to employ any of these weapons anywhere in the world at any time most effectively, not only is it necessary to control sea lanes, but also the total hydrospace. Only by total hydrospace dominance can the United States hope to carry out her national goals and meet her worldwide commitments.

The oceanic strategy becomes even more obvious if we recognize that national directives prohibit U.S. armed forces from striking first. Thus the deterrent forces of the United States must be able not only to conquer the enemy on the second strike, but must also be prepared to do so with no chance of failure, however remote. And so, as shore-based installations become more vulnerable, no matter how hardened or semimobile they become, the only certain placement for a system to deter premeditated attack seems to be beneath the sea in United States submarines. The oceans are becoming the nation's first line of defense, and their control must be the keystone of the military planning and budget expenditure.

The American people must consider the danger of a total war. Deterrence depends not only on the subjective feeling that the U.S. military is trying to create in the minds of the Soviets, but also the feeling that they are trying to create in the minds of our own people. Of the two, the second point is probably more important. The Soviet Union is a monolithic, tightly controlled society that relies very heavily on its intelligence networks. If these networks accurately report the strength of the U.S. armed forces and the mood of determination of our citizens, then a climate of caution is preserved. However, with the growing American breach in credibility and trust between the man in the street and his government and military representatives, the confidence in the military establishment is being eroded. And foolishly so, since unless the citizen supports the military establishment, a dangerous isolation is created. If he cannot rely on Congress and the president, he cannot be sure that either his safety or freedom will be preserved. In order to prevent "atomic blackmail" and the kind of bluffing and saber rattling that the Russians have mastered, it is necessary that the American people learn their true strength vis-à-vis their enemies, and particularly the Soviet Union.

"Force is never more operative than when it is known to exist but is not brandished" is as true today as it was when it was spoken by Admiral Mahan before the turn of the century. What has changed is the participation of the civilian populations in the risks and perils of war—and the consequent need for them to be aware of the advantages, risks, and perils involved. This is particularly true in a democracy, where national purpose may easily be subverted through fear and ignorance without national leaders being able to act decisively to prevent it.

During the last decade, the result of such a diminished public confidence in the defense establishment has caused hostile pressures to be exerted against the country's defense policies. Perhaps, as some critics claim, a fundamental reexamination of both the national strategy and the defense establishment itself is in order. But even if the problem of public confidence is unresolved, still we have not taken the position of previous generations and responded to this problem by slipping into a type of classic American isolationism. Instead, we have evolved an oceanic strategy that acknowledges the need for a continued defense of the Western Hemisphere and a number of other vital areas around the world. With this new conviction, our foreign and military policies begin to move closer to each other. There is no advantage in being able to negotiate from strength at a SALT disarmament conference unless our negotiators are able to take advantage of a position supported by a decided military advantage and a popular understanding. Americans must be aware of the stakes, the risks, and, most of all, the related military strength that would be involved in any enemy confrontation. Public confidence and determination can be built only on public knowledge and acceptance of our foreign policy.

It has been said that wars are the graveyards of the predictions concerning them. And, as we shall learn, since the days of the Continental armies, each generation of American military planners has made the same major mistakes in deemphasizing the extension of science into warfare—the effect of novel methods of warfare and of new weapons. The tactics and strategy of future wars were usually left to be improvised at the time of the battles. The scientific preparation and military decision-making which should have taken place well in advance of the confrontations simply did not happen for a variety of reasons. Some were major blunders and others trivial mistakes, but in the long run all of them amounted to the same degree of unpreparedness and resultant problems.

The situation is much the same today, but so far the United

States has not made the mistakes in pursuing the Wet Cold War that she has made in other areas of the struggle. Perhaps this is because the navy has not been challenged or pushed into the major confrontations that the other armed forces have experienced in the wars of insurgency and containment. But this undersea confrontation is coming—and the nation that survives will be recognized as the master of the world.

2 The Intelligence Community at Sea: CIA Adventures in the Glomar Explorer

The whole art of war consists in getting at what is on the other side of the hill, or, in other words, in learning what we do not know from what we do.

—WELLINGTON

Probably it has always been the prime requirement of a naval commander's intelligence activity to know in advance the strength and disposition of the enemy. In the early days of warfare, it was enough simply to know the number of ships the other side had, and perhaps the armaments involved. But as naval warfare grew more involved, the commander had to have more detailed information. It became necessary to know not only how many ships of different classes the enemy had, but also information concerning their firepower, speed, maneuverability, and seaworthiness. As tactics improved, it was vital to know how their fleets were dispersed and organized, and the best way to distribute friendly forces to counter the enemy's intentions.

From simple beginnings, the craft of naval intelligence has developed into an intricate exercise in determining the strength and disposition of enemy naval forces around the world in conjunction with other military forces. Such elaborate undertakings require painstaking, detailed work by hundreds and sometimes thousands of highly skilled professionals. In the most sensitive of military areas—submarine and antisubmarine warfare—it is crucial to classify and orient potential enemy forces and their available technology—their composition, equipment, and location of every one of their units and subunits—and their logistic support operations. The degree of detail required is considerable. For example, it is not enough to know how many submarines of what type the Soviet Union has at sea at any one time. Beyond this basic information, naval commanders need to know how these submarines are organized into units, how they will perform under any given set of attack-defense conditions, what their specific missions involve, both for offensive and defensive situations, and the aspect of the submarine force—when it appears hostile, when it appears defensive, and when it is carrying out some mission different from its normal purpose.

The knowledge of base construction, industrial production, and scientific research is equally significant, and the gathering of such information by intelligence staffs goes on continuously. For the most part, it is a routine and sometimes dull analysis of reports and magazine articles from a large number of open sources, as well as covert operations that range from spies to surveillance satellites. The entire intelligence network must have a current picture of the enemy's capabilities. As each small and seemingly unconnected item comes to light, it is included in the mosaic of information—referenced, cross-referenced, computer analyzed, and researched. Any intelligence bit may prove to be the vital piece of information which provides the solution to a troublesome jigsaw puzzle. There will always be gaps in information, and these gaps will create problems, particularly with submarine and antisubmarine warfare, the newest branches of naval science. There will continue to be large areas of assurance and small areas of ignorance—hopefully. But when a commander confronts enemy forces, he must have enough information to allow him to make a reasonable assessment of the efficiency, fighting capabilities, and technologies of the enemy, the tactics he will employ, and some history of what his foe has done before. This intelligence is necessary to form a shrewd estimate of their method of operations and the characteristic of their commanders. Without this knowledge, no commander can proceed to carry out his own battle plan with any degree of security.

Perhaps the two outstanding examples of intelligence in submarine warfare involve code breaking. The United States intelligence community broke the Japanese code on the eve of the Second World War and was able to provide submarine commanders with much specific information on the movements of the Japanese fleet and the sailing schedules and routes of the Japanese merchant ships. In the Battle of the Atlantic, which was critical to the survival of England, the British Ultra cryptographers broke the German code. The survival of Britain through the first years of the war was largely a result of this code-breaking operation. The code readers gave the British their only hope of overcoming the German U-boat at sea. In order to conduct effective ASW operations, the Royal Navy had to be supplied with almost exact information on the plans of the German U-boat commanders. The Ultra code-breaking effort supplied this information. German U-boat instructions on how and where to attack were intercepted and read, as well as the U-boat commanders' routine signals which kept the Nazi naval operations staff informed of their positions. With this information, British naval intelligence alerted ASW forces and not only warned of U-boat attacks against the convoys, but was able to alert the coastal command when U-boats came close enough to be attacked by land-based aircraft.

In spite of the Ultra information, in 1942 the U-boat campaign against British shipping was devastating. Finally it was assumed that the Germans had learned to read the British naval code —a fact confirmed by Admiral Doenitz after the war. When the British changed their code, the success of the ASW campaign resumed.

Checking U-boats in the Atlantic in 1943 was a classic example of naval intelligence cooperation between the intelligence groups and the naval operations divisions. Since the most dangerous areas for U-boats to operate were close to the British coast, the Germans developed a large class of supply submarine designated Type XIV, the "Milch Cow." These submarines acted as supply ships, carrying fuel and spare parts to U-boats at sea and allowing them to remain away from their bases for up to twice the usual operational time. The destruction of these Milch Cows was high on British naval priorities in 1943, so the code breakers located their bases and a program for their gradual elimination was effected. The submarines were systematically located and sunk over a period of time so that the Germans would not suspect Ultra's code breaking. With the loss of the Milch Cows, the German U-boat campaign was broken. British security was eventually relaxed to a point where ASW signals concerning the specific location of the U-boats were sent direct to Allied ships and aircraft, but by this time the battle at sea had been won.

The craft of intelligence has played a large part in the Cold War, particularly the supersecret war under the sea. Not only are the Russians and the Americans concerned with maintaining their own security from each other, but they also seem to work under tacit agreement that other powers will not be introduced into the secrets shared by the Russian-American intelligence community. The U-2 flights over the Soviet Union were a well-known surveillance technique, grudgingly accepted by the Russians until they were publicly disclosed and world opinion made it necessary for them to react. In the same fashion, the arming of the ocean bottoms and techniques which involve placing weapons in the sea are maintained in the highest security status, even when one of the superpowers is sure that its program and intentions are well known to the other. This effort to maintain a sort of intelligence "entre-nous" situation, excluding China, Israel, the United Arab Republic, and a long list of other dangerous, volatile countries from access to more than the barest amount of "need to know" information, is one of the few bright spots in the murky business of espionage.

Like all military intelligence networks, the Soviet system is patchy and erratic. Even its prime information sources in the generous Western press cannot be relied on to produce much of their most sought after information. Soviet intelligence keeps a round-the-clock watch over Chinese and Western communications traffic of all kinds, but its most modern computers cannot predict all of the sections of that traffic that should be decoded and read. Decoding radio and cable traffic and breaking the codes is a haphazard affair in which brief successes are followed by long periods of failure. There is no way of ensuring a consistent flow of information. As covert operations grow more risky and less effective, the Russians are finding themselves less informed now than they have ever been in the past twenty years.

After World War II, it was acknowledged that the British press was the most important overall source of military information for the German High Command. What was true for Germany is also true for the Soviet Union. But one of the major Russian problems is their classic mistrust of Western sources of intelligence. They simply cannot bring themselves to believe in information so casually distributed.

The emergence of the Polaris weapons system produced serious strategic intelligence problems for the Kremlin. In days when manned bombers were the delivery systems for atomic weapons, the Soviet intelligence system maintained a current picture of the strength and disposition of the West's atomic weapon potential. Thanks to the kindness of the Western press, they also maintained an accurate knowledge of America's atomic strength. But their knowledge of atomic weapons disposition has seriously deteriorated because they cannot track the underwater movement of the United States Polaris submarines, while the United States can easily track their own SLBM submarines. The emergence of underseas weapons systems may be a major peace-keeping factor between the Soviet Union and the United States, but it has also caused a breakdown in Soviet intelligence networks. The uncertainties and problems of Soviet intelligence now appear as both a stable and unstable element in a world struggling to keep atomic peace. The Kremlin can now make miscalculations it was not in danger of making five years ago.

This element of instability reflects a new ambivalent policy in the United States, at once more deeply concerned with the activities of its own intelligence community, but on the other hand moving ahead with new and massive weapons programs like Trident and the cruise missile.

The Russians did not realize the extent to which the United States was willing to involve itself in Vietnam, and are now concerned about the Middle East and Korea. Gradually, as new and more scientific intelligence gathering comes into use, the Soviet intelligence system has begun to fall seriously behind. When spies and dirty tricks would do the job, the Russians fared well. In the West there were always sympathetic left-leaning political organizations to provide assistance, or at least conceal the real espionage work of the Soviet professionals. But now the satellite and sonar surveillance networks are more important than planted microphones in embassy walls, and budgets to finance a *Glomar Explorer* escapade are far more significant than any highly classified information concerning America's Cold War philosophy.

Russia has not developed an astute intelligence corps which can assess the information in a detached way and impartially point out both the strength and weakness of Soviet positions. In the growing intelligence gap, Russian intelligence is not capable of quick and versatile action. Its spies may be in a familiar element, but the intelligence officer who attempts to give an objective, balanced view of the Soviet intelligence lag vis-à-vis the United States may run into insuperable difficulties in exercising his craft. Faced with censorship by his superiors, the Russian intelligence officer may not be able to tell a full and accurate story. Thus the Kremlin leaders will continue to base their military and political decisions on increasingly less reliable intelligence appraisals of United States strength and policies.

The recent adventures of the *Glomar Explorer*—the massive CIA project to raise a Russian Golf class submarine sunk in 17,000 feet of water some 750 miles northwest of Oahu, Hawaii—is an illustration of how far U.S. intelligence will go to gain an advantage. The sheer magnitude of this effort, the sophistication of the deep-sea recovery system involved is amazing—particularly to those who have attempted to remove large objects from the bottom of the ocean. The mission was accomplished with such secrecy, dispatch, and—official reports notwithstanding—outstanding success as to cause shudders in the Kremlin and grudging admiration from even the sympathetic members of the scientific community around the world.

Before the *Glomar* feat, the deep-sea weight-lifting record was held by the *Alcoa Sea Probe,* which had raised 50 tons from 18,000 feet. The *Glomar* was designed to handle a payload of substantially more than 1,500 tons from below 17,000 feet—an increase in the state of the art of more than 30 times measured in weight ratio. But this was not a brute-force system; the weight advantage was gained by the skillful use of positioning, sea-keeping and lifting techniques rather than by simply constructing a derrick of immense size to do the job. Such a giant derrick would probably have failed because of sea conditions.

The intelligence community seems to have far less problems than the navy in having a ship built. The *Glomar Explorer* contract was signed in May 1971, the hull was delivered in July 1973, and the entire system was completed by May 1974. Considering all of the components required for a structure specifically designed for salvaging the Russian submarine, this construction schedule was truly amazing.

When the CIA decided to raise the sunken Russian submarine lying off the coast of Hawaii, it looked around for a convincing cover for its operations. It had to be technically feasible, but also larger than life—a concept so grand in size and aspiration that even the scrutiny of the scientific community would not "blow its cover." These men of covert genius decided to establish such a cover in the person of Howard Hughes, the flamboyant billionaire, the man who had pioneered in all forms of speculative endeavor. Hughes had built the all-wood Spruce Goose flying boat—a plane which cost millions and never flew more than a few feet off the water. Hughes had virtually bought the Las Vegas Strip on a whim. Hughes had made and lost fortunes casually. He was wealthy, eccentric, and had a scientific bent that prized the bizarre approach. If Hughes announced that his Summa Corporation was planning to enter the ocean-mining business in a typical Hughes fashion, his decision might create quite a stir in the ranks of the ocean-engineering community, but it would not put the Russians on guard. And, more important, it would not attract the attention of the liberal legislators in the House and Senate that the CIA regards as potentially more dangerous than the Russian secret police.

Eventually, of course, both the Russians and Congress might find out, but by that time the CIA would have completed its project, gained vital code and weapons information, and would be content to accept the consequences. As predicted, Hughes was de- lighted. The *Glomar Explorer* was built and sailed on a widely publicized excursion to Hawaii as the world's first commercial-size ocean-mining ship. The scientific community was told that *Glomar* was designed to harvest the potato-sized nickel and copper nodules from the bottom in large quantities. This was a reasonably feasible commercial undertaking. The Pacific's underseas recoverable metals are valued at approximately $3 trillion in nickel and copper alone. The competitors among the international mining interests that would vie with Hughes in the development of sea mines were in agreement that the 618-foot *Glomar Explorer,* with her advanced electronic and mechanical systems, had put the Summa Corporation well into the forefront of the industry. No one questioned the in- tent of the *Glomar's* mission. The cover was perfect.

There were political hazards beyond the CIA's liberal critics in Congress. Several international treaties supported by most of the nations with a stake in the development of the world's ocean bot- tom had prohibited such paramilitary operations. Periodically con- vened as a Law of the Sea Conference, these nations had been demanding through the Chinese lobby that exploitation of the seas' resources be put under the control of an international body and that profits be divided among all nations. The United States and major maritime powers had vetoed this concept, but with each new development in the Cold War at sea, the demands of these free- share lobbyists had become more vocal. The CIA recognized that if the security of the *Glomar* venture was not maintained, the United

States might face heavy pressure toward liberalizing underseas development. Still, with the prize it had in prospect, the diplomatic risks were considered worthwhile.

When the Russian Golf class submarine sank 750 miles off Hawaii in 1968, its position was pinpointed by the navy's Pacific CAESAR surveillance network. Homing in on the surveillance fix, submarines and other deep-probe equipment were used to locate and identify the submarine, mark its position with beacons, and determine the conditions required for recovery. With this information, the CIA requested funds for Project Jennifer—the raising of the submarine. Upon obtaining an authorization of $350 million, it received the blessing of Howard Hughes and carefully selected the company to design a recovery vessel to its specifications. The CIA relied on the magnitude of the venture to assure security, so Summa Corporation surprised the oceanographic mining community by precipitously leaping into the business and placing an order with the Sun Ship Building and Dry Dock Company of Chester, Pennsylvania for construction of a ship. The Lockheed Corporation's Missile and Space Vehicle Company was asked to design a barge and sea-floor-recovery equipment, and Project Jennifer was underway.

There were technical questions posed by the scientific community, but the Summa Corporation had hired a dozen experts in the field to answer such questions. Most of them believed that Hughes had, in fact, made this multimillion-dollar commitment to sweeping metals off the ocean's bottom. The German Industrial Association for Ocean Mining and the French Center for the Exploration of the Oceans both issued statements congratulating Hughes on the excellence of the *Glomar Explorer* as a recovery vessel, although privately they questioned the reason for enormous lift capacity and the overkill in design that the ship and barge combination represented. The CIA cover-up was so complete that even the subcontractors were taken in. Global Marine Development Corporation, which designed the ship in 1969, insisted that its mission was ocean mining and stuck to that story until the CIA admitted its involvement in the program.

Lockheed executives were more candid, perhaps inadvertently. They revealed that the barge designed to carry the sea-floor mining equipment was towed about 300 miles off Redwood City, California, outfitted, towed to Catalina Island, then sunk in 160 feet of water after the salvage equipment was transferred to the *Glomar Explorer*. The Pacific Towboat and Salvage Company, which held the exclusive towing contract for the barge, confirmed that the barge was never used to perform any mining or salvage function. Later Lockheed confirmed that the barge had no part in the actual submarine recovery operations off Hawaii, which further refuted the story of the method used in the deep-sea lift.

Paul G. Reeve, the head of the Summa Corporation's ocean mining division, had a difficult role to play. He was the CIA designate in charge of the operation, but also the publicity source for whatever information would be issued to the ocean-mining community concerning the exploits of the ship. Later, when the world press broke the story of the CIA involvement, Reeve would have that situation to explain as well. The CIA seemed to be under no illusion that an operation of this magnitude could be permanently disguised as a sea-mining venture, so it pushed to complete the recovery of the Russian submarine before the story broke. Sooner or later, Reeve would be the man left to do all of the explaining, and he was told to prepare himself by taking a flexible position.

The *Glomar Explorer* actually did pick up a hundred tons of nodules from the ocean floor and showed them as evidence of operations in the mining field. That was the extent of their mining operations, but the CIA felt the cover was complete when the Los Angeles County Tax Assessor went after the Summa Corporation for a $7.5 million tax bill related to the project. He was taken aside and quietly told that the ship belonged to the United States government and that his claim would not be honored. He was to stop making waves.

The *Glomar Explorer* was designed to raise and lower a grappling machine which weighed over two hundred tons in air and was almost as massive as the submarine it would salvage. It was equipped with a seawater hydraulic system and power attachments to grasp the wreckage and thrusters for fine positioning on the bottom. The grappling machine was transferred from a submersible barge to a central well in the *Glomar,* called the Moon Pool. The grappling machine was too big and heavy to be lifted aboard, so it was taken from below. The submerged barge on which it was transported was routinely capable of submerging and returning from a depth of 165 feet with a load in excess of 2,500 tons. The *Glomar* maneuvered over the barge and flooded its Moon Pool, slid back the gates on its bottom, and opened the Moon Pool to the sea. The towers on the ship stood over the steerable docking legs. When they were placed on either side of the Moon Pool, they would slide down until they penetrated the barge and mated with the docking pins on the grappling machine. Then the machine was drawn into the ship and the gates were closed. When the Moon Pool was pumped dry, the ship was ready for operation.

After the transfer from the barge to the ship took place off Santa Catalina Island, a few miles from Long Beach, the *Glomar Explorer* sailed for the mid-Pacific site. Everything had worked the first time. *Glomar* was a designer's dream come true—certainly a major advancement in the state of the art.

The *Glomar* was equipped with dynamic position equipment that made it possible to hover within a few feet of target site. To insulate the pipe-string lifting device from the strains caused by the buffeting of the waves, a derrick was mounted on gimbals so that the derrick and its pipe string remained stationary if the ship pitched. The pipe string itself was formed in 60-foot segments, each weighing about 18 tons. It was controlled by an automatic system of cranes and elevators. The pipe was selected from storage and delivered to the derrick at a rate of one segment every ten minutes. Each segment was screwed into a growing string of enriched gun-tube-steel links that was in turn raised or lowered by a lift system consisting of a double yoke, each half powered by a pair of hydraulic cylinders which grasped the pipe alternately, eventually paying out a 17,000-foot string.

The bottom of the pipe string terminated in a strengthening

device called a "Dutchman" and an apex block with a three-legged bridle which was attached to the grappling machine. Divers fastened the electromechanical cables to the outside of the pipe as the string let down. The seawater hydraulic device was operated by pumping water down the bore of the string. (The pipe also had a capacity for air injection when used to raise materials.) Seawater was pumped down to power the grapples, followed by air injected into the grappling machine so that part of the weight would be offset during the lift.

Allowing a 1.5/1 safety factor from the maximum lifting capacity of approximately 1,300 tons, a safe payload for the *Glomar* would have been about 840 tons, and a short-time loading capacity of over 1,500 tons.

So much for technical excellence. Now to the CIA rendezvous with the submarine. Was the submarine in one piece—or in separate sections? The CIA had to provide the designers with this information before the operation: where the submarine was located, how it lay on the bottom, in how many pieces, and what would be required to lift each section. The submarine was not in a single piece. Most submarines implode on sinking below their designed depth. The crumpled wreck smashes to the bottom at high speed, and the hull is usually shattered. Two United States Navy nuclear submarines—the *Thresher* and the *Scorpion*—had sunk, and both disintegrated. The *Scorpion* lies with her bow and stern broken off, and the *Thresher* is broken up into debris scattered over a half-mile radius. Locating both submarines had required extensive search efforts.

If the *Glomar Explorer* expected to find the Russian submarine in one piece, there would have been problems. The 320-foot submarine could not be accommodated in the 299-foot Moon Pool. However, the submarine could have been recovered intact by the *Glomar Explorer,* positioned beneath the Moon Pool, and brought to shallow water, where the submarine could be deposited for investigation by divers. Or, alternatively, the barge might have been used for a complete submarine lift. But here again, although the barge is 324 feet long overall, the interior of the barge is only

256 feet long. Obviously, the CIA knew exactly how many pieces it would recover, and it designed a system around a load well within the recovery system's capabilities.

Official CIA reports were guarded—scientists said "misleading." The press differed so wildly in its stories that it completely confused anyone attempting to study the operation. The estimates of the lift system were badly over- and underexaggerated, as were the weights of the pipe string and other components and the lift capacities. The CIA said that it found the submarine in one piece, but in the lift operations approximately two-thirds broke off and was not recovered.

Not true—and not even a credible yarn. Nor did the CIA intend it to be. It was a sop for the Soviets—a face-saving gesture. Assuming that the submarine was recovered intact, the flooded weight would be as much as 1,400 tons—more than the safe lifting capacity of the *Glomar Explorer*. In a system so carefully designed around a specific purpose, it is doubtful that the lift of such a fragile, heavy object would have been attempted without a built-in safety factor.

The CIA had several courses open to it: it could have announced the mission a complete failure, a minimal success, or a total success. Under the circumstances, the choice of a minimal success with a partial recovery was probably the most reasonable. In every leaked intelligence-gathering situation, from U-2 spy planes, to the surveillance of the Russian fleet during the Cuban confrontation, to the Castro assassination plots, the CIA has been less than candid in its belated admissions—and probably justifiably so, since its business is not public relations but intelligence. Thus the Soviet Union was given an out. The CIA announced that it had recovered no missiles, no code, no critical components—only three torpedoes and one-third of the submarine.

But even the most gullible ocean engineer would have a problem with the official CIA version of the operation. The *Glomar Explorer* spent a month on the recovery site in 1974, casually going about its business and taking whatever time was necessary with the grappling machine to recover as many pieces of the submarine as it required. The ship had time to make a half dozen or more lifts from the ocean floor and conclude its mission in a leisurely style since operations remained undetected under the guise of a Howard Hughes sea-mining venture.

The CIA turned over the ship and her system to the government for sale as "surplus" material; and soon after, the National Advisory Committee on Oceans and Atmosphere described the vessel as a national asset. This led President Ford to offer the ship and barge to the Scripps Institute of Oceanography at San Diego. William A. Nieremberg, director of Scripps and a consultant to the National Security Agency, was delighted and compared the achievement of constructing the *Glomar Explorer* with the Manhattan Project. Admiral J. Edward Snyder, Oceanographer of the Navy, said that the system was probably the greatest technical achievement in ocean engineering in his lifetime—high praise for those shadowy CIA figures who made it all happen.

Before Scripps received the ship, it was briefly offered for sale. The General Services Administration published a brochure prepared by Global Marine, the ship's contractor, and the Energy Research and Development Administration released information concerning the barge. This was much more information than the CIA had ever intended to have disclosed concerning the *Glomar Explorer's* capabilities, even though it put the scientific community in awe of the agency's technical prowess. But the way the CIA had determined position and weight of the load was far more interesting to the newsmen and military observers than the amazing feat of engineering which went into the construction of the *Glomar Explorer's* hoists and engines.

In the Cold War, the submarine has become the primary weapon for both superpowers. With intelligence the only check on the submarine's dominance of the seas, there will be many more adventures like the *Glomar Explorer's* recovery mission—ranging from underwater "playing chicken" to deadly serious espionage, from technological miracles to secret submarine combats. But all probably with far less publicity than was generated by the Howard Hughes–*Glomar* escapade, if the CIA has any say in the matter.

③ Strategic Weapons: The Keepers of the Peace

The creation at the will of the Party of a new Soviet Navy and its emergence onto the ocean expanses have fundamentally altered the relative strength of forces and the situation in this sphere of contention. In the person of our modern Navy, the Soviet Armed Forces have acquired a powerful means of defense in the oceanic areas, a formidable force for the deterrence of aggression, which is constantly ready to deliver punishing retaliatory blows and to disrupt the plans of the imperialists. And the Navy, along with the other branches of the Soviet Armed Forces, is successfully fulfilling its main mission—the defense of the country from attacks by aggressors from the direction of the ocean. The warships of our Navy are a threat to no one, but they are always ready to decisively repulse any aggressor who dares to infringe upon the security of the Motherland.

—SERGEI G. GORSHKOV
(Admiral of the Fleet of the Soviet Union, Commander-in-Chief of the Soviet Navy)

There is a curious paradox in the Cold War: after a certain point is passed, the worse things get, the better the prognosis. The increase in mortal danger creates a better chance for peaceful coexistence of the two superpowers. By putting enormous spaces and scattered populations on an equal or near-equal vulnerability, the peace is maintained. Because the hydrogen bomb's vast destruction and contamination would make both powers highly vulnerable, such a deterrent makes both powers immune to surprises in a standoff well understood by both sides.

The balance of power was the guiding principle of European statecraft in the seventeenth, eighteenth, and nineteenth centuries; no state would be allowed to become so strong that it could dominate the rest. When a country became too powerful, it was a common danger, and the others united against it. On the whole, the system worked. It did not prevent the outbreak of all wars; there were failures in the system, but they were minor. If the balance of power had not been allowed to slip out of unsteady hands in 1914, and if it had not been maliciously upset in 1939, both world wars might have been avoided. Germany probably would not have gone to war in 1914 if she had been sure that Britain would stand with France. In 1939, if Russia had not made her treacherous pact with Germany at the last minute, Hitler probably would not have marched. Now Armageddon has taken the place of treaties and alliances. Doomsday is sure to follow any serious diplomatic or military miscalculation; thus peace is temporarily secure.

The United States strategic forces to combat the Soviet threat were first conceived in the 1950s, and there have since been few significant changes in their makeup. The three basic elements of the force comprised the fixed land-based missile systems, the mobile submarine missile systems, and the strategic bomber forces. All three still serve under the same organizational structure and fall under the same command functions. They have been progressively improved to achieve maximum effectiveness and weight-of-delivery of atomic-warhead missiles, and where there is a commonality of technology it is employed—at least so far as the planners of the army, navy and air force are able to cooperate. But basically the strategic forces act independently, as though each had the sole retaliatory responsibility. The administrative and tactical employment of their forces are strictly maintained by the three services which first put them into the air and in the sea. Although the Defense Department likes to pretend that there is a master plan based on the combination of these strategic forces on a mission basis, in fact it is not really so; each service establishes its own priorities.

It is not necessary to the national defense that the three deterrent forces are compatible or complementary in their employment. Two might do the job—or four might be more effective. A certain amount of political, bureaucratic, and parochial influence has shaped the present deterrent scheme, and budget debates in Congress always bring forth new proposals. However, by and large, this triangle of strategic forces has persevered—perhaps because it is the ideal formula in the arms race, calculated to keep all the country's eggs out of one basket. Or perhaps because it appeases all the armed services, Congress, and the technical community.

A major difficulty in creating a nation's strategic forces involves discovering what the competitive foreign forces are doing, and either establishing a superior force or some method to counteract it. Such decisions are difficult for U.S. planners because the Russians tend to pursue the same policies with the same weapons simultaneously. At one point it was thought that the overall United States goal should be the obliteration of Soviet missile complexes; but as both countries escalated their missile developments and built up larger arsenals of nuclear weapons, it seemed more prudent to create deterrents to prevent an all-out nuclear attack rather than planning to reply to such an attack once it was made.

It soon became clear that the threat of assured destruction had forced the Soviet Union into a national policy much like that of the United States. On one hand, the Russians wanted to push aggressively toward expansion plans and goals; but on the other, they were constrained by the threat that provocation would precipitate a nuclear war with the NATO alliance. Soviet political moves were checked by the reality that they would be limited in pressing for a world communist state—just as our national leadership knew that there were limits on the rigid containment of Soviet ambitions. Neither side wanted any issue to escalate to a state of war. The stakes had grown too high, the issue was agreement or holocaust, and even the most bellicose militarists on both sides realized the awful consequences of a nuclear war. A strategic change was in order. The superpowers began to speak of building for deterrent and "bargaining-chip" positions at the negotiation table, new weapons development was slowed, and disarmament talks were begun.

Before a detailed discussion of the role of the Polaris and Trident submarines in strategic policies, it is important to understand the other two legs of the deterrent triangle: the fixed land-based ICBMs and the strategic bomber force.

The Titan and the Minuteman missile systems comprise the fixed ICBM system. Over 1,000 Minuteman missiles are now in silos at the ready, but they are believed potentially vulnerable to a first-strike attack. The Soviets were initially far behind the Minuteman program in technology, but as they continued to build hardened silos—silos protected with steel and concrete—and to imitate the U.S. program, they became a serious competitor in both sophistication and numbers. The Soviet ICBM force consists of approximately 1,000 SS–11 and 300 SS–9 missiles and warheads—designed in the same time frame as our Minuteman system, with minor tradeoffs in comparable payload, sophistication, and throw weight. Are they comparable to our missiles in multiple warheads (MIRV) and accuracy? Opinions are divided. The consensus seems to be that the Soviets are modernizing, but that their technology lags five years behind ours. Under current Soviet policy, as technology becomes increasingly complex and funds are diverted away from hardware production and into the laboratory, unless they achieve a major breakthrough, they are likely to remain behind.

Since antiballistic missile systems are presently banned, the Soviets have initiated a massive air-defense system. They continue to burrow into the ground in the kind of fallout-shelter mania that seized this country in the late fifties and early sixties. There is some indication that the Russians would like to have an ABM system, probably because of their national paranoia which remains dominated by fear of a first strike by the United States. However, it is doubtful that any future ABM capability would substantially offset the capabilities of Minuteman or future developments in the fixed-missile-system technology. This is not an area where paper projections will satisfy—to be a strategic factor, the ABM system would have to be perfect.

The long-range bomber continues to be an area in which the United States has a substantial lead, but the recent rejection of the B–1 bomber concept will reduce that military advantage. The Russian Backfire bomber program proceeds—and although there are calculations, studies, and analyses by the thousands that predict the performances and survivability of the manned-bomber force in the event of nuclear war, there is not much agreement on its total strategic impact versus counterweapons. Its survivability has been questioned despite geographical dispersing of the force and scheduling to make the planes airborne as quickly as possible. Present plans call for the use of alternate bases and flexible and mobile deployments so that much of the bomber force would probably survive a nuclear first strike, leaving hundreds of bombers immediately available for the subsequent attack, which would devastate Russia.

Military observers have always felt that new developments will favor the manned bomber. Air-to-surface missiles are making air defense extremely hazardous, low-level attacks avoid radar surveillance, and jamming of electronic countermeasures are rendering most present-day fire-control systems obsolete. Coordinated bomber and missile attacks would ensure that a large number of bombers penetrated enemy air defenses. Missiles targeted at these defenses would further reduce their effectiveness. Any reasonable calculation for second-strike capability involves at least a hundred aircraft reaching their targets in Russia, with each bomber carrying a substantially larger payload than any ballistic missile. Enemy destruction is fast becoming a calculation of a power function of overkill —total destruction squared or cubed, if such a figure can have any real significance.

The SALT agreements and the ABM treaty signed in Moscow in May 1972 formalized a mutual deterrent and defined the basic policies of the United States and Russia with respect to the deployment of antiballistic missile systems and defenses. These agreements also specified that the submarine-launched ballistic missile (SLBM) force constitute the primary deterrent of both countries. Such forces would be expanded at the expense of land-based missile systems.

The powers could not agree on the restrictions of antiaircraft defenses, multiple-warhead rockets (MIRV), or land-based missile systems. Apparently bombers and missiles were considered more vulnerable than SLBM submarines, so a compromise was written around the SLBM fleets, although searching questions were asked about why the negotiators chose to allow freedom and technological development in this area of strategic weapons. Certainly it was not a matter of expense; the fixed land-based system would have been the least expensive. Many observers said it was another negotiating victory for the Soviets; others felt it was the fear of the traditional role of the bomber with its delivery capability tested and significantly greater than either of the other two forces. In any event, the submarine was chosen as the mutually-agreed-upon deterrent: the Russians were free to try closing the wide gap posed by the Polaris, but Admiral Rickover was also free to begin his campaign for the Trident supersubmarines.

The United States force of Polaris submarines stands at 41, with approximately 650 SLBMs and 5,400 warheads. The Russians have a target of 52 submarines and have presently built almost that number, armed with approximately 950 missiles. In the absence of an antimissile system, the only Soviet threat to the SLBMs is the ASW forces—a very weak defense against Polaris-Poseidon, and probably an even weaker threat to the proposed Trident class of submarine.

However, if tactical ASW is not a threat, strategic ASW may be. Such a strategic capability could occur in several ways, some of them almost completely covert. While tactical ASW is identified in terms of specific purpose—to protect shipping or to dominate sea lanes, for example—strategic ASW consists of technological breakthroughs which come after years of secret R&D efforts—or an integration of many surveillance and detection systems in some new manner, coupled with an improved kill capability. A superior underseas surveillance system similar to our own CAESAR network could be developed by the Soviets. Such a system could locate all of our navy's missile-carrying submarines at sea during a very short time. If at the same time a shipboard- or land-launched system could be coordinated to accurately direct atomic missiles at these submarines with a high probability of kill, then the combination of these tactical systems would neutralize our deterrent SLBM force.

At one time the difference between tactical and strategic ASW was thought to be the difference between a long, gradual period of time in which attrition would reduce the enemy submarine force, compared to a first-strike capability which would eliminate the enemy's submarine force at the beginning of hostilities. Now the significant difference between the two is measured in a brief period of time; a future war between the superpowers is not likely to allow a gradual attrition. From the military point of view, strategic ASW bears little resemblance to any combination of tactical ASW programs, unless this concept can come together in a plan which destroys nearly all of the enemy submarines at sea— and then probably only after an initial attack by land-based missiles or bombers.

Long before military planners had approached the problem, Captain Nemo and Tom Swift were operating in the depths with amazing devices and radically new technologies. Some of these concepts learned in boyhood seem to recur in proposals from the scientific community for new methods to detect and destroy submarines. Since the disastrous submarine campaigns waged by the Germans and the effective blockade of Japan by American submarines in the Pacific, ASW planners have struggled with the problem of challenging this weapon in its own environment. The results have been interesting, imaginative, and sometimes dramatic— but unfortunately for the maritime powers, largely unproductive until the CAESAR project came along. Infrared sensors were one of the more interesting technologies researched as a submarine detection system just after World War II, but tests proved it impractical, if not technically infeasible. Radar was effective against submarines when they were forced to surface frequently, but when modern submarines run underwater, there is simply no exposed outline for radar to detect. Laser concepts have been successfully used for very short distances under ideal conditions, but they are still classed as underwater oddities. The search goes on, but with far more failures than successes.

Thus we return to the constraining medium through which acoustic energy must pass: the long distances of the ocean with its noises and inconsistencies. The detection of underwater sound requires highly engineered equipment which can analyze foreign sounds while eliminating all the indigenous noises that confuse identification. Military scientists have been successful in developing systems for passive and active acoustic detection, bringing each to a high degree of sophistication. But there is still always the threat that some new development in submarine design or operation may render them less effective, and, in a short time, as totally obsolete as the "ashcan" depth charge or mortarlike "hedgehog," the ASW mainstay weapons of the postwar period.

Military planners must work within the limitations of different ASW approaches, constantly trading off advantages to eliminate disadvantages. Their goal is a technological breakthrough that would give ASW forces the advantage for a long period of time, but this is less likely than achieving a gradual, marked superiority in the use of all tactical ASW methods.

The submarine lends itself to an extraordinary countermeasure that is not possible with any other strategic weapon. At sea, the nuclear submarine may simply be trailed continuously by ASW forces—submarines, surface vessels, and aircraft. This creates a degree of vulnerability, but in no way significantly reduces the submarine's capability for a first-strike missile launch. Continuous active trailing at close range with active sonar is possible, but involves precise operations that would certainly be detected by the submarine. Employing such trailing operations around the world and following a large part of the SLBM fleets would be difficult, expensive, and would certainly violate the intent of any arms agreement which contains a mutual-deterrent scheme. Trailing does allow the United States a substantial advantage, however, since the Russian submarines generate more noise than ours, and the shorter range of their missiles requires their submarines to come relatively close to the United States in both the Atlantic and Pacific before they are in effective range. The Soviets must exit through the Greenland, Iceland, and Scandinavian passages, which facilitates tracking. During wartime, mining their routes would be relatively simple. The United States is now operating with 2,500-plus-nautical-mile Polaris A–3 and Poseidon missiles; at these ranges, the Russians cannot presently establish an effective passive sonar detection network. When the Russians finally achieve the 6,000-mile missile to match the 6,000-mile range of the Trident missile projected for United States submarines, they will still be at a disadvantage in the Atlantic and Pacific, both in detection and first-strike capability.

In the Second World War, when United States faced the island empire of Japan, we looked to the operations of many attack submarines to sink naval vessels and surface shipping. Eventually, our submarine blockade strangled the Japanese by denying them shipping routes. This was much the same tactic the Germans used against England in World War I and World War II. But in a war with Russia, the United States would not have an enemy that depended on sea routes as did the Japanese; although the Russians must assume the role of the Germans and attempt to cut off shipping from the United States to Europe in the Atlantic, and to Japan and Australia in the Pacific. Thus the United States concentrates on the SLBM fleet while the Soviet Union balances its requirements between a SLBM fleet and an attack submarine force.

In order to feel any confidence in dividing their efforts, the

Russians must assume that they will never be faced with the prospect of a first strike by the United States SLBM fleet. Although this seems like an elementary consideration from our point of view, a history of the Cold War and the Soviet actions clearly demonstrate that the paranoia in the Russian character which drives them to seek what we consider world domination also involves a distrust of all other nations. After a thousand years of warfare, repulsing one and then another invading military force, the Russians are not inclined to trust any powerful nation. Regardless of their analysis of western philosophy and politics, they will never be completely satisfied that the United States will not resort to a first strike, given some set of provocations. Consequently, the Russians must continue to balance their underseas forces with the prospect of carrying on a war after a preemptive attack by the United States—countering both submarine and surface forces.

If the ICBM system is fired as a first or second shot, the holocaust will take place within a very short time. A bomber force will be over enemy targets in a matter of hours, expected to avenge the damage to its own centers of population. After these three weapons strikes, an extended conventional war that would pit submarine against submarine or ASW task force against the SLBM fleet of either country seems unlikely. Therefore it seems unrealistic to argue the survival of a carrier task force at sea against nuclear bombardment—interesting but academic. And yet, for some opaque reasons that must be more political than reasonable, naval planners continue to request large appropriations to prepare for such eventualities. Their requests reinforce the strong belief, based on historical precedent, that the admirals are always prepared to fight the last war over again.

If it cannot be reasonably conceded that the SLBM force will effectively be countered in any future conflict, it is even more difficult to introduce the concept of strategic arms control. Short of the simplistic problem of eliminating the first-strike capability, the SLBM seems to play only a deterrent role. But with the apparent inability of both Russia and the United States to safeguard against either the land-based missile or bomber threat, it is difficult to conceive of a response to a super-SLBM system like Trident. Its tactical effect is immediate: employment of SLBM submarines in a future war would be so brief that it would render any ASW response futile. By the time a major ASW effort could be mounted, the SLBM force would long since have fired its missiles, and the continuing holocaust would be the responsibility of the surface missile men and manned bomber commands.

Any flexible deterrent requires a force capable of causing second-strike destruction. Its magnitude influences the degree of deterrence. It is particularly difficult to classify deterrence by relative standards, since only the provocation of an all-out nuclear attack would involve a nuclear response by any major weapon. To exert a meaningful degree of flexibility, a weapons system must be completely invulnerable. It must have a secure command and control system which is not subject to delays and fail-safe against release except by top-level command. And it must also be able to retarget on short notice, with missile accuracy precise enough to be delivered on target with little damage to adjacent areas. The fixed land-based missiles, the manned bomber, and the submarine-launched ballistic missile all have tradeoffs with respect to flexibility: the submarine-launch system rating highest in terms of invulnerability, the fixed system in terms of communications and control, and the bomber in terms of maximum delivery of payload on separated targets. Assessed as a counterforce based on second strike capability, each system will have unique advantages and disadvantages. In terms of both flexibility and counterforce, all three strategic weapons are substantial. There are no major defects in present designs and none anticipated in their design progression over the next decade. All three can survive a first attack in sufficient numbers to deal a counterblow which would deter either superpower from first-strike considerations.

Certainly the major long-range factor is cost, and here there are deceptive considerations. The most misleading comparison is the simple cost per missile. By far, the Minuteman system provides the lowest cost per missile as measured over the last decade—but surprisingly, the submarine-launched ballistic missile is a close second. Manned bomber costs, including support facilities, troop training, and other related costs, are substantially higher than either.

Both Russia and the United States have elaborate networks of tactical nuclear missiles, and the important moves in the East-West chess game must be based on the evaluation of these systems. But exercises that are based on paper studies of future combat situations are of dubious value; relative overkill and postholocaust statistics have no great weight. Russia lags behind the United States in total deterrent-force capability and is projected to remain behind for the foreseeable future. Its bomber force is inferior and smaller. The Soviet submarine fleet, although substantially larger, is largely obsolete. And as the ICBM multiple, steerable warhead technology increases and the cruise missile program progresses, the Soviets will trail the United States even more. Only by a radical change in their economic priorities will they remain within hailing distance. In what is almost an academic exercise, the differences in geography make throw weight and accuracy of the fixed-base system of the two countries a standoff. So we have the United States far ahead, and the Russians hard pressed to stay in the race.

It is reasonable to assume that the superpowers will continue to pursue all three strategic weapons systems, each independently involved in establishing its progressive capability in terms of retaliation. These weapons systems seem divorced from the political considerations and national aspirations of the two countries; they progress almost independently of political rhetoric and arms-limitation discussions. Even with growing Soviet reluctance to convey any indication of their willingness to risk mass destruction, there is no letup in the strategic arms race. Facing whatever is represented by the growing threat of China together with a substantial NATO force, the Russians may well be reexamining their own strategic policies and giving much more serious consideration to what will happen outside the United States in the next decade. But it would take a turnabout of major proportion to cause either country to let the other gain a substantial strategic weapons advantage—at least not intentionally.

There are situations which could result in major changes. The

SALT agreements on offensive weapons could freeze the strategic forces at their present levels. Not likely, but possible. Certainly such a freeze would serve to accent improving technologies, and with an increase in technology the competition would shift to the relative quality of the two competing systems: to transfer the arms race from a gross armament to a research and development competition. Such a competition could be far more serious in terms of a real threat to man's survival; new weapons more devastating than the hydrogen bomb are certainly the next step for science.

The possibility of any agreement involving large reductions in weapons systems is remote. However, the new large mobile land-based system now in development will place a heavy strain on the budget for technical developments required to maintain a bomber system and a submarine system. If a mobile land system becomes tactically superior to anything presently employed, it would also determine the United States' strategic policy. The spectrum of options presently provided by the bomber and submarine forces would be reduced, and the variability built into the present three-system deterrents would certainly be lost. Since insecurity immediately results from the vulnerability of any system, SALT-type agreements are meaningless in terms of the true military balance. Either government that allowed a major discrepancy between its strategic weapon capability and its opponent's would be disgraced.

It may very well happen that Russia cannot maintain competition in all of the three deterrent systems and so may decide to concentrate very heavily on one and neglect the others. The best bet is probably the acceleration of a mobile ICBM land system—a cheaper and more viable choice for the land-locked Russians. They may maintain a deterrent force in either of the other two, or at least keep abreast of the technology. The United States would have to follow a similar course, although it is difficult to imagine the air force giving up its heavy bomber program or the navy reducing its strategic submarine SLBM force. Reexamining the scorpion-and-tarantula-in-a-bottle phenomenon, it is difficult to believe that powerful nuclear weapons will ever be used by either country, but it is just as difficult to believe they will ever lay them down.

Strategic policy is often determined by political considerations and emotional involvement, both within the country and without. To reduce arms or influence the selection of weapons, a mutual trust of a most extraordinary and unlikely kind must exist between the United States and Russia. Certainly, as time goes on and technology expands, the prospect of what one country will be able to do to another on a first-strike basis becomes a more awful prospect. However, there has been no serious arms reduction program proposed by either superpower, and reducing the warmaking capacity of either country seems very remote. Planners hope for the best but prepare for the next generation of strategic weapons, willing to limit hardware but unwilling to restrict research and development of new superweapons or to appreciably reduce present weapons inventories.

In projecting ASW strategy, one of the important considerations is how limitations on it will finally be decided at a SALT conference or other arms-limitation forum. So far antisubmarine warfare has been generally ignored, and limitations on the buildup of SLBM fleets have not been subjected to the close scrutiny directed at the land-based missile complexes and bomber forces. The day is coming, of course, when not only submarines but also ASW will come to the bargaining table, probably with the same recommendations as the intercontinental ballistic missile defense systems—both a limitation on the active components and some consideration on regulation of the defense measures.

To evaluate strategic antisubmarine warfare, we first have to decide whether the SLBM would be an effective first strike against the enemy's submarine force and antisubmarine force. Certainly there is some impact from all strategic weapons on all other weapons systems. But the primary targets of the SLBM in any thermonuclear exchange would be land-based: first the fixed or mobile ICBMs, then the bomber bases. Using sea-launched missiles against airborne bombers is presently feasible, but any future flat-trajectory missile would not be effective enough to prevent most of the bomber force from taking off and carrying out its missions. At present, the SLBM can seriously impair the enemy's ability to retaliate, and although the SLBMs would extensively damage a fixed

ICBM system, their major targets would be the industrial and urban population centers within the Soviet Union.

Even ignoring a first strike, there is still the problem of balancing the growing United States SLBM technology, and some future control of strategic ASW will probably be imposed so that the powers continue to have confidence in their sea-based deterrents. There must be an assurance that their submarine fleet would survive any preemptive threat; control of the methods of anti-submarine warfare for longer engagements is far less significant. In considering global controls, it is difficult to imagine a major conflict between Russia and the United States in terms of anything less than thermonuclear warfare; if an attack on the submarine fleets occurred, such a war would certainly follow. But an all-out thermonuclear exchange is a subject that cannot be easily or rationally approached. So, instead, the arms-limitation negotiators from both sides prefer to concentrate on simple and specific measures and generally divide them into two categories: military hardware, including research and development, and operational controls. These fundamental approaches are intended to provide at least a starting point in the discussion of arms inventories and proposed limitations. For example, ASW hardware controls might include limiting the number of attack submarines; operational controls might restrict the ability of one nation to track and trail the SLBM fleet of the other or employ any tactics that would limit the major threat of the deterrent weapons systems. Thus the present SALT agreement emphasizes ASW in that SLBM submarine construction is frozen by agreement while attack submarines are unrestricted and continue to be built in large numbers—presumably unbalancing the equation, but still offering no solution.

The real problem of reducing arms or creating a parity is much more complex than periscope counting or operational limitation. The great threat is the insonification of the oceans—the deployment of so many large fixed and mobile active sonars that submarine operations would be endangered. To some degree there are limitations in the sea-bed locations of sonar implantments. However, this is an area in which technological breakthroughs are happening all

the time, and it seems only a matter of time until new developments allow barrier sonar systems similar to the radar DEW line
and BMEWS systems to be installed on all sea mounts or wherever
the ocean bottom will permit. The CAESAR project is a long step
in this direction. But no program of limitation has been recommended to curtail the employment of long-range sonar intelligence
systems. Thus Soviet SLBM submarines are vulnerable, and their
deterrence value may be largely neutralized now. Our SLBM submarines could be threatened at some time in the future.

Reliable arms limitations would require quotas for antisubmarine warfare ships, planes, helicopters, and the active and passive
sonars used in large surface ships, and also for sea-bed-mounted
devices. It might be very difficult to arrange a coordinated ban
which would be effective enough to have any realistic value. In
limiting tactical ASW—both passive and active—monitoring techniques are not yet well developed or reliable.

The submarine fleet is going through a rethinking of cruise
missile capability as the air-breathing, short-range missile becomes
an inexpensive, potent, thermonuclear-warhead-delivery system.
And even further out, there is the pilotless drone aircraft which
could be launched from submarines, a kind of Mach II robot that is
beginning to assume the proportions of a true aircraft, including a
range of missions from kamikaze bomb carrier to aerial dogfighter,
performing like manned aircraft. Cruise missiles are becoming
larger and more sophisticated and the robots, called Remotely
Piloted Vehicles (RPV), have extended their capabilities far beyond the simple drone. Missiles and drones are now used for
missions such as rocket launchers, laser-beam artillery spotters, and,
of course, as hydrogen-bomb carriers. But no matter what additional missiles are carried aboard, the basic threat of the SLBM
submarine will remain the same: the ICBM and its strategic offensive impact.

The most important single tactical antisubmarine warfare consideration is the continuous trailing and the active tracking of the
SLBM submarine fleet. There are a number of proposals ranging
from the simple agreement by both nations to stop continuous

trailing to the establishing of sanctuaries where missile submarines could operate and ASW activities were forbidden. But open ocean sanctuaries provide very little safety, since they would be subject to passive sonar monitoring. Also, as acoustic technology advances, few open ocean locations will provide protection against the first strike. Even if they could be made secure, such sanctuaries could be employed only in peacetime; with any threat of war, the submarine fleets would disperse to the best tactical positions for carrying out their missions. But sanctuaries have the advantage of a compromise, of sorts, and perhaps a first step in recognizing that some protection against a preemptive ASW threat is necessary to assure both countries' confidence in their SLBM deterrents.

ASW limitation has been introduced at SALT, and at least a first-phase limitation of ASW activities has been informally debated. Here the United States should be prepared to stand behind only those proposals consistent with our own security, rather than continue a policy of providing confidence for the Soviets. Although they continue to increase their number of vessels, the Soviets are falling behind in the technology important to ASW, and to negotiate away our expertise in acoustics and related technologies would be stupid and dangerous.

Unfortunately, one of the frustrations in negotiating ASW arms limitation treaties is that any proposals are bound to be complicated, difficult to negotiate, and subject to a gross public lack of information on what the negotiators are trying to accomplish. Although ranked higher in deterrent force than the land-based and bomber deterrents, the SLBM and its antisubmarine corollary seem destined to remain in public ignorance. Man's appreciation of the potential of the oceans in peace and war is still a long way off.

There may be a new deterrent weapon evolving—the air-breathing, torpedo-sized missile called Tomahawk, presently being developed by the United States Navy and Air Force in two versions: one which would be submarine launched, and the other which would be air launched. The United States' position is that the development and deployment of Tomahawk either in submarines or bombers would not constitute a strategic weapon. The Russians strongly disagree and insist that Tomahawk be discussed at SALT II. In its ,final design, the Tomahawk will have a range of over 2,000 nautical miles and can be mounted to fire from a B–52 bomber wing or an attack nuclear submarine.

Technologically, cruise missiles are relatively old; the Russians have developed a number of designs in the 100-mile-range class. But nothing like this first Sea Launched Cruise Missile (SLCM), the Tomahawk, now in limited production, has ever been developed. Piloted by an inertial navigation system called TERCOM, programmed with taped digital maps, and relying on a number of intelligence-gathering sources, including satellites, this missile follows the contour of the terrain at low altitude, making it difficult to detect by radar and other surveillance. But the most significant feature is Tomahawk's range: it will exceed 2,000 miles and carry a nuclear warhead large enough to wipe out anything, save the most protected enemy sites, with pinpoint accuracy. It is cheap, relatively easy to mass-produce, and employs the most sophisticated advances in electronics and aerospace technology. In short, Tomahawk is the ideal American weapon of the 1980s, and one which the Russians will be hard pressed to match in design or production.

The United States has unilaterally given up two important strategic weapons in 1977: the B–1 bomber and the national ABM system, both Spartan and Sprint missile emplacements. There is speculation that some of these concessions were meant to pave the way for a hard American stand on cruise-missile development at the SALT II meetings. Plans for the modification of 90 United States Navy attack submarines for the Tomahawk and most of the United States bombers for the Air Launch Cruise Missile (ALCM) within the next three to five years have been drafted. No Soviet proposals or offers of compromise should be allowed to lure us away from that program.

4 The Wet Cold War Begins—Phase One

*As long as capitalism and socialism remain
side by side we cannot live peacefully—the one
or the other will be the victor in the end.*

—LENIN

At the end of World War II, the Russians made a serious miscalculation which caused them to build submarines that would soon be obsolete. They felt their sea forces must be able to counter the United States amphibious forces that had island-hopped the Pacific and invaded Europe from the north and south. To counter this threat, the Russians built small, limited-range submarines that posed no threat to the maritime routes in the Atlantic and Pacific—in fact, operation outside of the Arctic Sea and far eastern Soviet coast was difficult because of the transit time involved. This mistake cost the Soviets years of fruitless labor.

Our experiences in the Korean War made the deterrent capability of the B–29 bomber questionable. Although the B–36 was being introduced as an intercontinental atomic-weapon delivery system, it was too vulnerable to the Soviet fighter-interceptor network to be relied on. The medium-range B–47 bomber was put into production and planned as the backbone of the Strategic Air Command until the B–52 and the B–60 bomber fleets were operational in the early 1960s. The B–47 was capable of extended massive retaliation because a reliable method of in-air fueling had increased the limited range of the bombers. A network of alliances set up by Secretary of State John Foster Dulles assisted the air force and the navy in establishing forward bases much closer to the Soviets. NATO was operating well in Europe. The SEATO pact covering Southeast Asia was signed on September 18, 1954. The CENTO alliance covering the Middle East established a series of treaties between 1955 and 1959, and the ring of bases around the Soviet Union was completed by treaties with Spain, Morocco, Libya, Saudi Arabia, Formosa, and Japan. The SAC fleets of B–47 bombers could fly from bases all over the world while the U–2 high-altitude reconnaissance planes were operating from covert fields in Turkey, Pakistan, Thailand, and Formosa. The Russians were slowly being hemmed in.

Whether the disparity between the Soviet Union and the United States with respect to army, air force, and navy capabilities was real or illusory, the Russians fell back on a strategy of nuclear retaliation which was probably more creditable than the match-up of armies and fleets put forth by the intelligence community and military observers of the day. For all their braggadocio, they did not want a contest in arms on any front.

The submarine construction programs and the general buildup of the Soviet Navy were slow in developing, primarily because the Kremlin emphasized army superiority and assigned priority to its weapons. The army was shortly to lose its top priority to the missile men, but these were still the days of Red Army dominance. Then Stalin came to realize that the navy would figure prominently in the moves of the Cold War, and in 1950 the Soviet Navy was taken out of the Defense Ministry and an independent Ministry of the Navy was created. This action was much like the United States Army Air Force move from under army control and establishment as a separate service. On January 20, 1951, Stalin appointed Fleet Admiral Kuznetsov as Minister of the Navy, and Kuznetsov began his new lease on life, after a period out of favor with the Kremlin leaders. Under Stalin's patronage, Kuznetsov began drafting ambitious naval plans which resulted in the Sverdlov class of cruisers and the Skoryi class of destroyers in the early 1950s and W and Z classes of submarines later on. Kuznetsov coordinated the planning and development of the Russian fleet more effectively than it had ever been done in the past. Until Stalin's death on March 5, 1953, the navy had a high priority in weapons funding, particularly in submarine construction. Stalin's death created a power vacuum in Soviet leadership; and a troika consisting of Prime Minister Malenkov, Party Secretary Khrushchev and Secret Police Chief Beria assumed temporary leadership. Military planning was shelved until a final power struggle determined a new leadership which would dictate its own military programs.

With the help of the Red Army and particularly Defense Minister Zhukov, Party Secretary Khrushchev was able to take control of the government later that year. Because he took power with the help of the Red Army, the army marshals were once again in full command. One of their first acts was to reintegrate and subordinate the navy to the Defense Ministry—in effect, to reinstall army domination of navy building programs, particularly submarine construction.

Whenever the Russians preach peaceful coexistence, there is usually some priority which prohibits their extending their weapons arsenal. In 1953 Malenkov preached restraint in the Cold War and pushed hard for the assignment of priorities to the consumer industry at home. To some degree, he also attenuated the Soviet military buildup being directed by the Red Army. Khrushchev finally eliminated Malenkov with the help of the military high command, and the priorities shifted back. Construction of the Sverdlov class and Skoryi class cruisers and destroyers and the submarine building program resumed, to be coordinated with a developing Soviet nuclear potential. The Soviets were working to produce a standoff missile capability as quickly as possible, and the navy buildup was central to their plan.

At the end of the Korean War, the United States assessed the sea power of the Soviet Union. Not only had the Russians achieved a significant buildup in surface forces, but they had also pushed ahead in accelerated submarine and ASW construction. The W class submarines were now operating successfully and being mass produced. These were diesel-powered craft of approximately 1,050 tons, designed around the technology taken from the German Navy at the end of World War II. Also in construction were the Z class boats: similar, but slower and heavier at approximately 1,900 tons.

The submarine threat posed by the Soviet fleet was reported as significant since it impinged on NATO's dependence on supply lines from the United States. The Soviets had mounted their first sea threat—and that it was taken at all seriously by the NATO naval planners spoke more for the Russian intent than the real challenge it implied. Senior officers in the United States Navy recognized that the submarine would be a problem in any future war, just as it had been in past wars, but privately the admirals were not awed by numbers of Russian submarines. Future threats would involve modern submarines, and the admirals had detailed information that the Soviet forces were verging on obsolescence.

The antisubmarine-warfare techniques and tactics of the 1950s were the same as they had been during the Second World War, and not really much different from the First World War. The fleet units available for hunting submarines were primarily the World War II class Sumner and Fletcher destroyers. Construction was begun on new destroyer and frigate types whose primary mission would be antisubmarine warfare; but these would not be available in adequate numbers for several years, and their tactics would not be developed for an even longer period. The assumed effectiveness of the NATO antisubmarine-warfare forces was as bogus as the paper submarine fleet of the Soviet Union; a classic match-up of paper tigers that lasted throughout the decade.

The destroyer, the airplane, and the large surface ship competed on a continuing basis for the primary role in antisubmarine warfare. In 1949 the navy had begun the construction of a hunter-killer cruiser, the Norfolk, for single-ship antisubmarine-warfare operations; but later analysis indicated that this approach would be too expensive, and plans to construct additional cruisers of this type were dropped. A smaller frigate type, the Mitscher class, was designed, and four of these ships were built by 1954. But again, by the time they were operational, these vessels turned out to be too expensive and not tactically sound for antisubmarine-warfare missions. Finally, the designers returned to their primary antisubmarine-warfare choice—the destroyer—as the long-term best bet for the pursuit of submarines from the sea surface until the surface-effect skimmers were a reality.

The construction of the first modern antisubmarine-warfare destroyers began with the Dealey class in 1951 which evolved into the Forrest Sherman class in 1953. In the next five years, 13 of these types were launched and performed to expectations. In addition, 34 of the older Fletcher class destroyers were converted into submarine killers (DDK) or destroyer escorts (DDE).

Western planners assumed that the underseas threat from the Soviet Union would proceed along classical lines: the Soviet program would threaten the sea lanes and fleets around the world. But they were wrong: the initial Russian submarine construction program was intended only to counter an invasion threat—a massive amphibious assault on the Soviet Union similar to the invasion of Normandy. The Russians constructed approximately 85 percent of their submarine fleet as medium-sized and small boats, with no delusion that they could control any of the main Atlantic and Pacific shipping routes. They might have proved effective against an invasion launched from the Baltic or Black Sea, but the Kremlin was unsure even of that.

The United States Navy's balanced-fleet proponent was Vice Admiral Daniel Gallery, a World War II hero who argued persuasively that to extend the deterrent force—if that was to be a national goal—the most effective plan involved constructing a nuclear-powered aircraft-carrier fleet capable of launching high-speed mobile bombers. He went so far as to suggest that if necessary, the planes could be ditched close to the coast on return flights, and the crews could be picked up by submarines. To demonstrate Gallery's point, a Navy P–2V Neptune long-range reconnaissance plane took off from the deck of the carrier *Coral Sea* with a simulated atomic bomb. The tests were successful, and carriers of the Midway class with four Neptunes embarked were assigned for atomic-bomb deployment. Later, smaller and lighter atomic bombs became available and the A–2 Savage was deployed in Midway class carriers, later to be replaced by the A–3 Sky Warrior, a jet bomber specifically designed for an atomic-bomb mission.

The Korean War proved once again that the carrier was a multipurpose weapon. Carriers were modernized; by the end of 1956, carriers of the Essex class were equipped with reinforced flight decks and steam catapults for deploying jet aircraft. In the second construction phase, the ships were provided with modern angle decks and hurricane bows. Eventually all of the Midway class carriers were fitted out in similar fashion, and the fleets had carrier strike groups permanently attached. At the time, the Second Fleet and Sixth Fleet were operating in the Mediterranean and Atlantic, the First Fleet in the Pacific, and the Seventh Fleet in Southeast Asia—all built around the carrier-task-force concept. The new larger carriers of the Forrestal class joined the fleet in 1955 and were fitted out to accommodate supersonic A–5 Vigilante bombers.

The carrier had fought off its opponents many times and won the funding battle in Congress. Congressmen like big pork-barrel projects worth many millions; carriers and battleship construction were very popular appropriation items. The air force watched the carrier task force prove itself in sea-control missions in the Korean War. With no choice, the generals reluctantly deferred to the navy's new strategic role. Despite rumbles from the submarine lobby, the carrier fleet entered the era of the fifties still the queen of the seas.

Meanwhile, the Soviets cast around for a nuclear-warhead-delivery system which could use the platform they had on hand— the conventional submarine. By miniaturizing the nuclear warhead, their torpedo designs would have worked and probably developed into their sea deterrent system for the decades of the fifties and sixties. But the cost of such a program was prohibitive: Soviet planners felt that even if the weapon could be developed, it would be limited to delivery by the slow electric-diesel-powered long-range submarines of the Z class and dangerous only to ports and coastal cities. Therefore the Soviets soon turned to experimenting with the German V–2/A–4 rocket fired from launch tubes towed by submarines.

At the end of World War II, the Russian military surveyed their potential postwar enemies and decided that the United States Navy's aircraft carrier-supported task force was their major foe.

They observed the activities of the Sixth and Seventh fleets with their carrier strike groups operating in the North Sea, Mediterranean, and Western Pacific and they changed their priority from an antiamphibian to an anticarrier program of defense. This developed a conflict in the mid-fifties between Chairman Khrushchev and Admiral Kuznetsov, prime architect of the Soviet high sea fleet. The political problem was resolved finally by the Red Army, which supported Khrushchev. Admiral Gorshkov, Kuznetsov's pupil and Commander-in-Chief of the Black Sea Fleet, was elevated and given the task of countering the new threat to the Soviet Union posed by the American carriers. His first effort was mounting missiles on Soviet destroyers, and by 1961 ten ships were fitted with missile-launching capabilities. But even with nuclear-tipped missiles, surface ships were not the answer, as the Russians knew, even as they were effecting the modifications. Submarines that could accommodate such missiles were needed, and the Soviets watched the fantastic progress of the United States Navy's Fleet Ballistic Missile development program in awe and admiration.

The early Russian Shaddock missile, SS N–3, was originally developed for coastal defense. It was slightly modified for incorporation into a W class submarine with a missile launcher that could be raised on an angle of approximately 14° placed in the upper deck behind the conning tower. By 1960 five additional W class submarines were fitted with such launchers, installed wideways on the upper decks behind the conning tower. Beginning in 1961, the missile tests proved moderately successful, although the sea trials of submarines demonstrated that deep-sea operations were severely impaired by missile-firing operations.

Next, the W class submarines were cut in two and equipped with a center section containing four erect tubes within the turret bridge, which permitted improved submerged operation, since the tubes presented less of a profile. This was called the W "Long Bin" class. It was regarded as a stopgap design and was soon discarded.

The first J class submarine was completed early in 1962 and was soon scheduled to replace the W class as a more stable launch platform. Two Shaddock twin launchers were included in the hull cover above the pressure hull, and a nuclear-power version was scheduled in the following generation of design. Still Russia lagged far behind the now-rapidly-building United States SLBM nuclear fleet.

The Russians inaugurated a generation of missile cruisers of the Kydna class armed with the SS N–3 Shaddock system. In order to accommodate the expanded building program, the shipways of the Zdanov shipyard in Leningrad were enlarged, along with the Severodvinsk yards on the Arctic Ocean and the Komsomolsk yards in the Far East. Russian building made up in numbers what it lacked in skill, and the surface fleet launchings began to increase at a satisfactory pace.

Still, the Soviet naval strategy was not fully resolved on an appropriate response to United States naval power, especially the carrier task force. The main Soviet thrust was to build a standoff capability against the carrier groups—a three-wave tactic. The first wave of long-range reconnaissance aircraft would maintain contact with the approaching carrier groups, to be joined by Badger jet bombers and later augmented by nuclear-powered submarines with torpedoes. The second wave would consist of missile-armed submarines complemented by conventional torpedo-bearing submarines which would be deployed in a broad barrier across expected carrier routes. In 1958, in anticipation of this policy in the Mediterranean, submarine facilities to accommodate W class submarines and submarine tenders were constructed in the Albanian port of Valona. The third wave would consist of missile-armed surface ships prepared to fire long-range missiles under the air cover of Soviet land-based aircraft without coming into immediate contact with carrier groups. In this phase, necessary forward observation would be conducted by a fleet of W and Z class submarines.

Whether these tactics would have frightened off the carriers was never determined, of course; but the plan did begin a phase in

Russian naval development that placed major reliance on the submarine both as an attack weapon and a reconnaissance and long-range surveillance ship. In the future, until the advent of the SLBM, the screening and protection of other fleet units would be the prime responsibility of the Russian submarine.

5 The Making of a Sea Power

The world has never seen a more impressive demonstration of the influence of sea power upon its history. Those far distant, storm-beaten ships, upon which the Grand Army never looked, stood between it and the dominion of the world.

—ALFRED THAYER MAHAN

In order to evaluate the naval challenge that one country poses to others, we should consider how a nation becomes a major sea power. What are the fundamentals of sea power? What capabilities must a country possess in addition to those normally imputed to a great power: population, agriculture, raw materials, and industry? The requirements for a maritime power go further—they combine elements of shore advantage with afloat capability, and, of course, vision.

First, the basic requirements: territory with advantageous geographic characteristics; a large and aggressive population; extensive raw materials; the ability to produce food in the quantities required; either fuel or access to it; a stable national economy; a broad and diversified industrial base; a secure financial foundation and a competent leadership. Now add to those advantages the elements necessary for a sea power: a shipyard capability, naval and repair bases both at home and where required abroad in order to maintain its fleets. While it is possible for a nation to become a maritime power although it is weak or even totally lacking in some of the fundamentals, they must be compensated for by greater strengths in other areas. For example, reduced capability in the shore establishment can be offset by an outstanding afloat element. The United States has grown into a sea power by a balanced buildup of all of the elements in less than a hundred years, while the Soviet Union has achieved a secondary role by emphasizing a few elements over a much longer period. Today the two powers face each other; close to parity in some areas, but still with dramatic differences in their competing strengths and weaknesses.

The Soviet Union has committed itself to a policy of expanding its shipyard capability. The Soviets have not only rebuilt and overbuilt old yards but have built new ones in the Baltic and Black seas and located specialty bases and submarine yards in the White Sea and in Siberia. Together with their allies in the communist bloc, they presently build about 70 percent of their new construction requirements and obtain another 10 to 15 percent from Yugoslavia and Finland. This is a dramatic increase in capability from the 1950s, when the Soviet Union had most of its shipping built by Great Britain, West Germany, Holland, Italy, and Japan.

On the other hand, although the Russians are restricted with respect to naval bases and access to oceans required for movement of large naval fleets, they have not aggressively pushed the establishment of the kind of forward bases or developed the remote logistics tactics needed for naval supremacy in the Atlantic and Pacific. This lack of bases severely hampers their submarine operations. Until nuclear power becomes fleetwide and more effective, the limited sites of naval bases in continental Russia will continue to prove the most serious defect in the Soviet naval expansion plan. To some extent Russia has tried to move into the base race by establishing overseas bases in any location where a friendly government could be induced to cooperate. However, the results have been poor. Even in the Pacific, where Russia has maintained friendly relations with several socialist countries with base capabilities, those ties have not been strong enough to permit the construction of a large naval-base complex. The Soviets want and need naval facilities in the Caribbean for the support of Cuba, but still they have not established a strong forward-base system in the Atlantic. For the future, the African coast would appear to be the most logical location for Soviet supporting bases—but here again there do not seem to be any arrangements in the making to permit them to build the kind of large facilities they require.

The Soviet merchant fleet has increased tenfold in deadweight tons between 1950 and mid–1970, and has become a significant factor in world trade for the first time. The Soviet goal is to increase the amount of commerce carried in its own bottoms to over 80 percent in the next decade. But whether or not they achieve this goal, they now carry almost 50 percent of their foreign commerce in Soviet bottoms. This is neither efficient nor economical—but it is a propaganda coup for the Soviet system and economy. The Communists believe their ideology spreads with the flag, and nowhere is the flag more obvious than on Russian merchant ships. Thus they have pushed their merchant shipping efforts hard. But now they have reached something close to saturation; to increase their cargoes significantly, they must either suffer major inefficiencies or enter the world market to take on more general world trade. It will be interesting to see the effects of this competition on the maritime nations—particularly on Great Britain and Japan.

The Soviets will certainly continue to expand their fishing fleets around the world; fish is a staple of their diet. Russia has always had a major inland-waters fishing industry of great size, usually composed of small craft. But in the last decade the Russians have gone to sea in large, efficient fishing ships—deep-sea trawlers, whalers, and seiners that number over 4,000 and fish on all the world's major banks.

In a spectacular scientific program, the Soviets have mounted a well-funded oceanographic research effort, probably because they see the oceans as a future major battleground. They have set out to learn as much about operations on and under the oceans as their research funds can buy. Although they are badly trailing United States efforts in most areas of ocean research and engineering, with a large budget and tight organization, they have made satisfactory progress in developing underseas weapons and long strides in oceanography and related sciences.

Although it has moved from a reactionary policy to one of posing as a world naval power, the basis for Soviet naval strategy has not changed appreciably in the last 500 years. It is best summed up by the statement that Nikita Khrushchev made before the Central Committee of the Communist party at a time when naval expansion was being debated in the 1960s: "The U.S.S.R. is a continental power. Those who wish to unleash war against us or use sea power to conquer the U.S.S.R.'s superior land power will be compelled to cross great expanses of water. This is why we are creating a powerful submarine force. . . ."

Although the Russians are moving massively into the ocean, they have not basically changed their defensive strategy. Their naval power goals rely on a large fleet of submarines, primarily as defensive weapons. So much the better if the submarine is the weapon of the future in naval warfare in general; it suits their particular defensive needs. The Russians are realists. Although they recognize that even an SLBM missile-equipped defensive submarine fleet could prove totally ineffective in some future war where the antagonists rely on nuclear exchanges, still they are solving the only problem that they are capable of solving: they are preparing to fight a defensive war. In the event of an all-out nuclear war, they are counting on their missile capabilities and the extensive civil-defense programs that they have pursued over the past few years to ensure their survival. The Soviets do not plan to fight a conventional war of attrition at sea. It would be a form of madness if the Russians felt that they could compete with the United States by building a larger strategically offensive force; a blue-water, high-seas fleet capable of contesting the control of the seas with the United States and her NATO allies. Even the Soviet propagandists who would have us believe that this is a fact seem embarrassed when they rattle the naval saber; our own navy public relations staffs do a much better job on their behalf.

But if the Russian strategy is operating on the principle of this doublethink, it may be dangerous and even self-defeating for them. Nothing would suit the United States more than for the Russians to be stimulated into such a race; it is the dream of

Western naval commanders. This would create a situation where the Soviet Union was expending large portions of its national budget in a race which it could not hope to win, in a technology where she began so far behind that only a limited United States program would be necessary to keep a satisfactory distance in terms of both ships and weapons. If the Russians have taken the bait—as our propagandists would have us believe (and with the support of the Soviets to back them up)—then we have already won the Cold War.

However, if we recall the saber rattling that the Russians have indulged in over the past decade, it has never been with respect to the weapons they are serious about. The Russians do not brag about their defensive submarine fleet or their advances in ASW or their huge programs devoted to the exploration of hydrospace. They may mention their SLBM submarine deterrent, since the world recognizes the threat posed by such massive missile capabilities; but they are more likely to talk of their cruisers, their nuclear surface-propulsion program, their aircraft carriers, and their missile-armed frigates. They speak very softly about their deterrent forces—particularly the ballistic-missile submarine, which is very comforting to them as a dual-purpose strategic system. It serves as a deterrent and at the same time supports their concept of continental warfare, if not the all-out fight for the seas. The SLBM is regarded as superartillery supporting the Red Army, rather than as an offensive weapon designed to play any major part in a contest in naval supremacy. Warships are expendable; the SLBM fleet must remain secure.

In 1968 Soviet Chief of Staff Marshal Zakharov issued a challenge on all fronts: from the NATO forces in the Mediterranean, to the nuclear submarines at sea, to the hydrospace exploration, to the merchant and fishing fleets, to the surface naval forces. This broad challenge has become the rallying cry for Soviet naval propagandists: "The time when Russia could be kept out of the world's oceans is gone forever. The imperialists can no longer have them to themselves. We shall sail all the world's seas—no force on earth can prevent us."

But Soviet declarations are reminiscent of past bombasts. In a dramatic move for a country considered landbound, Russia has often turned to the sea. And always turned back. While showing the results of their surface-fleet construction program, the Russians were devoting the bulk of their technology to the development of weapons and armies to defend their soil. The navy was to support that defensive force, and never to risk itself by contesting foreign supremacy on the high seas. That strategy remains operative today.

Admiral Gorshkov, Commander-in-Chief of the Soviet Navy, has been quoted as saying that with its ocean fleet, Russia can now challenge any enemy on the open seas. Such bold threats are not unusual for Russian military leaders: they may or may not have any foundation in fact, and are often made more in hope and anticipation than reality. But it is significant that the Soviets make such pronouncements. Whether they are reality or wishful projection, they are the Kremlin's grudging acknowledgment that sea power is vital to its plans.

The Soviet Navy is much larger, stronger, and more sophisticated than it has ever been, and its progress in the last five years has been impressive. Soviet planning has emphasized submarine warfare, but has not neglected other areas of the fleet armament: surface-to-surface cruise missiles mounted aboard many classes of ships are one example. However, Russians grossly overstate their strength. Their inactive ships are listed on the fleet roster, while the United States fleet numbers discount the reserve fleet.

The Russians lack the sophisticated weaponry of the United States Navy. Their fleet may be inferior in major capabilities to the European NATO forces using American weapons and with access to U.S. bases. The modern Russian Navy is another example of the Soviet rush to armament in an area in which it probably does not expect to fight a war. The Soviets will match projections—paper weapon with paper weapon—or count actual weapons. But the necessary and infinite labors required to design a first-class operational cruise-missile system are lacking. In this area they trail the United States badly and are failing to close the gap. Their primary emphasis is on submarine-warfare-deterrent capabilities, mine warfare, and the defensive seapower necessary to keep foreign fleets away from their shores. Their naval threats are boasts; they would be quickly and decisively defeated in any war at sea involving their forces matched against those of the United States fleet. Their navy leaders know it; U.S. Navy leaders know it. But the citizens of both countries are presented another view: one which serves the political purposes of both governments.

Based on total tonnage, the Russian Navy today is second in the world after the United States. Its naval manpower is approximately 500,000, compared with the 700,000 of the United States Navy. But the Russians are badly dispersed. To maintain a full protective patrol, the Russian Navy must have at least four fleets and a division of forces between Atlantic and Pacific. The fleets maintained in the Baltic and Black seas lend themselves to easy blockade; those in the Far East are far inferior to our naval strength. And Russia lags badly in supplying and maintaining her forces at sea all around the world.

But the Russians are serious about the protection of their territorial waters. In recent years they have constructed new industries in the more remote areas of Siberia which will serve to support their military installations. These include iron and steel centers, large power stations on the Angara and Yenisei rivers, and missile factories near Vorkuta and on the Ob River and at Tiksi on the Arctic coast. In the absence of adequate rail facilities, the sea routes that supply these areas are of great importance and must be guarded and held secure by naval forces.

The Russians expect to use their navy in conjunction with air power; they believe that Admiral Doenitz and the German Navy lost World War II largely because of their inability to cooperate with the German Air Force. However, the more important interdiction of shipping will come from the cruise-missile-firing submarine; the surface fleet will stay at home.

The Russians are building a blue-water navy, but its intended use is still subject to great speculation. Admiral Gorshkov has stated that the navy is expected to be used in a general war and has certain assigned tasks: Polaris submarines, neutralizing the

United States carrier fleet and as a contributor to the strategic defense. Although the Russians would like to challenge Western maritime supremacy in the sense that they want to prevent the United States from being able to use the high seas as an extension of national territory for the deployment of strategic weapons targeted on Russia, they are realists and will not seek to gain supremacy of the sea in the generally understood sense of the term. For them to embark on such an endeavor would require a complete upheaval of their established economic and military policies; putting them in a contest they could never hope to win.

Are the Russians attempting to wrest control of the sea from the U.S. Navy? The very prospect secretly delights Western military planners who for years have tried to induce the Russians to play "follow me" in the arms race. Their wildest dreams are that the Russians would stray away from missile technology and follow the will-o'-the-wisp of naval superiority—chasing the United States and Great Britain, Japan, Italy, France, and other Western nations in the hope of dominating the oceans of the world. That this seems to be happening is a joy close to delirium for some Cold War strategists in the West. American admirals look grave and cluck their tongues over the Russian bear's putting to sea, but their chief concern is probably to keep from showing their satisfaction at the prospect of a naval arms race. The rubles it will cost Ivan, the facilities it will tie up, the unhappy surprises and disappointments in store for him, make our navy brass fairly shiver in delightful anticipation. The Russians have the budget, the desire. Encourage Ivan to take the plunge—and most certainly drown. Nothing would suit the Pentagon more. Unfortunately, it simply will not happen.

Certainly it is most interesting to observe the growth of the Russian Navy as a sensitive barometer of the strengths and weaknesses of Soviet technology and the current political persuasions, but no responsible Western military observers are seriously concerned because the Soviet fleet is visiting ports and showing the flag around the world—or alarmed that the Russians are building a small number of Kiev-type "pocket" aircraft carriers, or that the

Russians are maintaining a fleet of obsolete, conventionally powered submarines. What does confuse these professionals at arms is the large surface-ship construction and refurbishment programs pursued by both antagonists. Russia and the United States are building larger surface vessels—ignoring the fact that any future conflict between them will certainly employ nuclear weapons and make the larger ships most tempting targets. Cruisers and carriers will be the first to feel the effects of nuclear-tipped missiles.

There will never be a prolonged war at sea between Russia and the Western allies; such a war would have to follow an all-out nuclear exchange. Envisioning a protracted sea war after such a global attack and counterattack is unreasonable—as remote as a general confrontation of the fleets using tactical nuclear weapons without such a situation leading to an exchange of ICBMs, Polaris, and Trident warheads. So it is strange that there is any doubt in the minds of the American and Soviet military planners that a confrontation between the United States and the Soviet Union which involved any attack on major warships would not only result in the use of tactical atomic weapons, but also everything in the East and West arsenals, including ICBMs, IRBMs (Intermediate Range Ballistic Missiles), SLBMs, and whatever else was available at the time.

It is difficult to change public relations policies practiced for thirty years—and as the Pentagon goes, the military press seems to go. But there should be a more reasonable rationale presented to the American people concerning their military preparedness. They should be told the truth. If it is not possible to tell the whole truth, then let it be as much truth as is feasible and consonant with national security. The "Chicken Littles" in the Pentagon and the military press around the world do the military establishment a disservice; our sky is not falling.

The United States does not lag the Soviets in the political, military, or diplomatic areas. Let us not lament about our lack of technological progress or the size of the military establishment or the sophistication of our weapons. Instead, if lamenting is required, there is much to exercise us in our willingness to face difficult decisions; the gradual erosion of our will to win the East-West struggle; the gross inefficiency, waste, and duplicity of the government; and the lack of character, integrity, and ability of the men we elect to represent us. Our strength is great; our resolve is questionable.

Other than the refreshing candor of General Brown, the former Chairman of the Joint Chiefs of Staff, there is little truth or comfort to be had from military public relations sources. It is difficult to find men in government service or the military ranks who will call a spade a spade; no bigger or smaller or blacker or more significant than it really is. And that is all the American people ask—just the facts.

Whether we accept the Soviet goal of world domination or see them as paranoid about their own defense in a hostile world, still we must now recognize that the Russians are dedicated competitors of the United States at sea and will continue to be. There is simply no other way to establish the importance they seek in the world. If they intend to narrow the gap between their economic system and ours, they must go to sea, as hampered as they are by continental boundaries, an army-oriented military tradition, and the lack of adequate bases. The Russians must persevere and pursue a vigorous construction and research program in both maritime and naval operations in order to contest our primacy—so they believe and so we want them to continue to believe. Strangely, we have hit on one area of mutual agreement: an arena where both countries want to compete. And this could bode well for world peace and prosperity if this competition results in the vigorous development of the world's hydrospace as a source of food and minerals, and perhaps a future place of human habitation.

⑥ Sonar: Sensing the Sounds of the Sea

A sound so fine, there's nothing lives,
'Twixt it and silence.

—J. S. KNOWLES

In essence, sonar may be defined as a body of knowledge relating to the nature of acoustic waves in water. Sonar embraces many different technologies and covers the broad spectrum of activities involving operations of systems that are dependent on acoustic energy.

During World War I, submarine detection was accomplished simply by listening underwater with waterproofed telephone receivers, submerging a device designed to operate with air-carried sounds. The success of this primitive sonar was due more to the recurrent loud noise of the target submarine designs than the construction of the telephone. For any underwater transducer to function properly, it must operate with about 60 times the force and $\frac{1}{16}$ the displacement, or velocity, of a transducer handling energy at the same rate in air.

During World War II, British and American scientists brought together several techniques to help them utilize underwater sound for submarine detection. The British called this program *asdic;* the Americans, *sonar.* In concept, it was the extension of work that had gone on since World War I in acoustics and electronic detection.

The essential process on which sonar depends is as old as the laws of acoustics—laws that were well understood at the time

Columbus was investigating the New World. At the end of the fifteenth century, Leonardo Da Vinci made the following entry in his scientific journals: "If you cause your ship to stop, and place the head of a long tube in the water and place the other extremity to your ear, you will hear ships at a great distance from you."

Definitions of a modern sonar system differ only in detail. In the 470 years since Da Vinci wrote, changes have taken place in the "head of the tube" and in the "tube" itself, and in the methods of detecting what is happening at the other extremity; but these improvements are simply refinements of Da Vinci's system. In fact, at the time of Pearl Harbor, United States submarines were listening with "tubes" which differed very little from those described by Da Vinci.

Popular concept has the vast regions of the ocean below the surface represented by ultimate quiet, when actually even the most secluded parts of the ocean are noisy, comparable to the murmurings of a quiet forest. Something is always moving and causing sound, although much of the sound is noise without relevant purpose. There are sounds and noise from natural phenomena, the activity of marine creatures, and the operations of men under water. These sounds may exhibit regular recurrent variations which are identified with a repetitive process or they may be random; ship propellers compared to earth movement.

The presence or absence of any particular signature, whether it be a submarine sound or a whale, is a function of the signal-processing techniques used in conjunction with the detection equipment. The acoustic monitors transmit signals to some form of processing equipment, and it is on the merit of the processing phase that the efficiency of the total surveillance system is measured. Processing equipment must make optimum use of all of the signals it receives related to the submarine, while discriminating against the other related noise fields. The figure of merit for such devices is called a signal-to-noise ratio. There are a number of ways of optimizing this ratio, and the limit of the system is related to its ability to decide whether the signal is a target or a false alarm. A large part of the R&D involved in sonar work is devoted to this detection system. The efficiency of the processing equipment, the ease of use and versatility of the equipment and the subminiaturization of the circuitry in order to make it more rugged and mobile are the areas where the navy concentrates its best technical talent and a large share of its research budget.

There are constant motions in the sea caused by atmospheric and seabed activities, volcanic disruptions, marine animals, ships, and submarines—all of which create what is called the ambient noise level of the oceans. Very large disturbances can be generated by the flow of ocean currents, subterranean turbulence, and pressure differences. Each of these noises creates a disturbance on some part of the acoustic frequency band; volcanic activity creates noise at the lower end of the band, while ships moving in the ocean generate noise in the upper end of the band. Disturbances from different sources usually occur at slightly different band frequencies, so that it is possible to separate the noises and identify them. This noise identification signature is an important consideration in designing long-range acoustic surveillance systems. The detection of any particular body in the ocean—an SLBM submarine, for example—will involve not only receiving the acoustic signal generated by the submarine but also the elimination of all other noise phenomena which might interfere with receiving that signal and the identification of the signature.

Passive surveillance systems depend on the detection and identification of sonar signatures. A moving submarine will have one signature; a tanker proceeding slowly over the surface will have another; a cruiser at high speed will have a third signature; a carrier launching aircraft will have still a different signature. All these signatures are a combination of acoustic effects. They come from the wakes of the ships, their inherent noise, or the complex mixing of several characteristics which may identify one type from another.

The moving submarine will usually have two noise sources: its machinery, and the hydrodynamic noises generated as it moves through the water. Machinery noise is a mechanical oscillation made by the electromechanical equipment aboard a submarine—usually propulsion-related equipment that rotates and may become slightly unbalanced. Turbine blades and gears, reciprocating pumps, and other cavitation noises (sounds of fluids flowing into the closed systems of the submarine) also produce pronounced acoustic impulses. The main component of the hydrodynamic source is the propeller. It generates a continuous sound generally in the higher frequencies, which comes primarily from a cavitation causing air bubbles to form at the tip of the propeller blades. These bubbles eventually collapse with a characteristic hiss. Since this noise is directly related to the maneuvering of the submarine, these sounds are very convenient to categorize. Each propeller has its own beat; its signature not only identifies the target, but often it is effective in measuring target speed.

There is also a hydrodynamic noise caused by flow-induced vibrations along the submarine's surfaces as it runs submerged. This is a minor detection factor, since it is low-level sound difficult to differentiate from ambient noise. But it is continuous so long as the submarine is in motion.

A system limitation in detection is caused by self-noise; that component of sound in the spectrum received by the hydrophone which is generated by the motion of the hydrophone itself in the ocean. This noise must be accurately determined since it will differ for each hydrophone, depending on its mounting. The component of this noise is called flow noise and will be present whenever the hydrophone is moved in any medium. This interference is most limiting at high speeds and is produced by the passage of air on the external shell of the hydrophone. The noise will change, depending on conditions, but it must be known under all conditions to compensate for it in the detection system.

Detection is a twofold problem: first trying to locate a submarine at a maximum range, then closing to sufficient accuracy to enable the weapons available to effect a kill. Most long-range methods involve some system of global surveillance, which includes everything from espionage within a country, to casual sightings by merchant ships and planes, to passive detection by complex computer systems connected to bottom-mounted arrays of hydrophones. One of the difficulties of sonar detection is the relatively slow transmission of sound. Modern high-speed submarines can maneuver and be far away from an ASW-launched weapon if the fix provided is not adjusted for some type of movement. Accurate and continuous reading is possible from dunking sonars— devices that are carried by antisubmarine helicopters and provide a continuous signal by simply following the sound. Because the helicopters are mobile, when conditions are favorable, they can maneuver to extend their listening devices below the thermal layer and pick up a relatively undistorted sound signal. The helicopter can hover close to the ocean surface and move at a speed equal to that of the submarine. The long-range sonar equipment mounted in hull-formed "bubbles" are the heartbeat of the ASW team on destroyers. Variable-depth sonars are similar to the dunking sonar of a helicopter but much larger and more powerful. They are lowered from a ship's stern and measure sounds below the blanketing thermal layers that otherwise hide submarine operations. There are many versions of submarine detection sonars; their design differs principally in size, power, and the method used to place the transducer in a listening position.

There are literally hundreds of ASW contractors developing new and more sophisticated sonar equipment. Think tanks like the Bell Telephone Laboratories, the Rand Corporation, Arthur D. Little, and MIT provide solutions for the problems of overcoming submarine evasion and cover tactics. Detection devices, from laser photographic impressions to satellite monitoring, are evaluated. Any device that will pick up the kind of change in state caused by a submarine is thoroughly researched.

Today acoustics is the basis of both submarine and antisubmarine warfare: the single most significant element upon which all undersea warfare activity depends. When the submarine was first developed, its security lay beneath the surface of the ocean where it would not be seen. Today its security lies in its ability to avoid being heard.

7 Submarines: The Evolution of the Ultimate Weapon

*I would not put so many dollars and so many
people into such a good target. Come to think
of it, I would not put anything on the surface
of the ocean—it's too good a target.*

—EDWARD TELLER, discussing a surface fleet

For a story of what submarines can do, there is no
more stirring saga than the World War II tales of submarines that
sank over a thousand ships in the Pacific and crippled the Japanese
economy. In one series of patrols during a nine-month command of
the U.S.S. *Tang,* Commander Richard Hetherington O'Kane sank
30 ships. The *Tang,* a 300-foot fleet boat, carried a crew of 88 men
and 24 torpedoes.

The career of the *Tang* probably represents the finest hour of
a submarine craft in World War II. The *Tang* had sunk 17 ships
in four patrols, and when she left Pearl Harbor in September 1944
on her fifth patrol, O'Kane expected to improve that score substantially. Skipper O'Kane had served under an outstanding commanding officer, Commander Dudley W. Morton, who performed
such feats of daring that he was a standout even in that group of
extraordinary heroes, the U.S. submarine skippers. When O'Kane
heard that Morton was missing, he vowed to take revenge in the
only way a submariner can: to sink as many enemy ships on the
patrol as his torpedo complement would allow.

The thickest Japanese shipping area was the Taiwan Strait between China and Formosa—filled with Japanese convoys shuttling

back and forth to reinforce the Philippine Island garrisons. Large naval forces were gathering to fight the decisive Battle of Leyte Gulf. Enroute to the convoy lanes, the *Tang* sank two freighters and trailed a formation of a cruiser and two destroyers, but was forced off by gunfire. Two nights before the Battle of Leyte Gulf, O'Kane attacked a formation of three tankers and two transports by running ahead of them and turning broadside to pick them off one at a time. As the convoy approached after dark, the *Tang* sent two torpedoes into the lead tanker, one into the second, and two into the third. The first ship exploded and lit the horizon while the other torpedoes were on their way. The transports saw the submarine in the glare of the flame and turned to ram it. O'Kane was on the bridge and had no time to dive; he stayed alone on the conning tower and maneuvered to escape. But the would-be rammer had concentrated on the submarine to the exclusion of the other ships. When O'Kane maneuvered the submarine out of the way, the ship lunged past and headed for the sister transport, unable to stop. O'Kane sent four torpedoes after them and watched while the two ships collided. A few minutes later, the four torpedoes found their mark—one at a time, at ten-second intervals—converting the transports into a sea of flaming wreckage. The *Tang* had sunk the entire convoy of five ships in less than ten minutes.

The next day, the *Tang* slipped up on another convoy guarded by a destroyer screen, alert to the submarine threat that had destroyed the convoy the day before. O'Kane tracked the convoy until he was sure of its course and makeup, then singled out the two leading transports and a tanker. Slowly, almost casually, the *Tang* took position, fired two torpedoes, waited, fired two more torpedoes, then fired two more. O'Kane watched as all the torpedoes hit. He surfaced and fired three more torpedoes—then began to run from the oncoming destroyers. He fired another torpedo and struck a tanker, and another and struck the tanker again, just as the first pursuing destroyer was running by it. The destroyer was tossed by the explosion and slowed to recover while the *Tang* ran to safety, loading her last two torpedoes in the forward tubes. One transport had been hit but was still afloat, dead in the water. O'Kane conned the submarine to a side opposite where destroyers were searching for his submarine and fired his last two torpedoes.

One went true and hit—but the last torpedo swerved and began to run a tight circle to the left. O'Kane was on the bridge with the deck crew. He realized the emergency and shouted a command to close hatches and maneuvered to try to escape the erratic torpedo. It was no use. He watched the phosphorescent circle in the dark water run toward the submarine. The *Tang* moved away too slowly. Her last torpedo, the twenty-fourth fired, struck aft and destroyed three compartments of the submarine. O'Kane was thrown into the water with the nine members of the crew who were on deck. The *Tang* sank slowly, then with a boil of air from the bow, finally disappeared. O'Kane and the survivors swam to shore; the skipper himself very nearly made it to the mainland before he was picked up by a Japanese destroyer.

The crew that remained aboard the *Tang* went down in 180 feet of water off the Taiwan Straits. After settling on the bottom, Japanese destroyers depth-charged the submarine for hours. Finally the thirty survivors in the forward compartment made preparations for escape to the surface. Amid electrical fires and slow flooding, they managed to open the escape lock, put on their escape lung apparatus, and started equalizing the pressure. Thirteen men went out the air lock before the gasket collapsed, and the seventeen men remaining aboard were lost to the fire and deadly gases. Only five of those who escaped were rescued; and of the fifteen captured, six survivors of the *Tang* sinking did not live through Japanese captivity. But nine did come home, including Commander O'Kane, who received the Congressional Medal of Honor, and, most important, held the record among his contemporaries for the most successful submarine patrol of the Pacific War.

If there is one thing obvious from examining previous predictions concerning the nature of submarine warfare, it is that such predictions are always in error; and judging by wartime experience, understated with respect to the eventual outcome. The most highly qualified naval and scientific authorities—people who spend their

lives in the process of designing and perfecting weapons systems—
tend to be mistaken in priorities, timing, and even weapon impact;
and the politicians trail them badly on all scores. Most naval
thinkers discounted the effect of the submarine before World War
I; in fact, only the Germans and Sir Arthur Conan Doyle seemed
aware of the possibilities at the turn of the century. Next the submarine was thought to have been rendered obsolete by sonar. Then
the submarine carrying hydrogen-bomb-tipped rockets was considered an unworkable arrangement. Next it was predicted that
these weapons would not be effective until well into the next century, and so on.

Perhaps planners have difficulty in keeping up with the technology and changing science because they tend to think in their
own specialties and consequently live in isolation from other technical disciplines. But now warfare involves men and machines,
politics, spheres of influence, timetables, gross national products,
together with maximum threats and countermanding deterrents.
And since it is very difficult to keep this entire picture clearly
enough in focus to know what is happening in any one technology
in the present, let alone predict the future, most professional military men rely on fleet exercises, war games, trials, experiments,
shakedowns, and performance tests to determine what impact a
weapon will have on the several types of warfare. But short of
actual battle conditions, there is danger in relying on such information; historically, it has always led to self-deception—like playing
the war by your own rules and assuming an enemy that acts as
programmed. And such results are always misleading, particularly
when related to warfare under the seas: the dangers have always
been different, the difficulties have always been harder to overcome,
and the casualties have always been more severe.

Realizing the problems inherent in speculation, planners still
must consider the future, and looking into the future, the employment of the submarine is the single most significant naval consideration. All of the old sea-power theories must now adjust to
modern submarine performance. The submarine has major advantages: it is silent, invisible, and undetectable except by special in-

strumentation, and in present operation it is able to go increasingly deeper into its protective environment. All schemes of detection appear to be limited to sound propagation; laser and infrared techniques hold promise, but sonar remains the only method that has provided any real hope of tracking the faster and more silent submarines operating today. As these submarines continue to improve and develop their operations, the antisubmarine forces must constantly alter their tactics. Although acoustic detection technology is pushed to keep pace and the desperate competition accelerates, still the ASW forces fall behind.

The nuclear submarine has proven to be not only a weapons system, but also the primary deterrent to an all-out nuclear war. Should a nuclear war start, the submarine will be the only weapon that can be relied upon to survive the holocaust and continue in effective operation. Consequently, the submarine has become the capital ship of the world's navies in terms of importance and effectiveness; and in the foreseeable future, as the nuclear stalemate between the United States and Soviet Russia continues, it could replace all other naval forces except those of the amphibious and close-naval-support units trained to fight the "brush-fire" wars.

There is a counterargument concerning the deterrent value of the submarine, or any "ultimate weapon." Poison gas and germ warfare were tacitly prohibited by the belligerents in World War II, and the Nazi dictatorship went to its doom without resorting to the use of these superkillers. The argument ran that the consequences of an all-out biological attack would be so suicidal that germs would never be deployed except in retaliation to enemy germ warfare. Similarly, the hydrogen bombing of Washington would certainly lead to the destruction of Moscow and Leningrad. Such devastating actions could not be considered by sane men, even in a state that was losing a major war. Therefore we must maintain our ability to fight conventional wars; it will not be possible for a losing side in war to regain its position by threatening to resort to thermonuclear weapons.

The leader of a German totalitarian state did not choose to use biological-warfare weapons. Although they were available to him, he ,chose to die instead. But who can argue that the world would ever feel safe if such a man should rise again and had at his fingertips the ability to launch an all-out atomic attack if he were thwarted in the use of conventional weapons. Somehow the situation seems different, and the risks even greater.

By and large, submarines have had their own way in World War I and World War II, at least so long as their logistics support lasted. In any future war, they could once again be the scourge of convoys and have the ability to interdict shipping in any area in the world, if the war lasted long enough. But in the age of thermonuclear weapons—there's the rub. The submarine has now clearly replaced the forces commanding the ocean; the battle fleet is a thing of the past, and the carrier is fading fast into the same category. As missiles and rockets become more accurate, the vulnerability of the carrier increases; with the advance of submarine technology that fateful day will come when even the conventional-force supporters cannot justify the cost of new carrier construction. These carrier advocates now hang their argument on a slim consideration: whether the use of tactical nuclear weapons would quickly and inevitably escalate into an all-out nuclear war. The future of not only the aircraft carrier but also most other surface craft rests on this question. But if one or the other side is concerned about the escalation and does not use tactical nuclear weapons, it must be caught in a fatal disadvantage. Continuing to build a surface fleet on the presumption that tactical nuclear weapons in some form will not be used against surface warships would seem most optimistic.

The world in which the submarine operates—the oceans which the superpowers vie to control—is divided into three distinct parts: the surface, above the surface, and below the surface. For military purposes, we may now assume that the surface is controlled by the area above it and below it more than by the vessels that operate on it, a departure from earlier strategies.

There is a tendency to move in two directions in submarine design: either to a small two- or three-man midget submarine or to large submarines capable of carrying cargoes and even larger missile payloads. In the future, the smaller submarines may be capable of carrying small nuclear warheads. The advantages of evading detection and greater maneuverability may make these small boats most effective, particularly in wolf-pack-type operations. Submarines are generally divided into three types: the fleet or attack submarines (SSN), the ballistic-missile submarine (SLBM) or (SSBN), and the conventional or patrol submarine (SS). Each of these submarines has a primary function, and although some weapons are common to all types, they differ in capacity and tactical purpose. The three types of submarine are evolutionary; the SS basic designs led to the SSN types, and a fusion of several technologies—submarine and missile—led to the development of the SSBN. Attack submarines, a class which includes fleet submarines, are the backbone of the Soviet submarine fleet. The Russians now have over 280 submarines in this class, of which at least 70 are nuclear propelled. This number changes, of course, depending on the phaseout of older types and the number of nuclear-propelled types under construction. In total number, NATO forces have 200 attack submarines, of which 67 are nuclear.

The attack submarine has a dual purpose: in blockades, it is capable of commanding the shipping lanes around the world, and it is also the most effective antisubmarine warfare weapon. Future ASW combat will certainly emphasize submarine-submarine duels. Both the United States and Russia are converting their submarine fleets to nuclear power; the cost of maintaining conventional submarines is simply not consistent with their projected performance as either a blockade force or ASW role or attack threat to enemy warships. Conventional submarine numbers are impressive but not meaningful; in any future war, they would be too vulnerable to be effective.

The design of Russian and American attack submarines is similar: they weigh 3,500–4,000 tons and are approximately 290–300 feet long. They are powered by pressurized, water-cooled nuclear reactors that drive steam turbines at submerged speeds of from 25 to 40 knots. The Soviets have shown a preference for arming their submarines with long-range cruise missiles and shorter-range tactical missiles, while the American vessels are generally torpedo armed. Both have a primary mission as antisubmarine-warfare hunter-killer attack ships, although the Russian subs have an important secondary function as carrier killers.

The main weapon of the attack submarine is the 21-inch torpedo. Its most modern version is the United States Navy's Mark 48, a wire-guided design that can home either by active or passive means with a range in excess of 20 miles. NATO forces are still using two older torpedoes, the Mark 8 and the Mark 23. The Mark 23 is a wire-guided passive homing device with a range of approximately 5 miles. These torpedoes are being replaced by the Mark 24, a British design which is comparable to our Mark 48.

The wire-guided torpedo is considered superior to the free-fired torpedo since it provides the optimum in both range and effectiveness. In the Mark 48 design, the wire is paid out from a torpedo whose computer is connected to the firing submarine's central computer and to the torpedo's homing system. Within the effective range of launch, the torpedo accuracy is very high; astonishing by comparison to the submarine torpedoes with which the United States Navy fought in the Pacific during World War II, when early embarrassing and disastrous undetected torpedo misdesign cost the lives of many United States Navy submariners in abortive attacks. These accidents made the Bureau of Weapons extremely sensitive to the operational requirements of torpedoes and other weapons carried aboard submarines. When a submarine goes into the lonely operations of the unsupported patrol, it must be ready with exceptionally reliable weapons—the navy learned that lesson well.

American nuclear attack submarines carry the SUBROC system, an underwater launch missile that maintains a rocket trajectory until it reaches the vicinity of the target, when it releases a depth charge. The charge follows a ballistic trajectory into the water and descends to a predetermined depth—say 1,500–2,000 feet—then explodes. The range of the missile is approximately 25 miles. The depth charge is either conventional high explosive or nuclear. SUBROC can be launched from the submarine's torpedo tubes which allows carrying interchangeable numbers of SUBROC missiles and torpedoes. One of the advantages of the system is that it creates no wake; enemy submarines cannot detect it by sonar since in its final approach it is an air-to-water missile. This missile with a nuclear warhead is probably the most devastating anti-submarine warfare weapon in operational use today.

Most of the nuclear submarines are fitted with the Raytheon design BBQ2 sonar system which employs the BQS6 active sonar with transducers in approximately 15-foot diameter at the bow. There is also a BQR7 passive sonar with hydrophones mounted on the forward side of the hull. While active sonar is ideal for fire-control purposes, it has a much shorter range compared to the passive sonar and also provides the enemy with easy detection. Passive sonars have been improved so that contacts are obtained at relatively long distances, and some improvement has been made in determining bearing with sufficient accuracy to provide continuous inputs to the fire-control computer.

The submarine's fire control is a central computer that receives input from all of the sensors and translates this data to the weapons positioning on potential targets. The operator selects the target and mode of attack, and the computer transmits information to the designated weapon—in effect, taking over the continuing problem solution. Fire-control systems are comparable for the United States and Soviet weapons, although the Soviet weapons are considered less sophisticated and probably much less accurate.

The Soviet anticarrier program concentrated on submarine-launched tactical-missile designs. They developed two types of underwater launched missiles: one with a range of approximately 25 miles and the other with a range of approximately 150 miles. This Soviet Shaddock missile is designed to operate outside of shipboard sonar range; although its initial target plot, particularly if determined by passive sonar or radar relay, is likely to be inaccurate. The missile's terminal homing device requires some midcourse guidance which cannot be effected by the submarine. Usually this is a submarine-aircraft team effort. The Shaddock missile is terminal homing with an infrared device and radio commanded to travel at supersonic speed.

The United States Navy uses a variation of the HARPOON design as a submarine-launched ship-to-ship missile. The priority for developing such a missile has been low; despite the publicity accorded the buildup of the Soviet fleet, in U.S. Navy circles their surface ship capability is discounted, and the weapons at hand are considered more than adequate to attack the Soviet fleets and shipping. However, NATO submarine commanders normally try to attack from well outside a sonar screen, which means relying on the ability of the passive sonar detection systems. Since conventional screening employing destroyers and helicopters is between four and six miles from the main body of the task force or convoy, any range beyond ten miles would probably be satisfactory to ensure covert launching and escape maneuvering by the submarine.

In terms of weapons development, the submarine has become preeminent in a relatively short time—there seems no limitation on its capabilities for the foreseeable future. It need only to continue to master its own environment to become even more powerful. Faster, deeper diving and more maneuverable submarines with improved communications and detection systems will continue to outstrip the antisubmarine forces and open an even wider gap between themselves and their natural enemies.

Russia has built over 350 submarines in the postwar period and the United States over 100—most of them nuclear propelled. Although the antisubmarine-warfare forces of the Allies triumphed over the German U-boats twice in the world wars, the record of the United States submarines against the Japanese was brilliant and stands as an example of the submarine's potential, given logistic support. The initial advantage has always been with the submarine —and until the battle of logistics and supply were lost ashore, the submarine always managed to evade the ASW campaigns.

Regardless of the change of submarine configurations or submarine-warfare tactics, one thing is certain: no surface fleet can ever rule the oceans of the world again. Those nations that are most dependent on the sea for their economic traffic and communication must view the era of the submarine with foreboding, regardless of their own fleets.

Although the submarine has been an effective weapon in two major wars, it is just that: a weapon for major wars. And it has not been successful in its overall battles with antisubmarine-warfare ships and aircraft, although this was due more to the logistical support of the submarine fleets than any superiority of antisubmarine weapons. But now submarines seem to have far outstripped even the most sophisticated means of antisubmarine warfare. They are faster than most surface ships and very effective in evading hovering aircraft. Once almost blind in its own element and relying on faulty navigational devices, the submarine is now sophisticated in both communications and navigation and has solved life-support-systems problems. It is as comfortable in its environment below the sea as the surface craft are in theirs, and sometimes more so. Weather is not a problem; submarines sail the oceans in winter and lie under ice caps. They remain submerged and on station for longer periods of time than their surface vessel counterparts can, and are capable of fighting any foe from a deep submerged position.

All the world powers are building submarines as their primary naval strike force; they are weapons which will give them command of the sea, to some degree. In the United States, Great Britain, and France, the submarine is built as a strategic weapon which can threaten nations whose population centers are far from the ocean. The Soviet Union threatens the United States and may also use its weapons against any of the Western powers—or even Japan or China.

But if missile-carrying submarines are the strike weapon and deterrent for Russia and the United States, they are even more significant for countries like France, Great Britain, and Japan, which require areas for dispersal of their weapons far greater than provided in their own territory. Russia and the United States have the expanses to accommodate ICBM systems; most European countries do not. These powers will disperse their missiles in the ocean and be less vulnerable to the enemy's near misses or hits on protected launch sites within their own borders. They can rely on the devastating effect that even the short-range missiles have if they are placed by submarines within range of critical targets.

In the past it was possible for even small nations to put a navy to sea and to look to providing a defense for its merchant fleet. With the development of the modern submarine, this is no longer possible. The missile-carrying submarines are beyond the technical or financial capability of the great majority of nations in the world; these nations are now left out of the race for domination of the world's oceans.

The difficulty of antisubmarine warfare is one of numbers; it takes many ships and planes and even submarines to attempt to locate and destroy each aggressive submarine. As submarines become more sophisticated, this problem will grow in complexity. There are ocean-surveillance systems and specially designed planes and satellites and mines and many other ASW weapons, but the numbers of these devices needed to adequately guard any country with a major coastline are something all out of proportion to the realities of military budgeting.

The submarine has been traditionally regarded as the prime weapon of the naval underdog—principally because of the success of the German Navy and their policy of unrestricted submarine warfare in both world wars. Eventually antisubmarine-warfare forces and economic strangulation curtailed the activities of the Germans, including their submarine fleet, and gave the Allied powers complete command of the sea. But it is doubtful that this will happen ever again; in future wars—even in Cold War action —there will be great areas of the world's waters which are in effect closed, interdicted by submarine and subsurface weapons.

Probably dating back to dim antiquity, the admirals have been essentially misguided, basically misinformed, and tactically unready to fight the next war. Recognizing these potential errors, it is still necessary to project a global-war scenario for the war at sea. But, based on historic precedent, we must recognize that doing so involves the possibility of being grossly misinformed.

Russian and American naval planners are strongly biased in the same way. Naval dogmas and tactics are accepted in essentially the same form by both superpowers, and the results of their programs tend to follow similar patterns: the structure of their analysis determines the results of their actions, which in turn determine the basis of their predictions.

For the time being, we are restricted to the thinking upon which present weapons systems are based. This concept divides all military activity into roughly three categories: the limited war, the general war, and the nuclear war. These are shadowy classifications with considerable significant overlapping; but these divisions hold up well enough to relate them to the war at sea where, contrary to both technological advances and historic precedents, we find naval planners preparing for a World War II–model general war, with slight variations. Just as there is no word for tiger in most Malaysian languages, because of horrible experiences with and dread of the animal, similarly there may be no word for all-out nuclear naval warfare in the lexicon of Pentagon tactical and strategic planners. The mention of nuclear warfare seems to raise the prospect of simpler threats closer to hand. So, as the Malaysians choose to discuss things other than tiger raids, military thinkers choose to design future wars around the comfortable pattern of the past. Nuclear-tipped cruise missiles taking out carriers and atomic-depth charges sinking SLBM submarines are messy considerations that pose problems with no neat solutions. Like tigers.

The recent flare-ups in the Cold War—the hot spots in Korea and Vietnam—were in no sense naval wars. They were not even worthy to be studied by the strategic planner as models of future conflicts. Riverine actions, amphibious assaults, blockades, and mining operations are routine tactical matters. The only significant factor in either the Korean or Vietnamese action was the use of the aircraft carrier, and given a situation where carriers were not available, the air force could probably have found ways of implementing the bombing, reconnaissance, and air-control missions. There has never been a test of naval strength between the United States and any other power since the Japanese war in the Pacific. Instead we have paper chases, data exchanges, and publicity standoffs. The threat of blockade on the high seas in the Cuban missile crisis sent the Russian shipping with its naval escorts back to home ports as soon as they could determine that the blockading ships meant serious business. And except for the nose thumbing and submarine trailing and a few contests of "chicken" between cruisers at 20 knots, the Cuban "confrontation" was the major naval event of the Cold War.

The present scenarios of general war, nonnuclear class, developed by U.S. Navy planners has Russian submarines thrown into the breach essentially as the Nazi submarines operated in World War II, to harass shipping lanes on a worldwide basis. This leads to a war of attrition between the submarine- and antisubmarine-warfare forces. Such a concept is clearly at odds with the realities of an all-out war at sea in which nuclear weapons would certainly be involved. The Russian argument that dooms the carrier to the role of a floating mortuary in wartime also dooms the conventional submarine as the easy prey of sophisticated ASW forces free to use any tactical nuclear weapons in their arsenal. Most of the United States carrier fleet and Russian submarine fleet would be dispatched quickly. Then strategic considerations become confused, and conventional tactics will go by the board.

The Russian submarine forces come to their present numbers and configurations almost as a holdover from Russia's post–World War II policies, when they faced future maritime enemies. At a time when Russia was able to react quickly, when there was little concern with a rising standard of living and more relaxed political leadership, plans were laid for a large conventional submarine fleet to prevent potential invasion. The inertia of this massive program has simply continued it to the present almost without change. This policy has left the Soviets in about the same position as the large carrier has left the United States; they have a magnificent fleet of obsolete submarines that look imposing in the paper calculations and are seen as formidable weapons to the military planners who are fighting the last war again. But actually, these submarines constitute a force which is unlikely to ever be used successfully in any war involving the United States fleet. Since now the Soviets are too far behind to catch up with the United States SLBM program or ASW technologies in the foreseeable future, their strategy must be to limit submarine and ASW progress at the SALT conference table.

The Russian Navy has very limited access to bases satisfactory for submarine operation. The difficulty of their transit to the open ocean would make a major submarine campaign totally ineffective in wartime—even with the large number of submarines involved. Although Pentagon briefings may set up the Russian Navy as a bogeyman of the largest proportions, most informed naval observers seriously doubt that the Russian fleet, and particularly the submarine force, is capable of extended operations at any distance from its home bases. The Russian Navy lacks logistics support forces for extended operations and forward bases, and this, more than any other deficiency, limits their sea-control effectiveness. The Russian Navy was established as an expanded coastal defensive unit and has grown out of this philosophy; pursuing a global sea-power policy will require the Russians to devote a large part of their naval budget to the nonromantic, utilitarian activities involved in the buildup of a logistics force capable of distant replenishment and base construction and fleet support. There is very little evidence that this kind of buildup is going on. The Russians prefer to fight a paper war with capabilities represented by large numbers of ships and submarines, the kind that count heavily in data tabulations and, standing without support, ignore the factors of obsolescence or functionality.

In addition to logistics support, there is the matter of training. By any measure, the average skill and experience and performance level of the Russian sailors is substantially below that of the United States forces, or even the NATO forces. Training has always been a serious limitation in the Russian military, and particularly in the Red Army–dominated navy. This is not a factor that shows up in the tabulation of naval strength, but it is as significant as ship numbers, and very nearly as significant as logistics capabilities.

Perhaps the most compelling reason for maintaining large conventional naval forces is the continuing hope that some technological breakthrough just over the horizon will strike a balance once more between the capabilities of submarines and underseas weapons and those of surface and air weapons. If this were to happen—if some new ASW weapon were developed and the problem of detection, location, and identification of nuclear-powered sub-

marines simplified—it would restore the carrier and the antisubmarine-warfare task force and the satellite-detection concepts to
their once-favored roles.

It would be much more viable to consider the buildup of a
balanced fleet. But this has not happened. The fast, quiet, deep-
diving submarines, equipped with nuclear weapons containing their
own long-range detection devices and enjoying the huge reaches
of the seas in which to operate, seem to be cast in the role of the
ultimate weapon. There have not been any major breakthroughs in
antisubmarine warfare since World War II which would create the
kind of parity that large-fleet planners had hoped for. And the
future prospects for such weapons are very remote. Thus, now the
pursuit of major oceanographic programs, submarine building,
and new technology developments may require the laying aside of
the surface-fleet-building programs. These are difficult decisions for
naval planners, particularly for those whose careers are involved
with surface fleets and naval aviation.

Navy men do not make such transitions quickly; they will bite
the bullet and suffer as long as possible before scrapping their most
cherished concepts. They will support a Trident program and give
priority to super-ASW-detection systems like CAESAR, but they
will also fight the reduction in surface forces so long as there is any
hope that somehow the carrier can hold its own against the threat
of nuclear-tipped missiles and the destroyer can retain its ASW
function.

8 Oceanography: The Efforts to Chart the Abyss

The Ocean: A body of water occupying about two-thirds of a world made for man—who has no gills.

—AMBROSE BIERCE

Over the past two decades, strides in oceanography and ocean engineering have gone hand in hand with advances in a wide range of scientific disciplines derived from modern technology; particularly the concepts of collecting, organizing, interpolating, processing, and classifying a large body of data. The collection of environmental data—temperature, salinity, ocean currents, radiation—is now vital to the accurate prediction of the world's weather, and particularly the surface and subsurface conditions of the ocean. To accumulate all this data, scientists are increasingly using new sensors and platforms. The aircraft and helicopter have become important data links—aircraft of opportunity (aircraft that accept the additional responsibility of monitoring and surveillance), are now used as frequently as ships of opportunity have been in the past. Over-ocean commercial flights carrying instrumentation for measuring atmospheric and meterological data and taking photographs explore millions of miles each week.

The underwater collection of data which is directly related to the operational capability of submarines uses all kinds of submersibles. Research submersibles offer greater capability; they place the scientists into the ocean for direct observation and contain many sophisticated instruments.

Knowledge of oceanography and related sciences is necessary to any count~y that aspires to maritime supremacy. Its scientists must know the environment in which their merchant ships and naval forces will operate. And as the navies become submarine oriented, hydrospace budgets increase and more basic and applied ocean research is funded by the major sea powers each year. The oceans hold the key to commerce, food supplies, weather forecasting, ore mining, petroleum, and navigation; increasing information about the oceans brings greater maritime wealth. Because naval success depends on such information, science is developing and expanding operating techniques necessary for survival below the surface and down to the depths of the oceans. The interrelated disciplines involved are becoming more complex and require ever more cooperative activities. The nation with the most knowledge of the seas is the most likely to control them; the Cold War is increasingly developing a technology race in the oceans at least as intense as that in space.

The Soviets have only recently been pushed into a full understanding of the vast potential of the ocean. Initially, their moves were not a projection of national power, but rather economic: to facilitate obtaining food for their enormous population and for world trade, as their economy became more developed. But Russia has no maritime background: the Soviets must fund a massive program to overtake the United States. This oceanographic priority has required that their scientific research be as dedicated, well funded, and as diligently pursued as it has been in missile development and space exploration. The United States has a substantial lead on the rest of the world in oceanography and, short of some great national indifference or depression, should maintain its present level of superiority. But the Russians must contest this condition or abandon their national goals.

Oceanography is a very old science and has been pursued by both the United States and the Soviet Union for hundreds of years. However, the push into the seas—the broad foundation of research which has solved so many mysteries and developed so many opportunities—has come about only in the last half century, and most of the important work has been done in the last twenty years. When there is a military need or economic benefit, new technologies flourish. As the nations become interested, funding becomes available. Expansion of the scientific horizon is a direct result.

When I was at the United States Naval Academy in the early 1950s, we were given instruction in oceanography, as well as navigation and exploration. But the Academy was one of very few such institutions in the world. Beyond the study of marine biology, there were only a dozen educational facilities in the United States that spent any substantial time on the application of technology to ocean problems. The Scripps Institute at La Jolla, California and the Woods Hole Oceanographic Institute at Woods Hole, Massachusetts were the pioneers in marine engineering, naval architecture, and oceanography. Now there are thousands of colleges and universities all over the world offering courses in marine sciences and engineering, the majority of them awarding graduate degrees in one of the disciplines. Many of the students are working under direct government grants on major investigation programs in the field of military sciences.

Hydrospace-related activities fit into a number of neat categories, most of them involved with one or another of the problems of security, economy, or the ability of the nation to increase its food and raw-materials supply. Generally, the most important areas of study include weather, transportation, aquaculture, mining, medical applications, fishing, desalination, and power.

The sea-air interface is a giant worldwide phenomenon that produces weather, and any global understanding of the weather must begin at this point. Over the years, weather prediction has become more sophisticated, based on a study of these sea-air and sea-land interfaces. Accurate weather prediction has become significant to the economic welfare and development of many nations. Weather bureaus are now able to predict hurricane and tidal waves. They also provide sophisticated information which serves as a guide for planes and ships—and, of course, submarines.

Fishing has become a major industry in the world's hunt for new food sources; farming the sea has become more science than chance. The knowledge required by fishermen is much the same as that required by navies operating submersibles or involved in anti-submarine warfare activities. The temperature gradients, sea states, and sea-bottom conditions are of as much interest to the Bureau of Fisheries as they are to the navy operational commands. The Russian and Japanese have outstripped the United States in taking food products from the sea; as the leader in ocean sciences, the United States is shamefully lacking in application of this knowledge. The fishing fleets of the United States should be the largest and most technically advanced in the world; the gathering of fish, food supplements, and agar are increasingly important in a world requiring more food and medicines. With a shade more enterprise and some incentive from the government, the United States could lead the world in fish production, particularly since the most lucrative market is in this country.

Related to fishing is aquaculture—the science of farming the sea. This technology requires controlled environments and the research of the characteristics of many species in order to properly supply their environmental requirements. Trout and oyster farming are already profitable and widespread; if properly treated and maintained, the yield per sea acre could be much higher than the most fertile land in the world. We already have the technology to begin widespread lobster and shellfish production in offshore areas; to succeed, we need only skill and investment.

Taking treasure from the sea is a very old occupation, but the science of mining the seas is relatively new. Still, already its applications are many and profitable; mining the seabeds for petroleum, sulfur, gold, tin, and other minerals is now economically attractive. A large, profitable dredging industry which recovers these diverse minerals from the ocean bottom has sprung from the experimentation and engineering of the oil companies that have learned to tap the large offshore oil reserves. It is now possible to recover manganese, cobalt, copper, nickel, and other essential metals from the ocean bottom, where limitless quantities of nodules and ores are available. The economy of many countries will be influenced by their ability to mine the oceans.

There are several commercial methods of removing minerals from seawater itself. Many metals can be distilled and filtered, just as salt has been for thousands of years. Since there are millions of tons of minerals dissolved in seawater, the development of a technology for their removal parallels the research directed at producing a relatively inexpensive method for desalinating seawater on a large scale. Fresh water can increase agriculture dramatically; the economic and social impact of a limitless world supply of fresh water staggers the imagination.

Medical research depends on new sources of biological agents for different approaches to problems that have not responded to other treatment. Drugs from the sea are now produced in large quantities, and research is rapidly developing more. There have been recent experiments using sea materials to cure certain types of cancer and heart disease, as well as hundreds of other ailments.

The world's energy supply of fossil fuels dwindles while the research necessary to develop power from the sea has barely started. Tidal forces, temperature gradients, and pressure-differential research may result in larger and more economical energy sources than the petroleum and natural gases that are now produced offshore.

With so much at stake, it is remarkable that in some areas of the development of the seas we occasionally lag behind the Soviets. Falling permanently behind would be far more serious than any temporary missile gap or periscope count of submarines. The implications of bringing in major new petroleum fields at sea or discovering an inexpensive method of harnessing the energy from ocean-temperature gradients would be significant beyond economic measure. The Russians realize this, and although their attempt to gain sea power in scientific fields is peaceful, still, the technical race is on.

⑨ Antisubmarine Warfare: Weapons and Tactics

In World War II ASW was confined to the escort ring of ships around convoys and task forces. Today, it takes in entire ocean basins. Tactical ASW {the strategy aimed at spotting the attack submarines} takes in a 200-mile radius at the very minimum. If we can't detect, track and localize submarines within several hundred miles of the fleet, our first indication that one is out there will be a missile coming at us several feet above the surface. No one part of the ASW system can handle it alone; it takes a combination of all of them, and it probably always will. Of the three fundamentals— detecting, localizing and killing, the toughest is detecting.

—VICE-ADMIRAL HAROLD E. SHEAR, U.S.N.
Head of Navy Office of the Director
of Antisubmarine Warfare

The U.S. Navy continually researches radically new concepts in antisubmarine warfare, but into the 1980 time-frame, the tactics proposed involve the same mix of ships, helicopters, patrol planes, and attack submarines as it is using today; guided and controlled by the same moored, suspended, and towed active and passive surveillance systems operated by personnel with the same level experience and types of training. The land-based four-engine prop P–3C Orion and the S–3A Viking carrier-based jet will continue to take the brunt of search operations, while the LAMPS (helicopter sonar surveillance system) operating from the fantails of destroyers and frigates will give the hunter-killer task force the ability to spot-fix-track and prepare to kill. In effect, this is the same ASW tactical mosaic developed shortly after World War II—with updating and technological advances incorporated, but no radical changes in organization or purpose.

SOSUS (Sound Surveillance System) and Project CAESAR will continue to be the backbone of long-range sonar surveillance. Within the next two years, this network of hydrophones and shore stations around the world will be augmented with SASS (Suspended Array Surveillance System) to improve reception by taking CAESAR hydrophones off the sea bottom and suspending them from hydrophone towers anchored to the bottom and cabled to the shore computer processors. There are performance advantages moving long-range surveillance systems off the bottom, but also some disadvantages in terms of the difficulty of installation and problems in cabling to shore stations. The SASS system will operate in depths below 15,000 feet.

The TASS (Towed Array Surveillance System) will be used as a mobile backup for both CAESAR and SASS. TASS is composed of sonar installed on submarines, destroyers, and frigates. TASS closes most of the Atlantic and Pacific gaps that CAESAR has not been able to monitor. The system has the advantage of being mobile, so that it can operate in the ocean shadow areas, which change from time to time.

To be effective, the SOSUS/SASS/TASS system must operate in real time (time independent of delays caused by the transitional processing of information), feeding an ASW command and control system that will coordinate all ASW communications and vector and coordinate all ASW weapons in an ocean theater, while presenting a kaleidoscopic, wide-ranging view of friendly and enemy forces.

Defense Advanced Research Projects Agency (ARPA) is the prime Pentagon think tank involved in advanced ASW concepts; it must place its seal of approval on any new system concept. The agency operates in concert with the Naval Electronics Systems Command (NAVELEX), where SOSUS is controlled and SASS is being developed. Since SASS will be an extension of the SOSUS technology, much as Trident is an extension of Polaris, there is no extraordinary hardware design breakthrough required. Cable techniques—particularly the installation of underseas cable—hydrophone elements, and the associated computer hardware and software are predicted in terms of CAESAR performance. Only the installation of the SASS presents a major problem, but only as a matter of scale.

Long-range planners look to new methods of quick installation for sonar systems: air-transportable designs which may be dropped to self-moor and transmit via satellite, or be installed by submarines and then covertly cabled to shore. There are designs in which an air-dropped system trails a cable which is later picked up and monitored by a submarine; the first-stage data processing is performed aboard the submarine before the information is relayed to the shore-based R&D projects.

ARPA is a strong force in the government: a combination of military scientists and engineers who coordinate military R&D prospects and theoretical scientists in many locations, from think tanks like Rand, to industrial laboratories like Arthur D. Little, to universities like MIT, including the advanced-research groups within each military service. ARPA spends over $250 million each year in non-covert funds and devotes approximately 10 percent of its budget to ASW.

Under the direction of ARPA, a broad base of civilian and military research is conducted. ARPA reports to the Directorate of Defense Research and Engineering in the Pentagon, an organization with the mission of maintaining technological superiority for the United States military over the Soviet Union and/or any other country in the world. Currently, the DDR&E major problems relate to strategic deterrents, and on this basis ARPA has become deeply involved in the development of sea-launched missiles. The agency must work both sides of the street; in two independent efforts, it supports the development of the SLBM fleet and also its destruction by ASW weapons. ARPA often has difficulty coordinating its huge military, industrial, and university efforts throughout the country, and entire programs are frequently subcontracted to industrial think tanks. But by and large, the ARPA network is the most effective, far-reaching, and well-funded scientific organization in the world. One wonders if an ARPA drive might not be capable of finding a cure for cancer or the common cold if so directed by the Commander-in-Chief, so substantial are its technical assets.

In submarine and antisubmarine warfare, the most important organizations are the United States Navy laboratories, the United States Navy Underseas Center (NUC) in San Diego, and the Naval Underwater Systems Center (NUSC) at Newport, Rhode Island. NUC works closely with the navy R&D contractors involved in long-range surveillance programs such as SOSUS and SASS and is also charged with the responsibility for support of the Pacific Fleet in ASW systems. NUSC has a similar mission, but concentrates more in the field of submarine communications and underwater-range technology. NUSC provides ASW support for the Atlantic Fleet. There is substantial cross-pollination between these two facilities, as there is between the Woods Hole Oceanographic Institute at Woods Hole, Massachusetts and the Scripps Institute of Oceanography at La Jolla, California—the two non-military ocean-research centers. In basic research, the Naval Research Laboratory (NRL) in Washington, D.C. undertakes the most sophisticated studies in acoustics and the physics of sound in the sea. NRL also studies physical oceanography, marine geophysics, ocean biology, and a number of other areas related to submarine warfare, to provide a foundation for ARPA's overall program.

The National Science Foundation cooperates with all of the research activities and particularly the Office of Naval Research. Typical joint projects involve the coordination of information in a computer and communications systems, the examination of weather and tide patterns, and the support of deep-ocean drilling. An NSF-sponsored research effort—Mid Ocean Dynamics Experiment (MODE I)—was a breakthrough in providing a comprehensive picture of water temperature, currents, and the effect of weather on the surface and subsurface of the ocean.

The AUTEC range (Atlantic Underseas Test and Evaluation Center) is the chief ocean laboratory for the U.S. Navy; the BARSTUR (Barking Sands Tactical Underwater Range) range on Kauai in the Hawaiian Islands performs a similar function in the Pacific, and smaller ranges allow test and calibration of submarines and weapons in the ocean environment in several locations from Keyport, Washington to facilities in the Azores. Basically, the concept involves a field of hydrophones installed over many square miles of ocean bottom which tests submarines, torpedoes, mines, sonobuoys, and other subsea weapons. AUTEC is located off Andros Island in the Bahamas, a 15- by 100-mile section running to a mile in depth in the underwater trenches. The range is too small for the big jobs and too big for the small jobs, according to some of the U.S. and NATO skippers who use it regularly; but for all of its installation compromise, it is probably the most effective underseas test facility in the world. The story of the tradeoffs, compromises, and international politicking that goes into the design of an AUTEC range is a thrilling and controversial story—a microcosm of achievements and avoidable failures, successes and gross errors; the amazing technical breakthroughs and operational disasters that are involved in weapons-system development in the hostile ocean environment.

Laboratories doing RDT&E work for the military have the problem of coordinating the massive amount of information generated by the scientists over ever shorter periods of time. The R&D community is involved in a galloping technological race, and breakthroughs occur with amazing frequency. The emphasis in certain fields of immediate interest sometimes threatens to unbalance the program as a whole, and ARPA has great difficulty in holding a firm control over the direction and budget for such preferred programs. Nowhere is this more evident than in the field of laser technology, a new field which is being carefully studied by both submarine and ASW weapons designers. Accurately directed high-energy laser beams are effective in many present applications, from range finding, to precision target selecting, to missile steering, to the death-ray type of direct destruction. The U.S. Navy is interested in rapidly applying this technology; the guidance of torpedoes and mobile mines is of particular interest. In surveillance, for example, the laser could solve the frequency-limitations problem. A submarine could implant an acoustic device and then lie in the vicinity to act as a first-stage processor, signaling to a satellite by laser in a covert, real-time communications system which would transmit an incredible amount of information, since the laser extends presence communications frequencies by at least an order of magnitude.

The advent of the SQS–26 shipboard sonar and the introduction of the 17,000-ton Spruance frigates which will be capable of carrying helicopters and perhaps VTOL aircraft is an attempt to provide fleet protection against the threat of attack submarines which mount cruise missiles. Ocean Escorts (DE) of the Knox class are another option. Smaller and more versatile than destroyers, these ships will carry the SQS–26 sonar as well as ASROC (Antisubmarine rocket weapon) launchers and a Dash helicopter and will mount the Sea Sparrow antiaircraft missile launcher.

Hunter-killer submarines are unquestionably the most deadly weapons in the ASW arsenal. To operate effectively against quiet, deep-diving SLBM submarines, it is necessary to be at home in the same medium; to be able to avoid the sound aberrations and sonar-range limitations of surface operation and take advantage of the ocean inversion layers and the seasonal changes in the thermocline. Hunter-killer submarines eliminate the shadow zones by entering them, just as their targets are able to do. More sophisticated weapons are available to the hunter-killer submarines than the aircraft or surface ships can mount. The deep-diving nuclear-propelled submarine has an advantage over surface ships, since an increase in speed at great depths will decrease cavitation noises and make the hunter-killer submarine quieter than a submarine close to the surface. The hunter-killer lurks below its target in the same tactic employed by interceptor pilots stalking the approaching bombers from a higher altitude.

The United States has in operation approximately 60 hunter-killer (SSN) submarines, principally the Permit and Sturgeon class, and 6 of these submarines are normally under construction at any time. The Los Angeles, a larger class at 69,000 tons, can travel at more than 40 knots submerged and has a depth capability greater than 2,000 feet. The navy has plans to build over 40 of this large class and is designing to combine size with more quiet operation. ASW planners budget for a fleet of over 100 of these new SSNs some time in the mid-1980s, with a speed greater than 45 knots submerged and a depth capability greater than 2,500 feet.

Deciding how the ASW forces might be used in combat by the United States, Russia and other nations is difficult. In order to accept presently projected operations, we have to depart from logic—or to pursue logic, we have to make some rather extraordinary assumptions. First of all, consider that the ASW forces of most navies have been designed to prevent hostile submarines from using the oceans to the detriment of the nation's security in time of war. This involves patrolling the coastlines, protecting merchant vessels engaged in maritime traffic, protecting surface vessels engaged in naval operations, protecting naval supply operations, and a number of related tasks—essentially the same kinds of activity that were pursued in both world wars, the only conflicts in which the submarine played any significant part. During peacetime or limited conflict—Korea and Vietnam, for example—ASW operations are confined to training, monitoring, testing, intelligence gathering, designing equipment, and building systems and platforms. In effect, since World War II, the billions invested in ASW by both superpowers have produced weapons that have never been involved in any situation even resembling actual combat. While the rest of the U.S. Navy fights, the ASW and submarine forces train and shine brightwork.

In wartime operations, the Soviet Union would assume the role Germany played in both wars; that of the submarine aggressor. Conversely, the United States would be cast in the classic role of defender of the sea lanes—the role that the United States and Great Britain found themselves in during both wars. However, neither role really fits or squares with reality unless we accept the next war as a conventional, protracted struggle between the United States and the Soviet Union—certainly a questionable assumption. But given this condition, where do the antagonists fight without escalating the war into a global conflict? If we look at any theater— Europe, Asia, Africa—at no point do the two forces oppose each other directly. Rather, the Soviet Union sits behind its borders, and the United States creates a trip-wire type of containment policy. Any expansion by the Russians into other areas would initiate the use of the tactical nuclear weapons the United States has introduced at key points around the world. If the war escalates by trip-wire stages, the use of tactical nuclear weapons would certainly provoke a counterattack, and such a war would quickly escalate into a hydrogen-bomb holocaust.

Then where does that leave us with respect to the ASW forces? The Soviets seem to have accepted this theory; their submarine and ASW forces are primarily designed around such a nuclear confrontation. Their two prime ASW tasks are to provide a counter for the United States Polaris and Trident fleets, and to defend their own SLBM submarines against attack. They are allowing their large conventional submarine force to rust in obsolescence and do not seem to be enchanted by the numbers of submarines on their active roles. They are building hunter-killer submarines to support Soviet surface units and missile-carrying submarines. The Soviet admirals do not seem to be concerned with blockade or the role of aggressor against merchant shipping. They see no clash of fleets in a total nuclear war context—only the exchange of thermonuclear warheads.

On the other hand, while the Russians plan for nuclear war at sea, the United States still appears to be concentrating its ASW program in the traditional areas: keeping the sea lanes open, assuring the safe movement of large expeditionary forces, and protecting the surface fleet. But how much of this protection will go on for any prolonged period in a war that quickly escalates to nuclear weapons? Certainly not enough to justify the massive ASW budget the navy requests each year based on a commitment to a variety of responsibilities ranging from carrier protection to the surveillance of the Soviet SLBM fleet.

Basically, there are two types of operation that can be employed by an ASW force:

(a) *Area Defense* involves denying access to large portions of the ocean to the enemy's submarines. This is an offensive operation which attempts to secure large sea areas against submarine activity by attacking all submarines which try to enter this area, and is accomplished by patrols of land-based aircraft, roving hunter-killer submarines, ocean surveillance by fixed arrays and, in general, a combination of ASW forces.

(b) *Point Defense* protects a particular point in the ocean— one occupied by a convoy or a task force or even a single large ship, such as an aircraft carrier. This is accomplished by organizing a task group and employing carrier-based and fixed-wing aircraft and helicopters to operate in conjunction with destroyers, frigates, and perhaps hunter-killer submarines.

Ideally, to have effective ASW control of the ocean, a navy should be prepared to employ both area and point defense, and the United States presently does have extensive capabilities in both areas. Air and naval patrols regularly cover the Greenland, Iceland, and Scotland passages in the North Atlantic in an area-defense approach to deny Soviet submarines easy access to the Atlantic Ocean. These tactics are very similar to those used against the Germans in the Northern Atlantic in World War II. Thus, in time of war, the North Atlantic would probably be secured very quickly. There are plans to seal off large areas of the North Atlantic with ASW mine fields and to monitor these mine fields with land-based patrol aircraft. The Captor mine and the giant surveillance arrays have been specifically designed for that purpose. In addition, wide-area surveillance is conducted on a regular basis. The CAESAR system and SSN hunter-killer submarines are combined in an area defense which monitors the activities of most of the Soviet SLBM submarines around the world. Such monitoring is an offensive weapon of the first order, since the intelligence gathered and the operations experience acquired adds to the remarkable tactical flexibility of this ASW program.

Point defense against submarines, particularly those carrying cruise missiles, must employ ASW platforms which can reach out far enough to prevent the submarines from bringing their weapons within an effective range. Helicopters based on carriers or destroyers are used, as well as carrier-based ASW aircraft, surface ships, and hunter-killer submarines. When the Surface Effect Ship (SES) fleet is operational, it may prove the most effective point defense weapon in the navy's arsenal. Unlike area defense, a point defense that is to be effective must remain defensive: not to defend a point as much as to defend a corridor and clear a wide area of ocean around the convoys which will allow them to proceed to their destination. ASW aircraft provide long-range surveillance, the helicopters short-range screen capabilities, the SSNs long-range acoustic detection, and destroyers wide-station screening. All of these ASW platforms carry offensive weapons and are capable of search-and-destroy missions.

The United States Navy employs the Mark 46 and 48 torpedoes as its primary ASW kill weapons. The Mark 46 is a lightweight twelve-inch-diameter active acoustic homing torpedo that has been tried and tested for many years and is a highly dependable weapon. It may be used from either aircraft or surface ships. The Mark 48 is a twenty-one-inch active/passive acoustic homing torpedo used by surface vessels. It has the advantage of being wire guided, with a pinpoint accuracy. It has a substantially longer range than the Mark 46 and is less vulnerable to countermeasures.

A peacetime ASW program bears little resemblance to wartime operations. In wartime, once located, the submarine is tracked until it is destroyed. In peacetime, the enemy's submarines—and particularly its SLBM carriers—require constant tracking. This tracking or trailing of submarines is more difficult than wartime search-and-destroy tactics; it is an arduous, continuing employment of sophisticated sonar systems and fleet operational forces. But it is probably the only effective peacetime method of antisubmarine warfare available to either the Soviet Union or the United States at this time.

There are four types of tracking: passive acoustic tracking by submarines, active acoustic tracking by submarines, active tracking by surface ships, and active tracking by aircraft. All of these forms are woven into conventional ASW tactics. Except for the improvement in technology and platforms, these methods have not changed from those developed for wide tactical employment in World War II. However, if the nature of the next major war will be an all-out nuclear conflict between the United States and Russia, then the ability to track submarines after their detection will be a trivial capability. The only submarines worth killing will be the enemy SLBM launchers, and then only on a first-strike basis. Therefore, tracking is an important peacetime tactic, but certainly not worth planning for the massive ASW effort a wartime program would require.

There are two families of tracking vehicles being developed which may be effective against even SLBM submarines. These trackers would be rigged to destroy the tracked submarine if it should attempt to use force against the tracker. In one design, the vehicle is an attack submarine; in another, it is a Surface Effect Ship. These trackers would require very little in the way of armament—only tracking equipment and destructive weapons. Their designs would emphasize speed and endurance, and there would be no need for the kind of quiet, efficient operation now required in the hunter-killer surface ships and submarines. Such a tracking system has no use in wartime, and as such becomes a weapon which is valuable to the extent that the Cold War is escalated to the point of actual conflict. In wartime, the Surface Effect Ship might have an ASW role in a long war fought with conventional weapons, but such a war of attrition must seem most unlikely even to the staunchest traditionalists in the Pentagon.

Based on President Carter's recent decision to support an extended cruise missile capability in lieu of building the Air Force B–1 bomber, the submarine fleet is rethinking its role. The cruise missile is an air-breathing, short-range missile that promises to be the submarine's most effective antiship weapon. And now in design is a pilotless drone aircraft which could be launched from submarines, a kind of Mach II robot that flies at twice the speed of sound and assumes the proportions of a true aircraft with a mission ranging from kamikaze bomb carrier to aerial dogfighter. Cruise missiles will become larger and more sophisticated, and drones will provide a new dimension in submarine defense against attacking ships and aircraft.

On August 15, 1945, in one of the last sea actions of World War II, Commander Kossler, commanding officer of the submarine *Cavalla*, was navigating on a lifeguard station off the coast of Japan outside of Tokyo Bay. At noon he received the word in a dispatch from Admiral Nimitz that Emperor Hirohito accepted the surrender terms proposed by the Allies. The message read:

CEASE OFFENSIVE OPERATIONS AGAINST JAPANESE FORCES. CONTINUE SEARCH AND PATROLS. MAINTAIN DEFENSIVE AND INTERNAL SECURITY MEASURES AT HIGHEST LEVELS AND BEWARE OF TREACHERY OR LAST-MOMENT ATTACKS BY ENEMY FORCES OR INDIVIDUALS.

The *Cavalla* remained on the surface in broad daylight 25 miles off the coast, patrolling leisurely and awaiting further orders. Commander Kossler decided that the crew should have a chance to toast the victory, so he ordered his executive officer to break out the medicinal brandy, mix it with pineapple juice, and give every man aboard a drink. The exec left to start the celebration and Kossler remained on the bridge, directing the submarine closer to shore. A few minutes later, a single aircraft contact was picked up dead ahead. Out of habit, Kossler rang up full power. The plane roared in and the officers on the conning tower watched in amazement while the plane dropped a bomb. The submarine swung wide to avoid it. The bomb landed a hundred yards off the starboard quarter, and the plane circled wide for another run. The submarine dove and stabilized at a safe depth. Skipper Kossler remembered the brandy ration and asked the executive officer about it. The exec shook his head. "Captain, we talked it over with the boys, and they decided to wait until the treaty was signed."

Half an hour later, the *Cavalla* surfaced and reported the incident to Admiral Halsey's staff in Task Force 38. Later that day, Halsey himself directed a message of caution to fleet units. As Commander Kossler remembers, it concluded: "If you see army planes approaching you directly, shoot them down—but do so in a gentlemanly fashion."

The ASW confrontation is no longer a direct-combat situation in modern warfare, and certainly not one that lends itself to an approach in gentlemanly fashion.

If it were possible to effectively counter submarines with anti-submarine warfare, then antisubmarine warfare would probably be the major task of the United States Navy. In both world wars, antisubmarine warfare has required the assistance of large fleets in order to cope with the threat posed by just a few submarines. Today the problem of effective ASW is even more complex: the hunters are suffering and will continue to suffer in the race to keep up with the hunted, both tactically and economically. New weapons are always planned and advances in technology could change this balance in the future, but the chances are slim; more probably, the submarine will widen the gap.

10 The Wet Cold War Progresses −Phase Two

History, showing us the life of nations, has
nothing to record save wars and revolutions:
the peaceful years appear only as brief pauses
or interludes, scattered here and there.

—SCHOPENHAUER

During the Khrushchev era, the Soviets continued to be obsessed by the concept of the carrier fleet, ignoring the much more vital threat of the nuclear submarine. Their principal naval developments were aimed at countering the carrier task force. By 1957 they developed the Badger, Bear, and Bison jet bombers and the supersonic intercontinental 103–M bomber. As the paper-submarine threat of five years before had grown in the minds of Western military observers, now a bomber gap was forming. The United States Congress authorized a massive expansion of SAC jet bombers, and the navy was given a go-ahead to build up to the strength of four large carrier strike fleets. NATO nations responded more slowly; being under the shadow of real and imaginary threats for so long had dulled their sense of panic.

Khrushchev showed off his missile technology to the amazement of Western observers in August 1957, when the first successful Soviet intercontinental missile was fired, to be followed closely in October by the launching of Sputnik. For all that these were small and simple efforts, they caused shock waves in every Western capital. In November the heavier Sputnik II was put in orbit.

Khrushchev had won an internal battle against Defense Minister Marshall Zhukov by supporting strategic weapons in opposition to Zhukov's emphasis on the operational forces. Zhukov stepped down, and the Russian space program pushed on to a number of firsts before the United States program decided to show off its technology. The Lunik firing to the moon in 1959 and Yuri Gagarin's first manned space flight in a Vostok capsule in 1961 were exploited to the hilt by Russian propagandists. A major missile gap was gravely announced by the Western military elite, and a responsive buildup of military systems and technologies was launched that soon catapulted the United States far beyond the Russians in all fields, including aerospace. After Khrushchev, the policy of goading the West was largely abandoned.

In September 1955 President Eisenhower attempted to set priorities in the military development of missile systems. The army was developing tactical rockets, the navy strategic submarine-launch missiles, and the air force strategic intercontinental missiles. Then the Suez crisis and the shock waves emanating from the Sputnik launching accomplished the kind of crash appropriations and development efforts in military programs that seem to be impossible in the Western democracies under any conditions other than crisis —real or imaginary.

As the arms race began in earnest, it became clear that the Soviet Union had failed in two of the three major deterrent weapons: the bomber and the intercontinental missile. The Soviets were also in a losing race with the United States in the development of the third leg of the deterrent triangle, the missile-firing submarine. The technological race between the Soviet Union and the United States was carried on in the fashion of three separate contests, and these separate contests—the ICBM, manned bomber, and SLBM— were carefully watched by military observers around the world. The rules seemed to involve both sides announcing experiments— then developments and tests—then displaying weapons on national holidays. Finally, improvements would be made, and the operational units would join the armed forces. What was not immediately detected was assumed or projected by military observers. There were false starts and imaginary leads, but on the whole the information was reasonably accurate, and over relatively short periods of time one nation or the other would be conceded a lead and awarded merit points. Sometimes the lead was based on a technical break-through or an outstanding program; more often it was measured in terms of assumed technology or simply activity in an area of interest. After World War II, both sides attempted to place missiles on submarines. But as long as the submarines were powered by diesel-electric propulsion, the weapon payloads would have to be launched quite near the enemy coast from platforms easily detected and at-tacked. It was necessary to achieve an undetected approach or to launch missiles far out at sea to avoid coming under enemy land or carrier bomber groups. Both advantages would be preferable, of course—and possible for a nuclear submarine, at least in concept.

From the first, navy planners intended to bring together the nuclear submarine and the ballistic missile. Their goal in the de-velopment of the atomic submarine was an impregnable launching vehicle for hydrogen-tipped missiles. In 1955 the General Dynamics Corporation was selected to complete paper studies on the feasibility of this union. The comprehensive report projected the development of an integrated submarine strategic offensive force based on the de-velopment of the atomic-powered submarine and a compatible missile. General Dynamics recommended a solid-propellant missile and predicted the design of a shipboard internal-navigation system for the submarine that would allow its use as a launching pad for pinpoint-accuracy delivery of nuclear warheads. GD was also op-timistic about the cost of the system and the time it would take to be put into operation. As a result of this study and a number of parallel studies made by MIT, the Rand Corporation, and others, in late 1955 the United States Department of Defense ordered a co-operative program among the armed services for the development of a ballistic missile. The goal: a missile with a range of ap-proximately 1,500 miles to be fired from a submerged submarine. The Soviet Union had just exploded its first H-bomb. The strategic situation was changing worldwide, and the design of a weapon which would provide a second-strike capability was of very high priority. A fleet of atomic submarines capable of delivering thermonuclear warheads from undetected locations constituted the logical reply to the argument that the Soviets would launch a preemptive attack in the hope that such an initial massive nuclear attack would give them victory in a single stroke.

The United States military-industrial complex seems capable of rising to meet any crisis. Thus, in the absence of a real crisis, either the Pentagon or one of the political parties creates the semblance of one. John F. Kennedy won a close national election on a platform which was cleverly based on correcting a nonexistent missile gap between the United States and the Soviet Union. He was politically committed to right that situation and restore America to first place among the nations of the world—the bastion of strength of the democracies against the forces of Communism, in general, and the Russians in particular. Kennedy promised to lead the country in a program of reestablishing a qualitative and quantitative superiority in weapon systems, and industry basked in the reflected prosperity of that program for many years.

The medium-range B–47 bomber was replaced by the B–52, and the medium-range Jupiter and Thor missiles were replaced by the Atlas and Titan ICBM. The solid-fuel Minuteman missiles gave America its first hardened-site missile arsenal and dramatically reduced the threat of Soviet preemptive action.

The United States had chosen the road to amassing a deterrent potential that would finally put the question of first-strike nuclear attack out of the minds of the Soviets. With the introduction of cost-effective weapons spearheaded by Secretary of Defense McNamara and his team, a fleet of 1,000 operational Minuteman and over 600 Polaris missiles was available by 1967—an amazing feat of coordinating United States industry and the armed services. Of course, some pet projects fell by the wayside, and many feathers were ruffled. Cancellation of the supersonic intercontinental B–70 Valkyrie bomber and the Skybolt missile system left their supporters alienated. But despite a sometimes hostile Pentagon, one way or another, McNamara got the job done.

To compensate the NATO powers for the cancellation of the

Skybolt missile, a multilateral nuclear force under NATO control was proposed. One ship under construction—the Italian cruiser *Garibaldi*—was fitted with four Polaris launching tubes. But before the missiles could be delivered, President De Gaulle's decision in favor of an independent French atomic force and submarine weapons caused the MLF project to be abandoned. Great Britain went ahead independently, and between 1963 and 1969 built four Resolution class nuclear submarines which would accommodate the Polaris missiles.

Russia's unfavorable geostrategic position required her military to quickly find a delivery system which would counter American naval power. There were two approaches the Russians could take: rocketry or submarines. The simplest antifleet action seemed to be a nuclear-warhead torpedo fired from a conventional submarine. But the Soviet weapons designers floundered and failed, and in the mid-fifties the program was abandoned. The Z class submarines available at that time would have difficulty penetrating United States coastal defenses, and a large fleet of submarines would have little chance to transit and prove effective against the antisubmarine warfare forces of the United States or NATO countries. Instead, the Soviets turned to some form of rocket—a rocket that could be fired from a submarine. This ultimate weapon—the missile-firing submarine—was a vision of the German scientists when they began working on their rocketry programs early in World War II. It was a two-step problem: first, to design a submarine that would carry a rocket traveling submerged and rise to the surface to fire off the enemy's coast; and second, to develop a longer-range rocket and a submerged delivery system which would not expose the submarine.

The United States Navy experimented with the Loon, a guided-weapon system developed from the German V-I rocket. During the period from 1947 to 1949, the Loon was successfully installed on two submarines, the *Cusk* and the *Carbonero*. In 1948 work was begun on the turbodrive missile Regulus, which promised to be superior to the Loon. In 1953 the *Tunney* was converted to launch the Regulus. A launch sled was built, and two Regulus I missiles were installed and fired.

The Soviets had a similar concept and developed a rocket based on German designs called the J-I. By 1954 they were experimenting with a supersonic rocket, the J-II. These rocket systems were developed as towed-sled vehicles; the sled was towed by a submarine.

The Soviets recognized the importance of atomic propulsion, particularly the design of an atomic plant that would be the proper size, weight, and power for use in the confined area of a submarine. After a series of failures, the Kremlin decided that the first prototype would be used in the icebreaker *Lenin,* and in 1959 the *Lenin* was commissioned and her test run on nuclear propulsion began. It was not satisfactory, and the development of a strategic nuclear-delivery submarine system was postponed until the problem of nuclear propulsion could be better related to submarine design.

In early 1956 two conventionally powered U.S. Navy submarines of the Greyback class were remodeled to include the Regulus II missile. A firing ramp was placed behind the conning tower to launch advanced supersonic missiles. Orders were placed for four more atomic submarines capable of firing the Regulus II missile, and the *Halibut* was converted from conventional to atomic power and received the Regulus modification. These submarines would have two additional missile containers, one on each side of the conning tower. The Polaris missile would greatly improve the range and performance of these weapons systems and would put our navy substantially ahead of Russian missile development, which still employed the Shaddock missile in external hull configurations.

In 1959, navy operations expert Rear Admiral William F. Raborn, Jr. took command of the project to give the navy a solid-fuel rocket. Existing designs were too weak for nuclear warheads to be fired over long distances, and liquid rocket fuel was unsuitable for use in submarines. The army had been directed to set up a joint program with the navy for development of the Jupiter rocket, and Admiral Raborn put together an industry-navy team that worked a production miracle. The task of producing a naval version of Jupiter was begun at the army rocket center in Huntsville, Alabama in early 1956 as a feasibility investigation. The missile had to be substantially shortened and tailored for shipboard use and made highly reliable and relatively maintenance-free. The rockets were tested in converted freighters and proved disappointing. To accommodate the modified army design, the submarine firing tubes had to be extended into the pressure hull. The submarine design would have to be increased to 8,000 tons, and the missile firing could only take place in semisubmerged conditions. Raborn could accept this compromise or hold out for a solid-fuel missile—a decision which would shape the capability of the United States submarine fleet for a generation. Raborn considered, shrugged off pressure from all sides, and recommended developing a solid-fuel missile. On December 8, 1956, with the blessing of the Secretary of Defense, the Polaris system and the now-famous Special Projects Office were born, to usher in the finest hour of the military-industrial complex.

The solid-fuel missile promised many advantages: smaller size and weight for the same payload and delivery range, together with safety and the ability to put more missiles on each submarine. The enormous disadvantage was the technological state of development of the missile; it was still largely unproven in tests, and it would be necessary to design a nuclear submarine around the untried system. It was a gamble not only with the missile program but with the submarine construction program as well. Raborn accepted these risks and advanced the proposed date for completion of the Polaris system from 1965 to 1963. Then, with the shock wave generated by the launching of Sputnik in 1957, he reassessed this deadline and advanced it to December 1960. It was a crash program by any standards, one which we will examine in detail in a later chapter as a classic of military weapons development. Rather than design the new class of submarine, Raborn accepted a Skipjack class boat —the *Scorpion*, already under construction—for modification. The *Scorpion* was cut apart at the shipyard and elongated so that a new section could be added to hold 16 Polaris missile tubes. The total modification increased the ship's displacement from 2,800 tons to 5,400 tons, but the nuclear reactor design modifications held speed reduction to less than 2 knots.

The development of the Polaris missile is the tale of outstanding military-industrial liaison. One after another seemingly insurmountable obstacle was overcome to keep the program close to schedule. The first submarine commissioning took place at the end of 1959. The key component—a radical new design of an inertial guidance system—was ready for testing early in 1960. The first SLBM nuclear submarine—the U.S.S. *George Washington*—made its maiden voyage on November 15, 1960, a month ahead of the "impossible" completion deadline set in 1957. By August of the next year there were five Polaris submarines in service. In March 1961, the submarine tender *Proteus* was assigned as the first mother ship for nuclear submarines and based at Holy Loch, Scotland. The Polaris program went on, creating a navy tradition of two crews —the Blue and Gold—which alternated on the two-month cruises. The *Proteus* was designed as a repair and maintenance vessel which would take care of not only the nuclear submarines and their missiles, but also the alternative crews of the submarines.

The United States Navy had found an Arctic blind spot in Soviet defenses much more significant to the Kremlin planners than the "weak underbelly" that Churchill once ascribed to the Axis powers in the Mediterranean. It would bother the Russians to the point of driving Chairman Khrushchev into a gamble which threatened the United States with missile bases on its exposed southern flank in the Caribbean. But the gamble failed and Khrushchev fell from power. Our Polaris submarines continued patrolling the northern waters off the Russian coast.

A parallel Soviet development program for the atomic submarine was initially based on employing aerodynamic missiles. In 1955 the SCUD class of weapons was developed as a missile for submarines and was followed by the longer-range SS–N–4 SARK, which was carried on the Z class conventional submarines. This submarine was designed to include a larger tower and two launch tubes to be installed vertically and extended entirely through the pressure hull, in a development similar to that of the early U.S. Army-Navy Jupiter project. There were delays and failures, and the first six submarines were not tested until 1959.

The Russian atomic-powered submarine program continued in

parallel with the conventionally powered, missile-firing submarine program. The H class submarines used a weapons carrier in common with the G class rocket launchers. Submarines were scheduled to be built at a rate of six per year, but the reactor development proceeded slowly, and the first Russian nuclear submarine—the *Leninskij Komsomol*—was not operational until 1961. In July 1962 this submarine succeeded in a polar surfacing similar to that carried out by the U.S. *Skate* in 1959, and the Russians made the most of this "better late than never" feat. But the technical problems caused further delays in the development of the H class submarines into their first operational period in late 1963.

The Russians continued to work on extended-range missiles, including the improved SS–N–5 SERB and converted the H class submarines to accommodate this missile system. The first successful submerged launch of a missile from a nuclear submarine was in 1964, after which the H class submarines went into patrol off the east coast of the United States.

The Russians were badly beaten in the nuclear-submarine-development race; into the 1960s it was no contest with the U.S. Navy Raborn-Rickover team. The Soviets had fallen behind badly. They planned to have over 100 submarine-based missiles operating at sea by 1960; instead, in 1961, they were operating a few submarines with the limited-range SARK missile. And the defenses against these Soviet submarines were overwhelming. Given the requirements of the submarines to launch from the surface and the need for a close approach to the target, the chances that a Soviet H class submarine would be able to operate undetected and effectively were small. The noise level of this generation of Soviet submarines had not improved significantly; their detection was relatively simple, and their position at sea was known to the United States Navy at all times.

The Soviets had banked heavily on their submarine program as a counter to the threat of American aircraft carriers. Then came the *Enterprise*—the first nuclear-powered carrier of the United States Navy—and the testing of the supersonic bomber A–5 Vigilante. Soviet leaders realized that they would once again have to reckon with the carrier threat—now more flexible and devastating than the carriers of the postwar era that had caused them so much concern. This new class of carrier had an increased range of aircraft which would permit operations at greater distances off the Russian coast. They would be effective beyond the range of Soviet missile ships and would require Soviet surface ships to venture beyond the protective umbrella of shore-based aircraft to engage them. The American ships carried supersonic, all-weather interceptors that would frustrate the mission of the Soviet long-range reconnaissance planes and would pose a threat to Soviet surface ships still out of missile range of the carriers.

To counter this new threat, the Soviets began developing surface-to-air and ship-to-air missiles. Air-defense systems developed for the Red Army were modified for naval use. The SA–N–1 system was installed in the cruiser *Dzershinski* and a lighter system, the SA–N–2 GOA, was installed on converted destroyers of the Kotlin class. The modification of the GOA system was later installed on missile cruisers of the Kynda and Kresta classes.

The J class submarines that had been designed as anticarrier surveillance vessels, as well as attack submarines, were also threatened by the new carrier aircraft. Their underwater speed against the nuclear carriers was too slow, and there were not enough of them in the fleet to make their deployment effective. Stuck with this gap in their defenses, the Soviet planners decided to convert a second generation of nuclear submarines scheduled for delivery in 1962. The conventional J class submarines would be modified in a crash program to produce them as quickly as possible. The H class reactor plant was modified for use in the new submarine, and three tube launchers were installed in the upper deck—changed to four twin launchers in later models. These submarines were called the E–1 and E–2 class and were a stopgap—poorly designed and armed with an aerodynamic missile totally inferior to the weapon systems under construction by the United States Navy.

Given the doubly difficult task of dealing with the strategic threat of aircraft carriers and the threat posed by nuclear submarines, the Soviet high command had responded with inferior submarines built to minimum standards. The Polaris A–1 missile with a 1,500-nautical-mile range would permit United States submarines positioned in the Arctic Ocean and eastern Mediterranean Sea to target on European Russia's missile sites and the Ukraine and Caucasus regions. The Soviets had no response.

The Soviet leadership reluctantly turned its full attention to naval combat and the related problem of ASW. With so little reliance on long-haul maritime traffic, the Soviet Union had simply ignored the problem of combating sea power. Soviet planners had been satisfied to simply copy the radar and combat-information systems that arrived on American lend-lease ships during World War II. But these systems were now totally obsolete for use against fast and maneuverable modern submarines. So the Soviets embarked on the design of new sonar equipment, ASW torpedoes and ASW weapons which could quickly be mounted aboard ship. A small submarine hunter-killer of about 350 tons was developed; the Poti class mini sub featured a combination gas turbine and diesel propulsion system and was armed with antisubmarine mortars and torpedoes. In 1961 the first antisubmarine frigates of the Peyta class were operational as diesel and subsequently gas-turbine powered. A successor model—the Mirka class—appeared in 1965 as a modern 1,000-ton warship equipped in much the same fashion as United States frigates of that time.

The Russians began putting antisubmarine equipment on all of the surface ships in the Soviet Navy and on merchant marine ships which would operate on the high seas. The Russian submarines were reequipped with new sonars which would extend the range of detection so that they might be used as attack and hunter-killer submarines. After 1958 there were still R and F class submarines being commissioned, as well as nuclear submarines of the N class. These, together with the G and H class missile submarines and the J and E class aerodynamic missile-carrying submarines, were the backbone of what the Russians considered to be their attack and hunter-killer capability. The Soviets had no adequate weapons for their surface fleet to deal with the antisubmarine problem; their submarines were the only effective ASW weapons. Therefore in

1962 they began constructing missile cruisers of the Kynda class and air-defense cruisers of the Kashin class. Priority was given to the Kashin class construction, which would be the primary Russian submarine-hunter. The failure of the Russians to recognize that the first Polaris submarines would be substantially improved in missile range and payload capability caused them to rush into a construction program for helicopter ASW carriers. The older destroyers in the Krupny and Kynda class were modified with helicopter landing pads on their quarterdecks, and the Russian fleet assumed an antisubmarine-warfare look—but it was a badly outdated response to the Polaris threat.

Military observers found it strange that the Russians would respond so compulsively to any new United States weapons system —given that they were intended as defensive weapons and would never be used in a first strike. But the record since World War II may have given the Russians pause. The United States has fought two major prolonged land and sea wars since 1945, and the Russians have engaged in none. The United States has been involved in many more armed interventions and taken part in and supported more foreign national defense buildups than the Russians, and United States technology in the name of peace and security has still continued to increase the lead over the Soviets in all fields of strategic and tactical weapon development. The Russians were constantly playing catch-up in military weaponry, always under the threat of American technology developing a superweapon. And slowly but effectively, the Russians had been ringed once more by a number of strong enemies: Germany, Japan, China, and others —some of them resembling the Mongol hordes and Teutonic Knights out of the past. Perhaps the Russian paranoia is somewhat justified—particularly as viewed East and West from Red Square.

In 1968, when the Israeli-Arab conflict seemed to be escalating beyond control, the Russians decided to show naval strength in the Mediterranean. Missile cruisers and helicopter carriers sailed through the Dardanelles as a task force at first thought to be amphibious. But careful observation disclosed that the helicopters were too small for troop transport. The ships were designed for ASW;

they mounted variable-depth sonars on their fantails and missiles that were clearly for only ASW purposes. Naval strategists were baffled. The extended range of the Polaris A–2 and A–3 to 2,000 and 3,000 nautical miles would allow the submarines to pick their firing positions well outside of the Soviet air-protection umbrella within which the Soviet fleet was constrained to operate. They would be firing their missiles from waters dominated by American naval power into which Soviet helicopter carriers and missile ships could venture only at the price of a very brief operating time before they were sunk or driven off. The design of Moskva-type ships to operate in a kamikaze fashion made very little sense. Such ships could only be deployed in the eastern Mediterranean with any assurance of protection if they operated within range of Soviet air bases. Once again it seemed to be a case of too little, too late, and of questionable design at best.

11 Russia Evolves a Naval Strategy

The nation that first learns how to live under the seas will control them, and the nation that controls the sea will control the world.

—G. V. PETROVICE
(paraphrasing Nelson's "Who rules the sea, rules the world.")

If we ascribe Stalin's reluctance to expand into the power vacuum left by the fallen Germans to fear of reprisal, we are better able to understand why he largely ignored the Russian Navy at the end of World War II. There was simply no need for aggressive sea power at that time. The navy's record was pale compared to that of the Red Army; the fleet had hardly seen combat. The Baltic Fleet was barely occupied and was almost completely contained in the Gulf of Finland for the entire war. The Pacific Fleet was inactive except for a few weeks fighting an already beaten foe. The Black Sea Fleet—the pride of the Russian Navy—had been through a series of minor skirmishes but had never taken command, even in the area where it had been numerically superior throughout the war. Only as convoy escorts did the Russian surface ships take any part in what could be called a contribution to the war effort. The White Sea Fleet cooperated with the Allies in covering the Arctic convoys for the last part of their run to the northern ports, a dull and largely uneventful task once the submarine threat was countered by Allied bombing and ASW forces.

The total effective strength of the Russian Navy in 1945 amounted to 3 cruisers of prewar design, 30 destroyers, also of prewar design, and about 100 submarines varying from floating relics of the 1930s to designs developed during the war and containing some of the elements of modern submarine technology. Considering these humble beginnings, it is remarkable that, in the short span of thirty years, the Soviets were able to build a navy larger in numbers of ships than any in the world except the United States. The resources required of this project in terms of men, materiel, and technical commitments were staggering, particularly when we consider the additional Soviet task of rebuilding the resources which had been ravaged by invasion and continuing the reequipment of the army and air force—not forgetting the development of nuclear weapons and space vehicles.

The Russians had learned a great deal over the years by copying the designs of their more technically advanced neighbors. Their best lessons in naval architecture came from copying German warships captured at the end of the war—particularly the German submarine. This allowed the Russians to start off at a level with the other world powers in the scramble to learn the German submarine technology, which was discovered to be superior to any other country, including the United States. During the early years of their postwar building program, the Russians attempted to obtain operational expertise from captured German naval officers and technicians. They did not subscribe to the philosophy generally circulating at the time that the A-bomb might make surface navies obsolete. Instead they expended enormous resources on building a defensive fleet which, even at that time, was programmed to be armed with conventional weapons. In an atomic-warfare age, when the exchange of nuclear weapons might settle a war in a few days, it seemed that a country like Russia should be concerned with missile and air power. She had never had the traditional security that a major sea power enjoys; yet the new Russian Navy was being designed to defend her coastline.

When the Russians began their building program, it was assumed that they would be happy simply with being able to contain a sea war in their own back yard, those areas near the Russian coast. They would rebuild the traditional Russian fleets in the

Baltic, Arctic, Black Sea, and Pacific, and use them to defend against the threat of seaborne invasion. Confirming this assumption was the Russian decision not to build any aircraft carriers—although the carrier had clearly become the replacement of the battleship as the capital ship for the great navies of the world. Instead the Russians copied the German policy of emphasizing the development of a submarine fleet and building conventional ships which had long been the backbone of their fleet: mine craft, torpedo boats, and larger surface vessels intended to act as raiders. Cruisers of the Sverdlov class were the largest ships the Russians would build.

The Soviet Navy emerged from World War II unscathed and largely unused—a seaward extension of the ground forces. While the Soviet military thinkers recognized that if the continued confrontation with the Atlantic powers which was then in the planning stages should ever result in warfare, some additional Soviet naval forces would be brought into play, still there was no program put forth to extend the navy beyond its initial defensive role. In 1946 Soviet military journals were publishing the papers of Admiral Kuznetsov and others who beat the drums softly for an increase in Soviet naval forces. They pointed out weaknesses and lamented quietly—as one did in the Stalin era—that a powerful Soviet Navy which could operate far from the homeland was needed. There was even a bid to construct a modern carrier force, similar to the one that had been used so effectively by the United States in the Pacific.

But Stalin could no more be persuaded of the need for the construction of aircraft carriers than he could be for the rest of the doctrine which would have moved the U.S.S.R. into a position to contest command of the high seas. At the time, doing so would have required an aircraft carrier building program and possibly even a battleship and cruiser building program. Clearly Stalin was much more concerned about the position of the United States with regard to the nuclear monopoly and the possibility of European concessions which could be based on the threat of a Red Army. Fighting the Truman policies of containment became the cornerstone of Soviet strategy. The buildup of a huge Soviet Army and tactical air support for that army—a crash program of developing first a bomber force and a missile ICBM capability—were the goals established.

The Russians faced a formidable foe: the United States Sixth Fleet in the Mediterranean and the Seventh Fleet in the Pacific coupled with the United States Strategic Air Command and an intercontinental atomic strike force of long-range bombers. This force more than counterbalanced the threat of the Red Army. Gradually, as Soviet expansion was limited in Europe by forces that relied heavily on the United States fleet in the Mediterranean, the Russians began to realize it was necessary either to contest the naval powers of the world on the high seas or develop a defensive and deterrent capability which would neutralize their sea power. A policy developed which has been attributed to Stalin and with slight deviations remains basic to Soviet military thinking. He viewed the navy as making its contribution by, "providing a creditable deterrent against a seaborne enemy attack . . . and having available forces adequate in wartime to defend the U.S.S.R.'s maritime borders. . . ."

Stalin's plan would provide naval forces sufficient to extend the Soviet Union's prestige and perhaps constitute some deterrent to the all-encompassing sea powers of the Western democracies, but would confine the Soviet Union's commitment to a moderate program of naval shipbuilding. Russia would develop marine technologies, merchant and fishing fleets, and whatever other ocean enterprise would stabilize and expand the Soviet economy, but Stalin would not juggle priorities in order to build a fleet at the expense of the army or air force.

At the time of Stalin's death in 1953, the building program for the Sverdlov class cruiser was halfway completed, with 6 ships in the fleet and 6 under construction. The Soviet shipyards had turned out 50 large seagoing destroyers of the Skoryi class in less than three years, and a dozen more were under construction. Submarines were being built at the rate of 12 a year, most of them small-tonnage coastal-defense diesel types. The accompanying technology development was substantial, and Stalin's plan to create a balanced fleet was shaping the immediate Soviet postwar naval strategy. A Naval Ministry was created in 1950 and provided the impetus necessary not only to engage in a building program but also to begin a major research and development program particularly in the area of naval missile weapons.

From the navy's point of view, Stalin died at just the right time. He had been a strong supporter of the admirals' wider interests and had given them considerable priority in the postwar period, but he was essentially a military conservative. Although he had made an important reformulation of doctrine that suggested that a capitalistic attack was no longer inevitable, it is doubtful that he would have pushed his argument to the fullest by abandoning his basic army-oriented position.

Although Khrushchev managed to oust Malenkov, largely on the grounds that Malenkov was cutting back too heavily on defense, Khrushchev still shared Malenkov's concern for the state of internal economy and cast a skeptical eye on the navy's massive building programs which had been projected in response to the threat of the seaborne invasion.

By 1955 Soviet military planners had conceded that the great threat lay in a surprise attack with nuclear weapons; in a naval context, this meant aircraft carriers. But if the Soviets were to respond to the threat, they had to reduce quantity and increase quality, primarily in terms of greater range and more lethal weapons. Khrushchev, castigating the navy as "metal eaters," favored any solution which would reduce the steel consumption of the shipyards and free it for other purposes. Khrushchev felt that the long-range cruise missile which had undergone common development for the services provided the answer. It had standoff capability for surface units and bomber aircraft and offered tactical mobility to the submarine while providing the platform for the nuclear warhead needed to neutralize the carrier. Because of the economic pressures and his own temperament, Khrushchev gambled that the operational application would be fully successful and appointed Admiral Gorshkov as Commander-in-Chief to push the program through.

In 1958–1959 the Soviet Navy underwent a painful assessment. The balance of maritime advantage had deteriorated sharply, and United States carrier-based aircraft now had range and payloads to launch nuclear air strikes on Russia from the south Norwegian seas and the eastern Mediterranean. The Soviet answer to the carrier threat was predicated on the encountering zone being within a few hundred miles of Russian bases—not a thousand miles away. The United States Navy was also building Polaris nuclear submarines, each of which could launch 16 missiles at a range of 1,200 nautical miles from a submerged position. But the Russian H class missile-firing submarine (SSBN) and the diesel-powered G class SSBN could launch only 3 missiles at a range of about 300 nautical miles—and from the surface.

Since the United States had already established ASW defense areas on each coast, with their own independent command structure, and task forces were permanently deployed at sea, the Russian threat was minimal; while circumstances of geography did not allow the Russians to adopt a similar policy as an effective answer to Polaris. Finally the Arctic cruise of the American nuclear submarine *Skipjack* showed the Soviets how badly they were lagging in terms of ocean science and in the technology of building nuclear submarines. Soviet planners firmly bit the bullet and admitted that the nuclear submarine and the carrier-strike aircraft now presented a strategic threat against which they had no effective defense. The Russian surface ships were likely to be sunk, the diesel submarine was too slow and short-ranged, and aircraft might never get off the ground to combat the carrier fleets. But the nuclear submarines armed with cruise missiles could overcome these disadvantages, and this reassessment led to a complete reversal of priorities in the allocation of nuclear propulsion.

The J class SSG was due to enter service about 1962, so it was a relatively simple matter to embody the missile system intended for this class into a hastily designed E class of submarines which were built around a second generation of nuclear-hull propulsion units. But the availability of nuclear propulsion made the J class itself superfluous, and the program was curtailed.

For whatever reasons, by 1959 it was apparent that even the

H class SSBN could not provide the assured response in terms of launch, and as a missile platform it compared very unfavorably with other strategic weapons—particularly the ICBMs then entering service. It was argued that the Soviet Navy had no future in deterrent schemes and could make no cost-effective contribution because the SLBM weapon did not offer the Russians the same relative advantages over land-based systems that Polaris provides the U.S. Navy. But the submarine proponents won the bitter battle and began building a force of SSBNs similar to the United States Navy's George Washington class. The clinching argument was that the Russian Navy could not effectively devise a counter to Polaris in an acceptable time scale, which meant that a Polaris submarine force held back from the initial missile exchange in a nuclear conflict would dominate. This would result in a United States victory if the Soviets had no comparable force. Reverting to the desperate policy of seeking to pose an equivalent threat, the Russians entered the race in a kind of catch-up strategy. Admiral Rickover, for one, was delighted with this competition.

In 1962 Khrushchev watched a missile fired from a submerged H class submarine. The range was only 600–700 nautical miles, but he was happy; Russia was still in the race. However, Khrushchev worried that the Russians could find no single ASW answer for the problem of countering Polaris and the American submarine force lead. Russian ASW submarines would lack the essential marginal advantage needed over their quarry, particularly in submerged performance, since they were not only slower and noisier, but also could not dive deep. This meant that northern Russia was vulnerable to the 1,500-nautical-mile A–2 Polaris missile, a threat the Soviets tried to meet by increasing their conventional ASW forces, both surface and air. The outlook was not reassuring, but then again, there was also nothing very original in the concept of ASW defense which the United States had been demonstrating for several years. However, while the United States was able to convert some of its older attack carriers to ASW operations, the Russians now had to build an ASW force almost from scratch. Then, even before the first unit could be laid down, Polaris 2,500-nautical-mile A–3 missiles were introduced. The Soviets realized that while air defense might discourage or even exclude Polaris submarines from the northern sector of attack, the Russian interior was now exposed to thermonuclear-missile attack from almost every other point on the compass.

12 Admiral Rickover and His Dream of Nuclear Propulsion

In October 1973 Chief of Naval Operations Admiral Elmo Zumwalt wrote this memo of a meeting with Mr. Nelson W. Freeman, chairman of the board of Tenneco Corporation, concerning Admiral Rickover's conduct at the company's Newport News shipyard:

"Mr. Freeman then proceeded to describe at length the inspection system which Admiral Rickover and the Navy use in Newport News. He stated that it has become so onerous and the management approach so abusive that he has ordered Newport to 'throw Admiral Rickover's ass' out of the plant if he shows up. . . . I said that in my view we were dealing with a problem in which, as a result of Admiral Rickover's management system, we were about to kill the goose that laid the golden egg. Admiral Carr [Clement's Executive Assistant] . . . stated that Admiral Rickover was only responsible for the nuclear part of it. Mr. Freeman said that anybody that thinks that doesn't know how the system works. I gave my view that Admiral Rickover does get beyond nuclear power and does

really run the entire shipyard involved in constructing a nuclear plant and indeed the Ships Systems Command with regard to nuclear ships. Under questioning from Mr. Corcoran, Mr. Freeman confirmed that Newport News had submitted a bid for a design of the Sea Control Ship which was about three and a half million dollars and that they had been 'blackmailed' out of it by Admiral Rickover and it had gone to National Steel for seven million, even though National Steel didn't have the expertise and had to hire architects. Mr. Clements appeared puzzled at this. I pointed out to him that Admiral Rickover's policy is to work against any non-nuclear-propelled large [war]ship. Mr. Freeman confirmed that Admiral Rickover was vehemently against non-nuclear-propelled ships. Mr. Corcoran made the point that there is nothing as dangerous as an old man with a dream, that Admiral Rickover is trying very hard to accomplish his vision for a nuclear-propelled Navy before he dies; but that he, Tommy Corcoran, sees much evidence on the Hill of great concern about the corners that Admiral Rickover is now cutting."

> *Sworn to no party,*
> *Of no sect am I;*
> *I won't keep quiet*
> *And I will not lie.*
>
> —ADMIRAL LORD FISHER, Royal Navy

British naval officers point out a similarity in methods, temperament and ambition between Admiral Hyman G. Rickover, USN, and Admiral Lord "Jacky" Fisher, RN, who had dragged the British Navy kicking and screaming into the twentieth century, then returned from retirement at seventy-three to build a submarine fleet for World War I. Fisher had feuded with First Sea Lord Winston Churchill, they disagreed on many policy matters, but a single catastrophe decided the issue of his accepting Churchill's request that he return to active duty. On September 22, 1914, the German submarine U–9 sank the British cruisers *Aboukir, Hogue,* and *Cressy* as they patrolled the Dutch coast. Of the 2,200 men in the crews, 1,459 died that morning. All Allied shipping was halted, and troop transports had to leave for France under convoy guard.

Lord Fisher reported for duty in October after the skipper of the U–9 had scored another success, sinking the cruiser *Hawke* with a loss of 500 officers and men. Fisher called a meeting of the admiralty officials and submarine contractors as his first official act.

"Gentlemen, I will make your wives widows and your homes dunghills if you bring any additional red tape into this business," Jacky Fisher told them. "I want submarines, not contracts." So began Fisher's War Emergency Programme which went on to design and build His Majesty's submarine fleet.

Like Fisher, Admiral Hyman G. Rickover, USN, has greatly affected and modernized his country's navy.

In November 1945, when it was announced that Fleet Admiral Chester Nimitz would replace Fleet Admiral Ernest J. King as Chief of Naval Operations, the U.S. Navy looked forward to a continuation of the vigorous leadership that had characterized its top commanders in carrying on the war. Nimitz and King were of like mind. They both were officers of vision and had stated that the navy must make major revisions to accommodate the lessons learned from combat. Nimitz promised to move aggressively into the field of new weapons development. To help in the transition, King ordered a board to review the strengths and weaknesses of the navy and make recommendations concerning weapons development in a report to Nimitz.

The board studied the impact of combat operations and in particular the characteristics of ship types and how their capabilities related to the missions they would be assigned over the first postwar decade. Submarines were studied most intensively—not because the board considered submarines most important, but because the role of the submarine had changed so radically from the time of its first use in World War I. United States submarine operation in the Pacific during the last year of the war was particularly significant because of its success and overall impact on the Japanese ability to carry on the war.

The board pointed out the dilemma of the submarine's performance: the same features that made it a more efficient vessel to operate on the surface impaired its performance as an underseas craft. For efficient surface and submerged operations, it was required to have two propulsion systems: diesel engines to provide high speed and long range for surface operations, and battery-powered electric motors for submerged action. Under the surface, the submarine was slow and depended on periscope observation. Below periscope depth, the submarine was blind except for a very limited acoustic detection capability. To achieve position satisfactory for a torpedo attack, the submarine usually had to surface and run for long periods of time, vulnerable to attack by aircraft or surface ships.

Radical design changes had been made during the war. The Germans improved their submarines by adapting a Dutch invention, the snorkel, a device that consisted essentially of tubes which extended from the submerged vessel, bringing air to its diesels and removing exhaust from them. The snorkel was not completely satisfactory; it was noisy and showed its exhaust. The Germans tried a refined approach, employing three times the number of batteries with a snorkel device to increase the submarine's submerged capabilities. Then they began the design of a submarine that would fire missiles while submerged. In addition to the snorkel, the Germans had begun work on closed-cycle systems in which oxygen for the engines was released from chemicals. German scientists were still adapting the submarine to new weapons and propulsion systems when the war ended.

The board drew a gloomy picture of submarine operations in future combat unless some method of substantially increasing the speed at which the submarine was capable of running submerged and the time that the submarine could remain down was found. If submarines could be designed to run submerged at greatly increased speeds, they would have an important part in any future war.

Nimitz himself was a submariner and well aware of the limitations of the craft. He had been briefed on the prospects of nuclear power which would make both surface and submerged operation on a single propulsion system feasible and was sensitive to the revolution in military technology that had developed during the war. He stated that the application of nuclear arms to the services would mean far more than the victories and politics that created the postwar world.

Since the discovery of nuclear fission in 1939, the U.S. Navy had faced the challenge of powering ships with nuclear engines— one of the earliest uses suggested. A nuclear chain reaction required a very small space—certainly a natural system for ship propulsion. But this transformation of scientific principles into practical engineering designs was a costly and difficult process; one that would require technical knowledge, management skills, and resources beyond those the navy had at its disposal.

The navy had very little part—and almost no voice—in the government's uranium-research project, and later the Manhattan Project. The Naval Research Laboratory (NRL) had worked on some of the projects, but in February 1942 President Roosevelt decided to rely on the army to build the plants and production facilities for the fissionable material and the atomic bomb. The navy's programs were gradually transferred to army control or phased out. But the NRL did make a major contribution to the program in its plans for a production facility for enriched uranium, which it gave to the army. The plans were used to expedite the production of Uranium 235.

In 1946 the NRL reported that it was prepared to design a nuclear-powered submarine which could be fully operational in two years. The advanced hull developed by the Germans for their closed-cycle system would be used. But the Navy Bureau of Ships (BuShips) examined the laboratory's plan and decided that neither the personnel or facilities were available to implement it. The bureau cast around for representatives to join in a government-industry project, a version of the Manhattan Project that would build an experimental power reactor. Contracts were placed for research on atomic power development as well as for a program of chemical and physical research into the properties of sodium-potassium alloys as a heat-transfer fluid in a gas turbine generator. General Electric was asked to design a nuclear-propulsion plant using a liquid coolant, and navy research groups began to examine other proposals.

When the navy began its liaison with the Oak Ridge atomic-energy plant, the top brass jockeyed to select a head for the project. Captain Hyman G. Rickover, a forty-six-year-old Annapolis graduate with a good technical background, was finally selected. Rickover was a Naval Academy graduate who earned a master's degree in electrical engineering at Columbia in 1929 and had had a brief tour in the submarine service.

Rickover was a loner at the Naval Academy, the type of serious, asocial midshipman who spends time with his books and is discounted as a man to know in the fleet. He graduated in 1922 and was placed in the engineering department of the battleship *Nevada* as a junior electrical officer. After completing his battleship tour, he was assigned to the postgraduate program in electrical engineering at the Naval Academy. Students in the navy were not held in high regard at that time; the officer who stayed in the fleet made his reputation as a line commander. Those who took advantage of postgraduate programs were branded technical types who would rise to commander or captain and huddle around in engine rooms or over drawing tables for their careers, but never command a fleet. Somehow this lesson was lost on Rickover, who proceeded from the postgraduate school to other courses at Columbia University's school of engineering. Perhaps he recognized that as a bookish Jew, his best and possibly only chance to rise in the navy in those days was by way of the new technologies. The navy was a caste system then—and perhaps still is, on a more subtle basis.

Rickover had applied for an Engineering Duty (EDO) designation, specializing in electrical engineering and propulsion. As an EDO, Rickover was assigned as assistant planning officer at the Cavite Navy Yard in the Philippines, and in 1939 was assigned to the Electrical Section of BuShips in Washington. There he spent the war as that rarest of naval professionals—an Annapolis graduate who could completely submerge himself in the detailed studies of electrical equipment without voicing any demand to go to war. He thrived on the pressures involved in building thousands of ships; the direction of design functions seemed to completely satisfy his naval ambitions. Rickover assembled a group of the best civilian engineers and officers he could find and plunged into the complications of wartime contracts, inspections, and procurement schedules. He showed tireless energy and a refusal to compromise that soon distinguished him from his colleagues who were restive with their jobs and anxious to get back to sea. His group found engineering deficiencies everywhere and often resorted to redesigning major equipment themselves. Rickover earned a reputation as a tough-minded, exacting contracts officer—one who was not lulled into the kind of security that a procurement officer enjoys in wartime.

As a reward for his wartime diligence, in June 1946 Rickover was nominated to begin his nuclear career with the Atomic Energy Commission (AEC) at Oak Ridge, heading up the BuShips liaison team. Rickover may have been chosen as a placeholder; he had spent twenty-seven years in the navy and seemed to be close to retirement after, in navy terms, a lackluster career. Well below thousands of officers with outstanding war records and demonstrated operational competence, he was nowhere near consideration for flag rank. But Rickover pressed on with his new assignment, possessed by extraordinary ambition and a burning conviction that nuclear power would revolutionize the navy. In this new technology, he probably saw the only opportunity to salvage his naval career.

But Rickover knew so little about nuclear science and the navy was so marginally interested in the program that the opportunity would be difficult to exploit. He suspected, in fact, that he had been assigned to Oak Ridge simply to get him out of Washington. If this was the case, it was one of the most fortuitous personnel reassignments ever made in the interest of eliminating an irritant. Rickover's devastating frankness and open contempt which antagonized his fellow officers were, by coincidence, exactly the traits that would make him a success in the unstructured military nuclear-power scramble.

The casual structure at Oak Ridge suited Rickover's personal style, but he felt it would lead to ineffective performance for the navy representatives. Consequently, he engineered the kind of ploy that would later become known as a Rickoverism. He had been openly critical of the procedures at BuShips, including the all-powerful fitness report, which determines an officer's promotion. But at the AEC, where he wanted power, senior army officers made out all such reports—until Rickover persuaded them to allow him to prepare the drafts of the fitness reports for the navy officers. BuShips had refused to grant him that authority, but the army was happy to have his help. Soon Rickover was awarded the job of roughing out the fitness reports, and his fellow team members soon acknowledged his new "leadership" role.

In another "leadership" technique, Rickover became master of the technical memorandum; he realized that in atomic energy his AEC position made him an expert in a limited area in which very few professional officers had chosen to become competent. This mastery of AEC jargon and the art of amassing a compendium of reports would serve him well. He developed a talent for taking contractors' ideas and "translating" them for his seniors. He made frequent tours of university laboratories, industrial-development facilities, and plants, picking up new material to feed his BuShip superiors at every stopover.

In the early days of the atomic-submarine program, the issue was not whether nuclear propulsion should be developed, but rather whether the potential impact of nuclear power on the navy warranted the kind of top-priority, high-cost program that Rickover and others were advocating. They wanted atom-powered ships right now. Immediately after the war, this small, aggressive group of naval officers put forward the idea of setting up a special program group, a type of navy Manhattan Project free of the control of any other authority. But the Atomic Energy Act of 1946 squelched their hopes. It placed the development of atomic energy in civilian hands and created an independent agency with broad, sweeping authority. Admiral Mills, Admiral Bowen, and others in BuShips had hoped to chart their own course; but now they recognized that nuclear fleet propulsion would have to be developed jointly with the newly formed AEC. Independent plans were scrapped, and BuShips made plans to establish an effective policy of liaison and cooperation.

The navy had difficulty in getting off the ground with the AEC because the commissioners had little or no background in either the technical or the administrative aspects of military-development projects. The Atomic Energy Act was to be implemented by the General Advisory Committee, a committee within the AEC, whose nine members included some of the most distinguished scientists in the country. Unfortunately, all of them were laboratory oriented. The navy complained that propulsion was simply not considered important enough by the commission—it was assigned a priority too far down a list topped with basic-research projects.

The AEC's actions were countered by Rickover, who began a guerrilla warfare to force the commission into a program for developing a navy nuclear-reactor engine which could be used for specialized fleet applications. Rickover was the power behind the throne, providing his seniors with information with which to bombard Chief of Naval Operations Nimitz, Navy Secretary Sullivan, and Defense Secretary James V. Forrestal, who in turn asked the AEC searching questions concerning their activities.

In parallel, Rickover went to the defense contracting community with the navy's message; he realized that there lay the greatest political clout. He worked his magic at Westinghouse, General Electric, Electric Boat Company, and many others—any major military contractor that would listen to his tales of the business potential represented by the construction of an atomic-powered submarine fleet. There was money to be made, Rickover told them —lots and lots of money. He played up the profit potential while simultaneously pointing out the military advantage of such a national asset. And many senior industrialists joined his crusade. They helped to finally forge an agreement of sorts between BuShips and the AEC, but it was an accord that Rickover was unhappy with for two reasons. First, it placed the submarine project in the hands of the Argonne National Laboratories and not the navy. Second, the navy would be permitted to participate only as observers.

Rickover complained bitterly that Argonne was a scientific and teaching institution, not an organization experienced in weapons development. His superiors countered by telling him that his group had been clamoring for engineers and scientists—not naval officers —to head up such programs. Now they had them. Rickover had no reply, so he used an uncharacteristic strategy: complete inaction. And without his cooperation, very little happened. As the navy brass fumed over the lack of progress, Rickover seized every opportunity to exploit the widening gap caused by inaction between the navy and the AEC. While the navy was happy over the arrangement with the Argonne National Laboratories in the beginning, Rickover made sure that this euphoria did not last long. He busied himself preparing an alternate plan for submission when the time was ripe. Meanwhile, he sowed the seeds of discontent and mutual suspicion among both the navy and AEC top brass.

When it was time for prime contractors for the propulsion program to be selected, there was a question of competition between the two foremost competitors: Westinghouse and General Electric. There should have been a decision, a choice of one or the other. But Rickover saw an advantage to keeping them both aboard, so he proposed that the AEC and navy launch parallel programs. This would require Westinghouse to develop a system based on pressurized water and General Electric to concentrate on a sodium cycle. Rickover pointed out that the Manhattan Project had benefited from parallel approaches. It would involve a more expensive—and possibly a more time-consuming—approach, but surprisingly BuShips and the AEC bought the dual-contractor plan. Westinghouse began Project Wizard and General Electric began Project Genie. Rickover was pacified.

As would happen many times in Rickover's career, it was the Soviet Union that helped out most when his program faltered because of funding and technical differences. The Soviets obligingly cut the Berlin land links with the West and threatened war. The U.S. Navy was asked to look into its war readiness program. Captain Arleigh A. Burke, the "Thirty-One-Knot" Burke of World War II destroyer fame, presented a report to his superiors that made much of the Soviet Union's threat and Rickover's case for atomic propulsion. The report grossly overstated the Russian capability based on the technology captured from the Germans and particularly the ability of the Russians to copy the German type XII deep-diving, snorkel-equipped submarine. Of course, the navy played the report as a trump card at AEC, calling in navy experts like Admiral Charles B. Momsen, of Momsen escape-lung fame, and Admiral Raymond A. Spruance, commander of the Pacific Fleet and one of the major naval heroes of World War II. They all spoke in behalf of the navy's interest in developing nuclear power and strongly recommended the creation of a BuShips section to expedite the program.

Admiral Mills, Deputy BuShips Director, strengthened Rickover's hand. Rickover was needed as a man who would threaten, cajole, and—where necessary—insult those who stood in the way of the program, without embarrassing or directly reflecting on his supervisors or the navy. Rickover could be cut off, dismissed, or reassigned at any time; but while he was in the AEC liaison position overlooking the AEC's activity, Mills knew Rickover would prove a bitter antagonist for anyone who took a view counter to the navy's position

Rickover won his two-contractor setup—taking both Westing-house and General Electric into the program and extending the navy's empire into their industrial plants throughout the country. He politicked for the creation of an atomic-reactor branch within the BuShips. Finally, when one was created, he shifted his command back to the bureau. Although he was not given full authority over reactor development at either the AEC or BuShips, he knew it would be just a matter of time until he could lay claim to both these responsibilities. His timetable for conquest was on schedule.

Rickover now did something that only a skilled practitioner in the military bureaucracy would attempt: he used his dual role in both the navy and the AEC to whipsaw each side—criticizing one to the other, leaking intelligence back and forth, and taking the initiative independently when neither the bureau or AEC asserted control in areas of disputed responsibility.

To deal with contractors, particularly Westinghouse and General Electric, Rickover established a very flexible organization. He had learned what could be done to control contractors operating without a definitive contract—particularly if the payment for goods and services rested on his goodwill. Rickover inserted himself between the navy project office and the contractor, in the role of arbiter, expediter, and quality-control czar. He became the bottleneck through which everything had to flow in order for contractors to be paid and work be kept on schedule. And while he was creating this position of authority, he was training a staff of like-thinking junior officers, schooling them in the ways of manipulation through conferences, staff studies, memoranda, and contractor-evaluation reports.

In 1949 Rickover was still involved in building the Westinghouse Argonne team. General Electric's efforts were left largely unsupervised, and this soon became a problem. General Electric's management was aware that the reactor concept they had been assigned had little chance of succeeding as the navy's choice for submarine service. The fault was not in their engineering approach, it was simply one of the laws of nature. The original assumptions based on limited data had proved wrong, and although the project would be interesting from a scientific point of view, it would yield very little that could be used practically in submarine propulsion. Rickover was not concerned by this blind alley; he wanted this development program to continue for the peripheral hardware it would develop. But General Electric's lack of interest in the project in favor of building civilian power reactors using the breeder design became evident. And because the company was now going through a decentralization of the overall organization, Rickover could not find a hot button to press to evoke a response from General Electric's scattered top management. Profit centers were largely on their own, in the company's decentralized approach, and as often as Rickover visited company headquarters in Schenectady and New York City, he was still unable to push his program. The Knolls Laboratory, where most of the General Electric atomic energy programs were being conducted, worked at a slow and steady pace that infuriated Rickover, but he seemed unable to change that situation or change the priorities.

A new phase in Rickover's career development began. Stymied by the Atomic Energy Commission and General Electric, he turned to Washington politicians. He met with Senator Brian McMahon, Chairman of the Congressional Joint Committee on Atomic Energy, and one of the sponsors of the Atomic Energy Act of 1946. McMahon was young, bright, and ambitious—eager to climb aboard the nuclear submarine program which Rickover described in such glowing terms. The Joint Committee in Congress included Congressmen Charles D. Durham and Carl Hinshaw, two staunch AEC supporters, and with this group behind him Rickover once again approached General Electric with the proposal that GE expand its activities into a number of programs in reactor development to which the Knolls Laboratory would give top priority. GE had many irons in the fire—departments of the company that had programs that required congressional support—so it reluctantly agreed to go along with Rickover's plans and pushed the Knolls efforts. The dual-contractor situation prospered, and Rickover was much impressed by the clout of a few congressional leaders in dealing with big business. It was a valuable lesson, and he learned it well.

Although Rickover himself was a basically unorganized manager, this lack of a fixed-pattern organization seemed to help him in dealing with contractors. All of the organizations he dealt with were different in structure and style: Westinghouse, General Electric, Argonne, Knolls, BuShips, AEC. Each had its own peculiarities and organizational practices. Since Rickover was uncommitted and unbound by any fixed structure, he could respond to each situation on an individual basis. He acted as though he were responsible only to himself, and this attitude was unlike any previous navy relationship the contractors had experienced. Rickover established a direct, free, personal, uninhibited contact with the contractors. Arms-length negotiations were maintained, but no aspect of the contractor's operation was immune from Rickover's inspection or criticism, and no member of the contractor's organization escaped his personal scrutiny and evaluation.

Much was gained, but must was lost, too. Under Rickover's sway, the organizations within Westinghouse and General Electric no longer bore a resemblance to the companies' efficient operations. A long tradition of maintaining independence from customer influence was the watchword of these companies. Each division was responsible primarily to its own management; there was tight accountability and responsibility, particularly in fiscal matters. Rickover sought to change that—to loosen this management structure and add to his own span of authority. In effect, he moved the contractors' organizations closer to his own until they were almost an extension of his project group. Then gone were the management and fiscal restraints. The programs suffered chronic cost overruns. Early and late, throughout his career, Rickover displayed a monumental unconcern for the taxpayer's dollar. As he interpreted his mandate, his job was to succeed quickly, and damn the financial consequences.

Although his methods were arbitrary—and later bordered on the unconventional—Rickover always considered himself an expert at choosing personnel. In the early 1950s he staffed the bureau's Code 390—his own reactor program group—with the best technical people he could borrow or steal from the navy, civil service, and the industrial-talent marketplace. Once assembled, the staff was bombarded with Rickover's requests to learn more, research more, and expand their own technical horizons. Even the clerks and secretaries were given instruction in the rudiments of nuclear engineering. Rickover took training very seriously, devoted a large amount of staff time to it, and was completely unselfish with his own time when it came to increasing the knowledge of his subordinates.

If Rickover had no social presence, he compensated with a commanding administrative presence—at least in his own office. He read everything, reviewed everything, and commented on everything of any import that happened in and around his headquarters. Rickover's quixotic character has been most in evidence over the years when he was given an opportunity to form a group, rather than simply acting as a critic. Offered any opportunity to create an organization—at the AEC, BuShips, or in the fleet—he displayed the same empire-building traits. He was much more a staff than a line commander; Rickover's world was circumscribed by the technical report, the contractor-appraisal form, the memorandum, the review and meeting. He was critical of the red tape in the navy and the AEC, but his own organizations were just as deep in it. He demanded paper work—and elaborately prepared paper work at that. It was said that he read every communication to and from his organizations. Rickover's BuShips clerks complained that they were required to submit a pink copy of everything they typed to Rickover for correction—even incomplete drafts and interoffice memos. He read them for bad grammar, careless expressions, vague terminology, and the wrong approach—what he called "poor administrative tactics."

Rickover saw his organizations as a loose confederation of people like himself, harried by an overwhelming number of technical problems and responsibilities, so dedicated to their own job and organization that they would put all thought of rank, protocol, or promotion aside. It was always the concept of "them against us" —the overbearing and technically ignorant brass, the grasping administrative officials, the devious congressmen, the profit-crazed contractors. Only Rickover and his staff were really attuned to the navy's problems. He conducted the nuclear submarine program in a different way but with the same attitude that Admiral Jacky Fisher conducted his building program—as a crusade with himself as the messianic leader.

Rickover's key managers often differed with him, but his sincerity was never open to question. His total commitment was striking and very successful. They followed him—sometimes confused, but always fiercely loyal. He flattened the pyramid organization that was based on military rank and civilian grades, eliminating precise titles and hierarchical levels to keep the technical exchanges balanced. He argued that titles were invented only to justify military rank and civil service grades; because some people had been around longer had no bearing on their knowledge or value to the organization. Engineers were constantly being reassigned, managers floated to different parts of the program. People who showed technical leadership were quickly promoted; those who did not were quickly dispatched.

In addition to being a free-form organization man, Rickover was a free-form technical-discussion man. No argument was ever closed, no question ever too stupid or embarrassing to ask—and ask again, if the answer was not satisfactory. Everyone—Rickover included—had to argue and win his own point on technical grounds alone. Silence in a Rickover meeting was interpreted as assent; merely accepting what was going on never precluded an engineer from reopening an argument at a later date, but he would be criticized sharply for his earlier silence. Rickover encouraged rough-and-tumble technical meetings. As wary as he was of the printed word, as much as he honored the report and memorandum, to the same degree he held little respect for published technical facts that could not be defended in the context of his own program. He was suspect of any technical data that was developed outside his own group; the NIH (Not Invented Here) syndrome was strong in any Rickover system of research and development and project management.

In 1950 Rickover's Code 390 was in the process of designing

and developing two models of a land-based prototype reactor for submarine service. The Mark I version centered around the use of pressurized water to transfer energy from the reactor to the propulsion equipment; the Mark A version, a radical sodium-cooled design, offered the possibility of attaining higher temperatures and a more efficient steam cycle. Westinghouse was assigned the Mark I Project; General Electric, the Mark A Project. Although the General Electric system seemed to offer several unique advantages, it was obvious from the beginning that Westinghouse had been selected as the favored vendor when the company was awarded the Mark I system. The Mark A was too promising to be overlooked, but it was a long shot. It did not offer the simplicity of design and straightforward engineering approach of the Mark I system. Designing around the use of sodium and beryllium meant that General Electric would be involved in extensive R&D efforts while Westinghouse was able to use state-of-the-art materials and techniques. "After all is said and done, it means Westinghouse is working with water and we are working with sodium," a GE official said.

Westinghouse was delighted, and General Electric was less than enchanted, but the laboratories of both companies hunkered down to serious research and development work and performed outstandingly.

When Rickover was in trouble he devised, improvised, and in some cases proselytized—but never did he come up with anything more unheard-of than the "Quaker Meeting" form of technical exchange. Often when laboratory scientists encountered Rickover and his staff, the exchanges were at first abrasive, later mellowing to a ripe acrimony that yielded to a cold hostility as time passed. Probably Rickover cared very little about deteriorating personal relationships unless it interfered with getting the job done; but the more disenchanted the scientists became the more reasons they found to avoid Rickover's people. To overcome these problems, the Quaker Meetings were established with the laboratory chiefs. They were ideal forums from Rickover's point of view, since they involved his people on one side of the room and the laboratory staff on the other in a sort of classical disputation forum. The rules of the meeting required that neither group speak unless and until the members could represent themselves as individuals, rather than as spokesmen for their organizations. There were long silences, and when tempers flared many meetings were terminated. But gradually the barriers of hostility and mistrust were broken down to an extent—and at least some of the misunderstandings and frustrations were eliminated. "Talk *with* me, not *at* me," Rickover would scream at the scientists, and finally they decided it was easier to try to deal with this strange man rather than suffer his wrath when he felt he was being ignored. In the beginning they assumed that most of Rickover's motives were hidden, that his cause had a political connotation, that he was simply trying to feather his own nest. And they became more convinced when he mouthed platitudes and stooped to castigating personalities. But when the Rickover approach of focusing discussions on purely technical issues was accepted, they saw his side of the argument— and while not in total agreement, they began gradually to move the program off dead center. By 1951 Westinghouse was on schedule—but General Electric was still a problem, and would continue to be throughout the program.

Transforming an ideal into a new type of naval vessel was a long and difficult process, one that required a lot of support from the navy's top brass. Rickover bemoaned the fact that many ships were designed and approved based on old Annapolis friendships or associations in the fleet rather than operational requirements. But he was never one to put down the political approach, and in 1949 he found almost the ideal solution to having the nuclear sub proposed and seconded at the CNO level. Lieutenant Commander Charles B. Momsen, Jr. was selected for a position in the Atomic Energy Division of Naval Operations. Young Momsen was the son of Rear Admiral Momsen, inventor of the Momsen lung and a revered naval officer. Thus it came to pass that Admiral Momsen, head of the Underseas Warfare Division in the Bureau of Naval Operations, was prevailed upon to request from the Chief of Naval Operations permission to analyze a closed-cycle nuclear-propulsion system for submarines. When permission was granted, Momsen appointed his son to the ad hoc committee, which received most of its information from the only available source—Code 390 of the Bureau, headed up by Captain Hyman G. Rickover. Needless to say, Momsen's report was glowing with respect to the future use of nuclear power.

"The advent of the true submarine, capable of unrestricted operations in a medium which covers $5/7$ of the globe may revolutionize the entire character of naval warfare," the report began—and became more rapturous of atomic power as it continued. The CNO approved Momsen's report in August 1949, and Rickover's program was made. With this stamp of approval, reactor development was placed at the top of the AEC military list—ahead of the air force's airplane engine and army's artillery.

Now Rickover was anxious to have General Electric commit its vast technical and industrial resources to the project, and beginning in 1950 he harangued GE management to join with the Electric Boat Company in forming a new team. Meanwhile Rickover began what would be a long career in personal congressional liaison. In February 1950 he appeared as a sole witness before the House Senate Joint Committee on Atomic Energy. He criticized conventional submarine capabilities and hinted broadly that the Soviet Union might be well ahead of the United States in reactor development. The congressmen were already worried about recent Soviet developments in the production of atom bombs; Rickover's warnings were well timed and impressive.

When Rickover was finally able to coordinate his two programs—Mark I for the water-cooled reactor and Mark A for the sodium-cooled reactor—they broke down into two teams: Mark I, directed by the AEC field officer in Pittsburgh, was contracted to the Bettis Laboratory and the Westinghouse Corporation to build a submarine thermal reactor at the National Reactor Testing Station, Idaho, for use in *Nautilus*, SSN 571, which would be built by the Electric Boat Division, Groton, Connecticut.

Mark A, directed by the AEC field office in Schenectady, was contracted to the Knolls Atomic Power laboratory and the General

Electric Company to build a sodium-cooled submarine intermediate reactor at West Milton, New York for the *Seawolf*, SSN 575, which would be built by the Electric Boat Division, Groton, Connecticut.

Both the Westinghouse and General Electric designs would be delivered in 1954.

The program proceeded, and Electric Boat made ready to launch the keel of the *Nautilus* in June 1952. Rickover wanted very much to have the kind of publicity splash that only the president of the United States could achieve; so he approached his friend Senator McMahon, still Chairman of the Congressional Joint Committee on Atomic Energy, and suggested he invite President Truman. McMahon was an astute politician and an aspirant for the vice-presidential nomination that year. By now a Rickover convert leading the crusade for a nuclear-powered navy, he agreed that a highly visible position was desirable. The keel laying could bring national attention to the AEC and the accomplishments of the Democratic-controlled Congress. McMahon telephoned the invitation to Truman, who accepted, appeared, and delivered one of his better speeches when he recalled the role atomic energy had played in his administration.

In the summer of 1952, Rickover prepared to face two major crises whose outcome would decide his future in the navy. He had managed to involve himself with the management of Westinghouse, to a great degree, and General Electric, to a lesser degree. At BuShips and the AEC he was respected for his talents; his congressional ties were growing stronger. But now he had a most difficult contractor relationship to hammer out with the Electric Boat Company, one that he felt would make or break the nuclear program. At the same time, he faced a Navy Selection Board in a last chance to be selected for rear admiral or retired.

Rickover had identified what he considered the problem at Electric Boat; it was the general manager, O. Pomeroy Robinson. Rickover had insisted that Robinson depart from the conventional feast-or-famine cycle of running a shipyard; and Robinson refused. Shipyards always retained a core group of employees in spite of the shipbuilding construction cycles, which were subject to wide oscillations. But only this group. Rickover wanted more specialists trained for his program and began instructing Robinson on how to run the yard—from hiring practices to engineering design standards. Robinson balked. He would not be pushed around. It was left to John J. Hopkins, president of General Dynamics, EB's parent company, to intercede. Rickover called on his friends at Westinghouse and General Electric and in Congress to support him against Robinson, and Hopkins eventually caved in to the pressures. He removed Robinson from his post and reconstructed the yard management in accordance with Rickover's recommendation. It was a touch-and-go situation. If Hopkins had not acceded to Rickover's pressure, the precedent might have rallied the managers in other contractor organizations who felt that Rickover was simply too overbearing to have to deal with. But, as had happened in the past and would happen many times in the future, Rickover was willing to sake his career on the turn of a card—and his adversaries were not willing to match the bet.

With the victory over General Dynamic's management notched, Rickover proceeded to confront a much more difficult situation— the navy's selection process. The Navy Selection Board had passed him over once; he knew they would not promote him now, and he would be forced to retire. It seemed hopeless to fight this system. But Rickover had become an expert in rallying from certain defeat, and he pressed on.

At one time, the navy selected officers based almost exclusively on seniority in grade. Then, in 1916, the selection-board system of promotion was established—a system designed to avoid chance and political influence. A selection board was chosen from senior officers—a procedure which placed the evaluation of officers in the hands of other professional naval officers. These officers were best able to determine which of those in lower rank possessed the experience and ability required for assignment to higher rank. Promotion was not intended so much as an award for accomplishment as it was to recognize an officer's capacity for greater responsibility. Over the years the navy had developed precise regulations for the methods used in selecting members of the board and for the way the board would function. The higher boards which selected admirals were chosen by the CNO, and when the board evaluated engineering officers, its membership was required to include three admirals with engineering specialties. So that the exchanges would be candid and the officers could speak frankly concerning their opinion of the candidates, the proceedings of the selection board were kept secret, and no official records were kept.

Selection by the board was tantamount to promotion, but subject to the approval of civilian authorities—the secretary of the navy, the president, and the Senate. And here Rickover and his supporters saw their only opportunity to save his career. Although Rickover's achievements and accomplishments had been widely publicized by the press and his friends in Congress, his work in the navy and the Atomic Energy Commission was not considered of extraordinary merit, and his reputation was not one that would have caused the selection board to choose him as an officer qualified for broader responsibilities. Giving him full credit in his job as a nuclear reactor project manager, still many of the traits he displayed in the job had no special bearing on his fitness for increased responsibility. In fact, in Rickover's case, his tactics and ruthless actions over the years seemed to indicate that exactly the opposite was true. As expected, the selection board passed Rickover over once again, in July 1952. He was fifty-three years of age and had been a captain since 1942. He had no extraordinary record. Now he was faced with retirement on June 30, 1953.

Rickover knew it was very unprofessional to politic for promotion beyond an acceptable limit; certainly no officer had ever taken on the whole promotion system which had worked so well over the years. It was unthinkable for an officer to fault the navy system simply to assure his own promotion. From a navy point of view, Rickover's career accomplishments were far inferior to many other officers who were passed over by the same board— many of them operations heroes in naval combat and men who had displayed extraordinary bravery and leadership capabilities.

Superior talent was one of the criteria for flag rank, and professional officers accepted the fact. But not Rickover. His only hope was in not following their example. He charged his staff to spread the word to the press, to Congress, to anyone who would listen, concerning his battles with the brass and their discrimination against him on that basis. The press was fed stories about his career as an "outsider," his hard days at the Naval Academy, his fight up every rung of the navy ladder. It was dirty infighting all the way. Once they became aware of what was going on, the senior officers in the navy vowed to stop it. They realized that although the promotion system was not sacrosanct, it had proven over the years to be the most effective method of choosing officers, based on their ability and service. An officer—especially a Naval Academy officer—was honor bound not to involve Congress or the press in what had always been an all-navy matter. The admirals were even more disgusted when they learned that Rickover's staff had been alluding to anti-Semitism as a reason for his being passed over. And these rumors caused members of Congress to recommend that the entire selection process be overhauled, since it was obviously faulty if an officer like Rickover was not promoted. The Rickover staff men had found a champion in the House of Representatives in Congressman Sidney R. Yates, and in the Senate in Senator Henry M. Jackson. The two exhorted their colleagues to "teach the brass a lesson" and they eventually mustered enough votes to be able to threaten the navy with holding up all 39 flag nominations, pending a complete investigation of the navy selection system.

Although many senior admirals were willing to fight, Navy Secretary Robert B. Anderson was not, and he directed the navy's capitulation. He wrote Senator Leverett Saltonstall, chairman of the Senate Armed Services Committee, that he would convene a selection board to recommend engineering captains for retention in active duty for the period of one year with a requirement that one of those recommended for retention be experienced in the field of atomic propulsion machinery for ships. It was both a graceful stall and an assurance that Rickover would be selected by the board convening in July 1953. To make matters worse, although the engineering officers on the board unanimously refused to vote for Rickover's nomination once again, the line officers on the board broke tradition by casting a majority vote for the Rickover boondoggle in the face of what had always been the board's deference to their engineering duty peers. Clearly a rigged jury and a permanent stain on the navy's escutcheon.

Rickover could be proud of his record. Seven years earlier he had gone to Oak Ridge as an engineering officer—shuttled aside to wait for retirement. Now, in 1953, he had exposed the navy's management system as unworthy, embarrassed the service, and created a situation that compromised the navy selection process from that time on. He had slugged it out toe-to-toe with America's leading industrialists and won every round—and now he was ready to assume the mantle of the czar of the nuclear navy—whether the navy or the AEC or Westinghouse or General Electric or anyone else objected or not. Some said he rode the wave of antinavy sentiment generated by the air force during this period and was on the air force and congressional side of the movement that crushed the admirals' revolt after the cancellation of plans for a large carrier fleet—in effect, a willing pawn of the congressional Democrats. Others said he was the military contractors' big-weapons advocate in BuShips. But whatever he was, he was first and foremost a nuclear-power advocate, always more interested in his nuclear program than politics or interservice rivalries. The air force was more than happy to support his efforts so long as the carrier remained second to the bomber in priority and budget considerations—and the congressmen loved the way he buffeted the brass. But it never mattered to Rickover whose ox was gored as long as his own program moved ahead.

On January 17, 1955 the first nuclear submarine—the *Nautilus* —sailed down the Thames River from Groton, Connecticut, from the Electric Boat Company's docks to Long Island Sound. Rickover stood on the bridge with the commanding officer, and, as the submarine left its naval escorts, he sent the historic message: "Under way on nuclear power." The nuclear age had begun for the navy, and Rickover would thereafter be regarded as its prophet.

This outstanding technological achievement—this nuclear reactor that performed beyond expectation—would profoundly effect the navy's attitude toward propulsion systems and revolutionize submarine warfare. That was important—all the politics and the money and the strife were petty details, so far as Admiral Rickover was concerned.

After the initial breakthrough, progress in building a nuclear fleet was steady, if not as spectacular as in the original freewheeling postwar period. Nuclear submarines went on the building ways, were commissioned, and joined the fleet. Nuclear-propulsion systems for surface ships followed, but proved much less satisfactory from both a cost and tactical employment basis. Congress finally approved funds for the nuclear-propelled supercarrier *Nimitz* over the arguments of most of the Pentagon military experts—but this program was more in the hands of the navy air lobby, and Rickover was not comfortable with these "brown-shoe" admirals.

With the nuclear program now routine, Rickover seemed to lose interest. Now, looking around for other worlds to conquer, he dredged up two challenges, but both far below the challenge of reactor development. One was the Chief of Naval Personnel, who demanded to be allowed to staff the nuclear navy. The other was Rear Admiral Raborn, who had been selected over him to head the Fleet Ballistic Missile program, and in effect became Rickover's boss. In Vice Admiral James L. Holloway, Jr., Chief of Naval Personnel (BuPers), Rickover saw a man that he could deal with and probably dominate—and so began Rickover's career in education. He attempted not only to reshape the navy's selection policies for the submarine service, but also to change the basic training of submarine officers.

The navy's submarine school in New London, Connecticut, had the sole mission of training personnel for the submarine service, but Rickover wanted to change that. He tried the same techniques of winning one chunk of authority at a time, and when the navy balked, he railed and refused to cooperate. A confrontation with the command at New London resulted in a Rickover strikeout; the school had trained naval officers for submarines from the inception of that service, and it held firm to its ideas and procedures. Rickover was stymied, but then, characteristically, he moved his own submarine school program—the nuclear-reactor school—from New London to Mare Island shipyard at San Francisco. Rickover let it be known that he wanted to be as far away as possible from the New London facility, which, he said, lacked an academic atmosphere and subscribed to standards much lower than were required for his students. He allowed his school to be coaxed back to the East Coast by an offer of the World War II training center at Bainbridge, Maryland; and, when he directed graduation exercises in July 1962, it was with the assurance from Admiral Holloway that BuPers would go along with his demand that he be allowed to select all personnel for the nuclear program. Reports of the Rickover selection system are bizarre, ridiculous, or sublime—depending on the source. They come from an opinion spectrum that includes President Jimmy Carter and ex-CNO Admiral Elmo Zumwalt, both of whom were "tested and selected" by Rickover. The methods were in the true Rickover style—eccentric, unconventional —but in the final analysis they apparently achieved the results he was after: officers turned out in his own image.

Whether he was impressed by the cut of Admiral Raborn's jib or the rumor of Raborn's navy clout, Rickover decided that he had met his match, and, for the first time in his career, did not storm the fortress of Congress for greater authority or cry foul because he had been overlooked for a senior position. Although Raborn went his own way and generally refused to accept Rickover's advice, the two cooperated when it counted. This cooperation led to the development of a solid-fuel, seagoing ballistic missile—a program in many ways more risky and technically difficult than the nuclear submarine.

The first atomic submarine was launched at the cost of $90 million—a beautiful, huge black weapon of destruction, capable of traveling more than 100,000 miles submerged, with a nuclear mass no larger than a baseball as a source of power. In 1957 a second atomic submarine was at sea trials and a third atomic submarine was about to be launched. By this time, the *Nautilus* had logged some 60,000 miles while averaging an incredible 19 knots per hour for a protracted period underwater and was scheduled for the first transit of the Arctic ice cap in the summer of 1958. The submarine made a transit from Hawaii to England, from Pacific to Atlantic, traveling submerged much of the time—a feat that was incredible to submariners who had lived with the limitations of the fleet boat in the Pacific during World War II.

During the next few years, polar trips were common. The *Skate* and the *Nautilus* made several, each time cracking through a thin skylight of ice to maneuver and develop operational procedures. Rickover controlled the complete program from selection of officers for the atomic navy to the selection of contractors for even the most minor equipment to be used aboard the submarines. Gradually he gave up some of the reins of command to other officers and technicians of industry, but always grudgingly. He became a political philosopher—an educational gadfly and a closer friend of those in Congress who needed a friend inside the Pentagon. He continued to push the development of the nuclear submarine, particularly against his implacable foes in the air-power and missile lobbies—and to antagonize an always-renewing set of enemies in the military, industry, and government. Now he castigated the shipyards of the country for building inferior ships as he had once denounced the manufacturers for building inferior parts. He criticized the educational institutions of the United States as being inadequate and inferior to those in other civilized countries around the world. He dealt harshly with any politicians who did not immediately espouse the religion of strength through sea power through the atomic-powered submarine navy.

With a new project—the Trident—and redesigns of the Polaris and Poseidon weapon delivery systems, Rickover continues to oversee larger and more versatile submarines. The Trident, his newest adventure in size, will displace 18,000 tons and operate as a fully mobile ICBM launching pad of 24 hydrogen-tipped missiles capable of submerged firing at targets up to 6,000 miles. Her reactors will be capable of about 400,000 miles—or eight years' cruising without restoration or refurbishment, and each of these submarines will cost something over $1 billion.

Certainly this brilliant, controversial, cantankerous man has created a colossus of sea power out of the force of his own indomitable personality. From the humblest beginnings, from an uneventful assignment and hampered by a lackluster war record, an officer who never had seen combat or any of the naval actions of his time came to be the single most outstanding success story of the Cold War navy. He is a man against whom all of the other Cold Warriors will be measured.

When Rickover recently observed that defense contractors didn't know ships from "horse turds," and that Congress should issue most admirals coloring books to while away their time, and that Annapolis was approaching the Ivy League standards in providing a totally useless education, the assorted military contractors and navy brass and college educator cliques once more railed against him. But his powerful friends on the Senate and House Armed Services Committees rose again to hold back the critics and skeptics. House member Jim Lloyd of California fired a broadside of mixed metaphors which may become the classic apology for this congressional darling and curmudgeon architect of the country's nuclear submarine fleet:

"Mr. Chairman," Lloyd said, "I am not prepared to sail into the teeth of Rickover's excellent batting average compared to that of the others with braid on their sleeves. He is a different drummer."

Sighted skeptics, sank same—the crusty and cantankerous septuagenarian Rickover and his friends are still able to outgun them all.

13 CAESAR: The Response to an Ultimate Weapon

My work on the Research and Development Subcommittee has consumed more of my time and effort than any other responsibility I have had in the Senate. The size and complexity of our military R&D exceeds one's grasp. The Pentagon wants $9.3 billion for R&D spread over three thousand individual programs and projects. My subcommittee has the responsibility of reviewing all of them. I feel sometimes as if we are wrestling with a greased octopus.

—U.S. SENATOR THOMAS H. MCINTYRE
(D.–N.H.)

If we ultimately lose the Cold War, our loss will probably have been caused by the inability of Western politicians to find new ways to communicate the continuing threats posed by the Soviet Union. It will not be because people in Western countries—particularly the United States—are not prepared to shoulder the burdens or are weak or disunified. They are resolute, but they are misinformed—grossly and chronically. The implications of the conflict under the oceans is well understood by both Soviet and American leadership—to the military men who pursue the cold and sometimes hot war in the ocean depths, and also to the politicians who have a part in directing it. But all this is kept from the public because the military feel it is easier to operate their programs in an atmosphere of secrecy—excluding unwanted contractors and covering up mistakes. They are comfortable only if they can spread a cloak of secrecy over most of their activities.

Politicians are notoriously inept and frequently stupid. Their tenures in office are often short. Consequently, the military tell them only so much as they have reason to believe the Russians already know and the American public will believe—information that is not critical to the security of their undertakings. Then politicians rattle off meaningless data or shoot from the hip in criticism or disclose what seems most beneficial to their vote-getting image. The public is caught between a wall of secrecy on one hand and obvious manipulation on the other.

Project CAESAR is a case in point. Stretching over twenty years, the navy's SOSUS (Sound Surveillance System) program of ocean instrumentation—and particularly Project CAESAR, the system of bottom-mounted hydrophones—has put the United States into a commanding position in the field of ASW. But even the most informed military observers outside the navy know very little about CAESAR—and what they know is so wrapped up in technology that they are reluctant to discuss the program out of concern for their own ignorance. The Russians know about CAESAR but play a game with the United States Navy in avoiding discussion of the entire field of covert ASW and long-range surveillance. Both countries are reluctant to discuss the general control of the seabeds, not only with each other but with all the countries of the world that have a stake in the oceans. CAESAR is simply the forerunner of the insonification of the ocean and the use of the seabeds—and eventually the ocean deeps—for warfare. As such, it appalls and frightens the nations of the world far more than the exploits of the major powers in outer space. The ocean has been every man's road to freedom and commerce since the dawn of civilization. Having one or the other—or perhaps both—of the superpowers arm and completely control the oceans of the world, is a concept that will take some getting used to, once the facts begin to filter out of the war rooms.

Like so many events that were to shake the foundations of war at sea, SOSUS activity and the CAESAR project began as an R&D exercise. In the early 1950s the United States Navy approached the Bell Telephone Company with a new concept of sonar—a combination of transducers in long string configurations stretching along the seabeds, tops of sea mountains, and continental shelves of the world. These hydrophones would use the long-distance transmission of sound in deep channels to monitor first hundreds of thousands—and eventually millions—of square miles of ocean, a procedure allowing the navy to track any craft on the surface or under the surface almost anywhere in the world. CAESAR was a very long step from the single operator listening to a "pinging" return from his headphones aboard a sonically noisy destroyer bouncing in pursuit of a submarine in World War II. CAESAR was a sophisticated system which would lay thousands of miles of complex underwater cables and hydrophone assemblies, first at key points along the Atlantic and Pacific coasts, later in other parts of the world. These hydrophones would be linked to shore-based data-processing equipment to complete the sonar network.

The Bell System went to work. It turned over the R&D part of the program to the Bell Telephone Laboratories and the cable-laying and deep-sea operations to the company's Long Lines Department that operated the C.S. *Long Lines,* the largest cable-laying ship in the world. In a year, the first system was ready for sea—a tailor-made miracle.

The CAESAR system combined several sonar techniques and equipments. Deep-sea cables were built to stay buried and operate reliably for twenty or more years in the ocean. Rugged new transducers could be laid just like the cables were designed, but most important was the sophisticated new computer-processing equipment that would reduce all of the ships and submarines in the world to individual signatures and run continuous plots on the traffic of the surface and subsurface of the oceans in the same manner that high-powered radar systems functioned to monitor the movements of aircraft and satellites.

Instrumenting the sea for military purposes was considered a most sensitive area—not only by the United States, but also by the Russians, who had their own surveillance systems covertly installed in the Arctic. It was obvious that the ocean depths of the world would be controlled by one or both of the superpowers—notwithstanding the efforts of the other navies in building atomic submarines or the publicized adventures of the undersea explorers. Conquering the total hydrospace of the world would involve enormous resources and the high technology available only to the Soviet Union and the United States. Other nations of the world would not find such a prospect comforting or acceptable. Thus, from the beginning, progress in CAESAR and its related weaponry was kept secret—discounted with respect to military implications and passed over quickly in disarmament and seabed treaty discussions or weapons-limitation negotiations.

In passive, long-range ASW surveillance, the United States Navy began years ahead of the Russians and has since maintained a substantial lead. The Russians have been attempting to duplicate the SOSUS system and CAESAR—in fact, Russian hydrophone strings have washed up on beaches in Iceland and have been discovered on continental-shelf areas close to the Soviet Union. Their technology appears to be far inferior and their site installation opportunities comparatively poor, but the Russians have begun to carve out their own barrier areas. Military planners project that by 1990 or sooner there will be a complete monitoring of most of the surface and subsurface of the ocean—much as there is now in space. Sonar installations similar to radar will monitor ship and submarine movements in real time. Its primary impact will be on naval strategic weapons; it will make the SLBM submarines vulnerable. Just as the bomber and missile are easily detectable by radar, which is the heart of antibomber and missile-defense systems, long-range sonar poses a similar threat to the submarine. The tracking and targeting of all of the SLBM fleets for destruction by land-based or carrier-based aircraft or by trailing attack submarines will then be possible.

But still the debate continues in Congress and in the press on the advisability of building multibillion-dollar aircraft carriers and submarines, without the public's being advised of the vulnerability of both these weapons. Naval air enthusiasts and submarine advocates debate pro and con about where the enormous Navy Department budget should be expended, but they agree on at least one point: all the recommendations are for larger versions of ships. Although these ships seem totally unrealistic in terms of future applications in a hot war, questions about them are seldom raised outside of navy or DOD forums. The problem is left to an inept Congress to struggle with or leave unresolved. The public is ignored.

Each year the National Security Industrial Association, a military contractors' group founded to support the Pentagon, holds a Washington meeting of its ASW Advisory Committee. The top ten projects for the coming year are announced, and the weapons builders then know where the navy would like them to concentrate, based on navy priorities in allocating funds. For the past decade, the CAESAR program has topped the list simply because it is the best ASW weapon—indeed, perhaps the only effective ASW weapon—against the Soviet submarine forces, which are becoming increasingly more sophisticated.

And this brings us to the most secret of the Wet Cold War battlegrounds: the covert operations of Russian ships and submarines attempting to locate and sometimes destroy CAESAR sites —Russian trawlers dragging to hook the cables and underseas craft patrolling to locate and identify the hydrophone strings. When they can make it appear accidental, the CAESAR cables are cut and recovered for study. But so far the Russians have not effectively copied the system—probably because they cannot match the Bell Telephone Laboratories sophisticated technology. And even when they have designed a CAESAR model that works, the absence of suitable sea mounts and continental-shelf locations on which the cables and hydrophones must be laid for maximum effectiveness will limit the Russians. Most of the best sites have already been taken, and the cable run to Russia would be a long and vulnerable link.

The CAESAR program is one element of the United States Navy's ASW surveillance arm—by far the most important, but designed to operate in conjunction with other fixed, mobile, and deployable systems. ASW has long been one of the areas of substantial and anticipated growth within the military, and there is no shortage of contractor firms willing to enter the R&D race in order to win lucrative production contracts.

But while most of the systems are primarily tactical, CAESAR was a strategic system from its beginning. If passive underwater hydrophonic arrays could be located on sea mounts and the continental shelves around the world, perhaps the total submarine problem might be simplified. Then the problem becomes not where the submarines are, but only the best method of tracking them down for a kill. And if nuclear weapons are employed, extensive tracking may not be required at all. Navy aircraft or attack submarines can cruise hundreds of miles away from a target, knowing its position and projecting its course and speed, with a nuclear-tipped homing weapon with a high kill probability targeted and ready. In a brief staging time, the entire Russian submarine fleet at sea could be threatened. And this goal of super-reliable long-range detection and continuous tracking is very near for the United States Navy, but only a distant and remote prospect for the Russian ASW forces.

The U.S. Navy's ASW budget for RDT&E (Research, Development, Test, and Engineering) and procurement has increased from less than $2 billion in 1965 to over $4 billion in 1977. With the Trident submarine development in early production stages, it is difficult to project expenditures; however, if Trident is partially replaced by a fleet of many more smaller nuclear submarines, the budget dollar surplus remaining will certainly go into new ASW procurements and increased sonar surveillance capability.

The East Coast CAESAR system was first successfully operated in the early 1960s and played a significant role in frustrating the Russian attempts to bluff their way into a missile-base position in Cuba. It has been continually upgraded; each succeeding president is delighted to learn of this remarkable capability. In the mid–

1960s we offered to extend the CAESAR system to friendly countries—those that would allow CAESAR terminals to be installed as part of the navy's overall world network. In Great Britain and Japan, systems were installed in the shallow coastal areas which had proven over the years to be the favorite exit points for Soviet submarines proceeding to the high seas. In 1967 there was congressional debate about extending CAESAR overseas, but testimony allayed congressional fears that control of the system would slip beyond the navy's reach.

Attempting to decide who is ahead in the submarine and antisubmarine competition is like trying to pick the National Football League Super Bowl winner before the season begins. Still, the brave and foolhardy do, year after year, and publish and proclaim their selection with a confidence supported by libraries of information and assisted by advanced data-processing techniques. But until two teams play out a season and finally confront each other, no decision is possible. All the preseason speculation is meaningless. As the play begins with the first game and continues to the championship climax, many things happen along the way that cannot be forecast: a quarterback breaks his wrist, a lightly regarded lineman becomes a defensive superstar, a coach resigns—an infinity of detail, all of which, to a greater or lesser degree, will affect the outcome of the contest.

In the submarine-antisubmarine forces corollary, we have similar uncertainties: the relative training of navy personnel, the rapidly changing technologies, the military budgets, the arms-limitation treaties, Russia's inferior weapons, America's faltering leadership, NATO's growing naval forces, China's SLBM construction program, and many more factors which will affect the East-West sea-power confrontation—a contest that may or may not ever take place. But there are two factors that weigh heavily in the present balance: the advent of the supersubmarine, Trident and the extension of the long-range sonar surveillance science in CAESAR and TASS and MSS, the large suspended and bottom-moored array systems. Their capabilities are on the increase, and the threat to Trident's massive ICBM capability is growing. The CAESAR-TASS-

MSS networks are making the oceans ever more transparent.

But now both weapons systems are on the same side—and for the foreseeable future the Russians will not have the capability, budget, or sea sites to match CAESAR-SASS undersea sonar systems, or to build a fleet of Trident class super-SLBM platforms.

As two teams face each other on a football field, the relative dominance of a great defense versus a great offense may be a subject for debate—but only if an unstoppable force faces an immovable object across a scrimmage line. If the highest-scoring offense and the toughest defense are on the same side, the argument becomes academic.

With CAESAR, Trident, SASS, Tomahawk, and the rest of the United States Navy's Cold Wet War arsenal ranged against any enemy, the outcome of any contest in the near future seems assured.

14 Admiral Sergei Gorshkov: The Russian Mahan

The constant upgrading of its readiness for immediate combat operations in the most complex situation is a most important pre-condition determining the development of the Navy. At the present time, when in a matter of minutes it is possible to reach major strategic targets and even to accomplish particular missions of the war in certain areas, the need is objectively arising to maintain the highest readiness for naval forces and weaponry. This is a consequence of the effect of the develop-ment of naval equipment and weaponry and also of the conditions in which navies have to carry out missions.

In light of what has been said above, the old well-known formula—"the battle for the first salvo"—is taking on a special meaning in naval battle under present-day conditions [conditions including the possible employment of combat means of colossal power]. Delay in the employment of weapons in a naval battle or operation inevitably will be fraught with the most serious and even fatal consequences, regardless of where the fleet is located, at sea or in port.

—SERGEI G. GORSHKOV
Commander-in-Chief of the Soviet Navy

Since 1945 the Russians' maritime threat has been assessed through their own eyes and attitudes, principally through the hardware they have introduced as a measure of the military assessments of their requirements. Design decisions had to be made for those units that actually went into service, and these long-range projections mirror the evolving nature of the Soviet military posture. Colored by their belief that they stand in national danger, the Soviet press has played on the theme of the West's control of the seas and the menace of attack from that sector. They point out that more than one-third of the total strategic strike potential of the Western powers is concentrated in a nuclear-submarine and aircraft-carrier fleet of the United States. Since the end of the war, this strategic situation which troubles the Soviets has continued to undergo a fundamental change. For the first time in their experience, their potential enemies are now the traditional maritime powers, and the nature of the threat to Russia since 1945 has gradually "gone to sea" even more because of changes in technology.

Russia has built the second largest navy in the world. Since she is not considered a traditional maritime power, there must be some unusual purpose for which this powerful force has been assembled. It is not the first time in Russian history that she sought to further her aims by the use of sea power—and until the war with Japan in 1904, her navy was used rather effectively, particularly against the Swedes and the Turks. But the dramatic victory over the Turks in the Battle of Sinope in 1853 was the last of Russia's successes; the outbreak of World War I found Russian ships and equipment obsolete, and when Lenin seized power after the Revolution, he decreed that Soviet Russia did not require a navy. In fact, so low was the Communist government's opinion of the navy that this doctrine was followed for ten years and the fleets languished.

The father of the modern Russian Navy was Admiral Nikolai Kuznetsov. In March 1939 he was appointed Commissar of the Soviet Navy and was entrusted with implementation of naval preparedness. He commanded naval forces in World War II, but in 1947 was retired for four years because of political difficulties connected with the integration of both the army and navy under a single Ministry of Defense. In 1951 he was reinstated and put together a program of naval construction and expansion. But in 1955, two years after the death of Stalin, after another political argument over army and navy authority, he was replaced by Admiral Sergei Gorshkov, his deputy.

It has been said that the Russians have no naval tradition, but this is not strictly true. Instead, a lack of tactical skill has characterized their actions in the past—a disorganization and reluctance to act—attributed, in part, to the army's dominant role. To change this perspective, the Russian naval forces were reorganized after World War II. Until 1932 the Soviet Navy was divided into the Baltic and Black Sea fleets. Under Stalin's policy of naval expansion, two additional fleets were formed: one in the Arctic, known as the Northern Fleet, and one in the Pacific. These four fleets are independent and self-contained. They have their own supply and repair organizations. The commander-in-chief of each fleet controls not only ships and aircraft attached to it, but also all of the coast defenses and divisions in coastal areas. Political control of the navy is exercised through the Political Director of Naval Affairs, who is subordinate to the Chief Political Director of the Armed Forces. A political assistant commander is attached to every ship and shore establishment; he is subordinate to commanding officers who, in addition to their naval duties, are responsible for the political attitudes of their officers and men. In the larger ships, political assistants are attached to the commanding officer and heads of departments. Every day these political assistants interpret the news of the navy and the world in terms of Marxist principles.

Russian naval officers are almost all regulars—as was the United States naval officer corps before World War II. They are not permitted to leave the service before the maximum retirement age for their rank. They enter into naval cadet school at age ten, and competition for these appointments is keen because of the high pay differential between officers and men. The officer class is reminiscent of the old czarist days, although political supervision is ensured by the political assistant commanders—a system which has hampered the Russian military since the Revolution. This political auditing prevents Soviet flag and commanding officers from exercising full authority; it is a double-banked control which allows very little scope for initiative.

Fleet Admiral Gorshkov has been called the Russian Mahan by naval-power advocates in both East and West; he is a man who has been a flag officer longer than any professional in any navy in the world. Gorshkov was appointed Commander-in-Chief of the Soviet Navy in June 1956, replacing Admiral Nikolai G. Kuznetsov, who was forced to resign in a dispute with Khrushchev. Kuznetsov lost the faction fight between the army and navy, a power struggle in which Khrushchev used the army's support to seize command of the party and government and do away with the troika leadership that had governed Russia after Stalin's death. Somehow Admiral Gorshkov, Kuznetsov's first deputy, survived the political wars and became the head of the navy—the youngest in Russian history. Gorshkov is durable and capable, able to roll with the punches and adapt quickly. He is not only a naval officer but also, to a large extent, a politician—a Rickover without bombast. Most important, Gorshkov has survived countless purges and power plays.

Sergei Gorshkov was born in 1910 in the city of Kamenets Podolski in the Ukraine. He attended the Frunze Higher Naval School and graduated in 1931, a vintage year for the Soviet and United States naval officers who were to lead their country's naval forces in the Second World War. After a number of early assignments in destroyers in the Black Sea and Pacific fleets, he was cited by Admiral Kuznetsov, then Commander-in-Chief of the Pacific

Fleet, as a particularly bright young officer and given a destroyer command. In 1938, while commanding a destroyer division as captain, second rank (equivalent to commander in the United States Navy), Gorshkov's promising career suffered an almost fatal setback. After the military purges of 1937–1938, Gorshkov stood to benefit from Stalin's bloodbaths. Most of the high-ranking naval officers had been executed; promotion of junior officers was certain to be rapid. Gorshkov remained politically aloof and worked hard at his command. He was placed in charge of the commissioning of the new destroyer *Reshitelny* and personally directed a towing operation to move the destroyer to a fitting-out base. A storm drove the towing ship and destroyer on the rocks near Cape Zolotoni, close to Vladivostok. One man was killed, and the matter was serious enough to be brought to Stalin's attention. Gorshkov's commission was about to be revoked, but Admiral Kuznetsov went to Moscow to plead for him, and no court-martial action was instituted.

Returning to the Black Sea Fleet, Gorshkov again took command of a division of destroyers and completed the advanced line-officers' course at Voroshilov Naval Academy. When war broke out in June 1941, Gorshkov had command of a cruiser division of the Black Sea Fleet based in Sevastopol. He saw action with Rear Admiral Zhukov in the defense of Odessa, where troops and naval forces fought desperately under Stalin's orders not to abandon Odessa under any circumstances. Gorshkov was now a captain, first rank (equivalent to a captain in the United States Navy), and commanded naval infantry in a landing force defending Sevastopol, and later Odessa. In one of the few successful early Soviet actions against the Germans on that front, Gorshkov was able to contain the German offensive for two weeks before evacuation was ordered.

In 1941 Gorshkov was promoted to rear admiral, his reputation made by the single action at Odessa. He was placed in command of a flotilla of the Black Sea Fleet but continued to direct amphibious operations and infantry actions, including the Russian retreat from Odessa and the evacuation of the Kerch Peninsula in

May 1942. His ships were credited with protecting the sea flanks of the Red Army retreating to the Caucasus. Later Gorshkov led several amphibious operations on the German rear forces which slowed their progress enough to allow the retreating Russians to escape.

By 1942 the Azov Sea was completely controlled by the Germans. They had swept away the Black Sea Fleet. Remnants of the fleet including Gorshkov's command were hidden in small ports, unwilling to take any offensive actions. Gorshkov was appointed Deputy Commander of Naval Matters in the Novorossiysk defense district, where the army and navy had joined to prevent the German forces from advancing to the Baku oil fields. The Germans continued to advance until February 1943, when the Soviets, under Gorshkov's command, began to counterattack near Novorossiysk. After continual assault by Russian troops, the Germans finally abandoned the Novorossiysk front. During this period, Gorshkov's principal responsibility was supervising the transport of troops and military supplies across the Kerch Strait. In 1944 he was still a rear admiral, now commanding the Danube flotilla which supported Marshal Malinovsky in the advance that carried through the Ukraine, Romania, Bulgaria, and eventually into Hungary. Then the war ended.

Gorshkov assumed command of a squadron of the Black Sea Fleet and in 1948 was promoted to chief of staff of the fleet. Compared to many Allied naval commanders, his war record was mediocre; his experience more closely related to amphibious-assault and naval-landing-party operations than command at sea. But the Soviets had few naval heroes in World War II, and very little to go on in selecting postwar commanders based on their wartime records. In 1951 Admiral Kuznetsov was reappointed Commander-in-Chief of the Soviet Navy in a political reshuffling that gave Gorshkov command of the Black Sea Fleet and resulted in his promotion to vice admiral.

In 1955 Gorshkov was appointed First Deputy Chief of the Soviet Navy. He remained aloof from the power struggle between the troika that replaced Stalin, but managed to let his sympathies be known. He claimed to be a submarine advocate rather than a large-surface-ship proponent—philosophically placing himself squarely on the side of Khrushchev and against Admiral Kuznetsov, his superior of many years. Khrushchev won the party and state leadership and appointed Gorshkov as the Commander-in-Chief of the Soviet Navy in June 1956, commenting that Gorshkov was a good combination of sailor and diplomat, had a reliable political background, espoused the submarine and missile technology, and was from the Ukraine—all of which were endearing qualities to the new chairman.

During the Khrushchev era, Gorshkov remained discreetly in the background, writing an occasional article or speaking at a Navy Day function, and completely satisfying Khrushchev as a defensive-fleet, submarine-oriented strategist. Gorshkov was awarded the Order of Lenin for services to the state and in 1962 was appointed to the rank of fleet admiral. Gradually Gorshkov seemed to be brought to the opinion that although submarines and defensive measures were important, the Soviets should have a larger navy, including even capital ships. When Khrushchev announced plans to scrap 90 percent of the Soviet Navy's cruisers, Gorshkov was able to persuade him of the need for some larger ships, and so the Sverdlov class cruisers were kept in service and the construction program for missile destroyers was continued. Gorshkov's policies were vindicated in the eyes of the Russian hierarchy in 1963, when the Cuban missile crisis clearly demonstrated that there was simply no way for a second-class sea power to confront the United States in the Atlantic with any hope of success. So Gorshkov, who had been a submarine advocate with no submarine experience, now became a large-ship advocate with no blue-water experience. Still, there was something in his message that pleased the communist leadership and he survived Khrushchev's fall.

In 1965 Marshal Zakharov honored Gorshkov for his wartime leadership of the Danube flotilla and he was publicly proclaimed one of the leading heroes of World War II. He began appearing in key places and was in the reviewing stand at important functions and at state dinners was seen in the company of the right Com-

munist Party bosses. Gorshkov's star was again on the rise, reflecting not only his personal situation but also the new emphasis on
the navy in the scheme of Russian military forces. In 1967 a new
rank was created for him, similar to the U.S. Navy's five-star fleet
admiral, and Gorshkov was encouraged to become the poet and
promoter of the Red Navy's cause in the government.

Gorshkov's message was one of continued warning to the West
—uncharacteristically polite, but all the same, in a saber-rattling
vein. He told the Western powers that it was only a matter of time
before the Soviet Union would be supreme at sea. Once he had
supported the submarine as the ultimate weapon, discussed oceanography as the science of the future, and doomed the aircraft carrier
in that classic Russian tendency to write off what they could not
copy well. Now he was the leading advocate of a large-ship navy—
including even small aircraft carriers.

As a navy propagandist, Gorshkov served admirably. He had
a flair for straightforward position and even a turn of phrase
which most of the Soviet propagandists lacked. And he was
preaching to the baptized; his messages were addressed primarily
to the naval leaders of the world who happily reciprocated by re-
inforcing his claims of Russian naval strength, since it was in their
self-interest to do so.

Beginning in 1970, Gorshkov wrote a history of the Russian
Navy in World War II. This was almost as arduous a task as would
have been the making of heroes from the French fleet during the
Napoleonic era. But Gorshkov claimed that Soviet sailors were in
fact soldiers, and more valuable in conducting landing parties and
amphibious operations than fighting the Germans at sea. His writ-
ings were published in Soviet military magazines, and instantly
seized on for reprinting and comment by publications of naval
interest in the West. Gorshkov was critically acclaimed as a military
writer—not so much for his style or content but because he was
the only voice Western critics could hear concerning Soviet naval
matters, and they wanted to keep this communications channel
open.

If there is a hero in the modern Russian Navy, and particularly the Soviet submarine program, it must be Admiral Gorshkov. As the chief spokesman—if not the architect—of the new Soviet policy, he has pushed for those weapons most likely to terrorize and frustrate the West: submarines, missile ships, ASW light cruisers, and destroyers.

There are other Soviet officers rising in the ranks who will probably be more significant than Gorshkov, since they will face more trying times with both the United States and China. Nevertheless, Gorshkov's career must be considered remarkable. He survived the purges of the thirties and the political infighting of the sixties. He rose from being a whipped naval officer in war to become a hero in peace. And, most of all, he managed to stay on the correct side of the defensive vs. offensive fleet argument for forty years. Gorshkov joined the Communist Party in 1942 and juggled the extraordinary positions of elected Soviet official, member of the Communist Party Congress and the Central Committee, and professional naval officer—pursuing both a military and political career simultaneously. He is a forceful writer and has managed to present the West with arguments strong enough to convince many that the present Soviet policy will challenge the United States for supremacy at sea. As long as Gorshkov has a forum in the Soviet military journals, he will continue to add to his laurels and delight Western military observers who support big fleets.

15 A Casualty of the Cold War: The Thresher Disaster

O Death, old captain, it is time!
Raise the anchor!

—BAUDELAIRE

The sudden deaths of explorers, innovators, and researchers who probe the extent of geographic and scientific boundaries has always held a special fascination. These men demonstrate a different kind of heroism, not made of wars, or great political victories, or social uplift. It is the kind of courage that is difficult to classify; men doing their jobs in the face of obvious danger, day after day, until the danger becomes commonplace and is all but ignored. The astronaut goes into space time after time and then faces an impossible reentry situation. The lone explorer never returns from the jungle. The test pilot loses an ongoing battle with gravity. But perhaps the most awesome are men who go down to the depths of the oceans in diving suits, bells, and submarines to explore those last vast frontiers, men who work in the abyss to master the hydrospace.

From the beginning of her short career, the *Thresher* was a very special submarine—designed by the U.S. Navy's best engineers with the advice of the navy's top submarine commanders. Her single high-speed hull would combine the most advanced sonars, together with a design that accommodated the latest deadly weapons. This submarine was the answer to the missile-firing submarines that were being built in the Soviet Union. The sixty years of submarine technology and the experience of the United States

Navy in two wars were combined to develop the *Thresher*'s design, the weapons she would use, and the tactics she would employ. As a modification of the Skipjack class, she was a hunter-killer weapon designed around sonar detection equipment, operating to optimize her sonar systems' performance. The *Thresher* represented the navy's commitment to carry the ASW offensive against the Russian submarines by the development of one of their own kind: a killer submarine. Her primary mission was locating and destroying other submarines—no matter how deep or fast or quiet they were running, or in what part of the world.

Later some called it a mistake—certainly, in view of the consequences, it might have been—but the *Thresher* was the first of the lead ships for any of the classes of submarines to be built by a United States Navy shipyard. The Portsmouth Naval Shipyard in New Hampshire was selected over the Electric Boat Yard in Groton, Connecticut—the yard that had been first with the Nautilus, Seawolf, Skate, Skipjack, Tullibe and George Washington class submarines.

When Commander Wesley Harvey took over as skipper of the *Thresher,* she was going through an overhaul at the Portsmouth Naval Shipyard—a process of removing the kinks from her shakedown cruise and trying to determine whether the design of the large forward sonar unit would require modifications. Every first design of a new class is a risk, and in a submarine where there is small margin for error, the risk is compounded. Therefore, extreme precautions are taken during this evaluation period. In the course of the overhaul, 875 different work requests had been processed—jobs the shipyard was responsible for completing before the *Thresher* would put to sea again. According to later reports, for the most part, they were completed and signed off as satisfactory—but there were questions about a few items that were never resolved.

There may be colder parts of the ocean than the waters off the Piscataqua River where it empties into the Atlantic Ocean near the Portsmouth Naval Shipyard, but they must be very close to the Arctic. At 3:45 on the morning of April 9, 1963, the *Thresher* began making preparations to go to sea. The control rods that would start the reactor were arranged, and the atom-splitting process of the sustained nuclear reaction was begun.

The nominal crew of 104 men was increased to 129 by the addition of casual observers and yard inspectors who decided to go along to check how their particular areas were functioning. One ship's officer, Lieutenant Raymond J. McCoole, was excused because his wife had sustained an eye injury and finding someone to care for their five children was a problem. A young chief machinist's mate, Frank D. Stefano, had been dispatched to Washington for a tête-à-tête with Vice Admiral Rickover in preparation for further assignment in the nuclear-power program. It was not a time for high drama, just a casual operating day off the New Hampshire coast. The *Thresher* wallowed along in company of the submarine rescue ship *Skylark*—the escort during her diving tests and the communication link with shore stations. The *Skylark*'s skipper, Lieutenant Stanley W. Hecker, was later cited and threatened with court-martial for his conduct during the *Thresher* affair—specifically for his failure to issue an early report concerning the probable sinking.

After the loss of the *Squalus* in 1939, when 26 men were trapped and drowned, the U.S. Navy had been very strict about rescue ships accompanying all submarines on shakedowns and postshipyard overhaul operations. The *Squalus* had sunk in 240 feet of water; the rescue chamber carried by *Skylark* was capable of taking men off a submarine to depths as great as 850 feet. If operations were conducted over the continental shelf—that submerged coastal area where the water depth is less than 600 feet—the *Skylark* would be able to use its rescue equipment to remove anyone aboard a sunken submarine.

The *Thresher* made her first shallow dive to check for minor leaks and test major equipment performance, then surfaced after the dive, wallowed awhile on the surface while Commander Harvey exchanged information with the skipper of the *Skylark*. Harvey released the rescue ship and directed a rendezvous again with the submarine the next morning for deep-dive tests which were to be conducted some 200 miles east of Cape Cod, Massachusetts. These tests would be conducted beyond the limit of the continental shelf in an area where the bottom drops to 8,000 feet and more, since the *Thresher*'s diving capability was greater than the 600-foot continental shelf could accommodate. The *Thresher* continued her drills during the day, making a full-power run and several maneuvering runs.

That night the *Thresher* dove into deeper water. Commander Harvey transmitted a routine radio check to the Atlantic Fleet Submarine Force Headquarters at Norfolk, Virginia, and early the next morning the *Thresher* came to periscope depth about 10 miles from the *Skylark*. The submarine held depth for a short period of time—then submerged on what would be her last dive.

An hour later, the *Thresher* notified the *Skylark* by underwater telephone that she was preparing to dive to test depth—the maximum depth at which she was designed to operate. Before entering the navy yard for the nine-month overhaul, she had been to test depth over forty times during the shakedown cruise. However, submarine skippers are under strict orders not to go to test depth except in cases of dire emergency—which ordinarily means only evasive action from enemy attack. As the submarine dives beyond test depth, the hull builds up enormous pressures which often rupture pipes and fittings. Eventually, at sufficient depth, the hull splits. The submarine floods in a matter of seconds.

The *Thresher* was intended to stay near test depth but not exceed it—to advise the *Skylark* of her course, depth, and speed, and to make a routine fifteen-minute radio check while operating. Such telephone messages are recorded in logs, along with significant operating information both on the submarine and the rescue vessel. During the subsequent court of inquiry proceedings, the *Skylark*'s log was carefully examined and the messages analyzed. But they shed no light on the tragedy.

At approximately 7:45 A.M., the *Thresher* reported to the *Skylark* that she was beginning her test-depth dive, and five minutes later reported that she was below 400 feet and checking for leaks. Things were progressing normally when at 9:00 the *Thresher* reported, ". . . have positive angle . . . attempting to blow up."

A few minutes later, the sonar operators of the *Skylark* heard the sound of air escaping under high pressure. Sonar interrogation at 9:14 drew no answer, and communication with the *Thresher* was lost.

Lieutenant Hecker received a last message at 9:17, too garbled to be understood, except for the distinct words "test depth." Then there were sounds familiar to those who had manned hydrophones in World War II—the muffled roaring of a submarine breaking up, compartments collapsing, air escaping under pressure. The *Skylark* patrolled the area, dropping hand grenades as a signal for the submarine to surface. Hecker informed New London that he had lost communication with the *Thresher* and described the sounds of disaster. He was told to remain on station and await assistance.

So the search for the *Thresher* began—a search that would take months before any signs of the submarine were located. By 3:00 that afternoon, Chief of Naval Operations George W. Anderson had been alerted to the *Thresher* "incident," and he set up a hotline circuit to New London. Secretary of the Navy Fred Korth called an emergency meeting of his staff, and later in the day, President John F. Kennedy, the first United States president to have served as a naval officer, discussed the prospect that the submarine might be lost and possible tragic ramifications with his naval aide.

Since the *Thresher*'s last reported position was off the tip of Nova Scotia, the Canadian Navy was asked to stand by to assist— and from the crews assembled for the Canadian submarines, word leaked out that a United States submarine was in trouble.

The massive search involved thousands of hours for navy rescue ships, frigates, destroyers, and even the submarines *Seawolf* and *Seaowl*. The destroyer in which I served with Task Force 77 in Korea—the U.S.S. *The Sullivans* (DD537), was a part of the rescue operation, which was taken over on April 11 by Rear Admiral Lawson Paterson Ramage, Deputy Commander of Submarines in the Atlantic. Ramage was one of the most decorated submarine commanders in World War II and the Chief of Naval Operations' personal choice to head the rescue mission.

The Russians complained that since the sinking took place close to the Gulf Stream, the newly charged atomic reactor would contaminate the Atlantic waters. A host of oceanographic research ships began to operate in the area. The *Allegheny, Chain, Conrad, Gilliss, Mission Capistrano, Prevail, Requisite,* and *Rickfell* all saw service in support of the rescue operations. *Atlantis II* was the most advanced oceanographic research vessel in the United States at that time—a floating laboratory operated by the Institute of Oceanography, Woods Hole, Massachusetts—equipped with excellent depth-recording instruments and advanced sonars. The unmanned, obsolete submarine *Toro* was used in a search operation. To approximate the sinking, she was rigged with a large sonar reflector and towed to the search area. Under controlled conditions, the *Toro* was sunk to approximate the sinking of the *Thresher.* Through sonar tracking, perhaps the *Toro,* as she sank, might lead to the *Thresher* or parts of her hull.

Then *Atlantis II* began locating cameras close enough to the bottom to take pictures of any unusual-looking debris, and the first pictures located rings of the type used for sealing hydraulic equipment aboard submarines. Then more wreckage was photographed, and finally pieces of pipe, air bottles, and metal plates, from which a probable site for the sinking was established.

The *Trieste* was the only navy manned vehicle that could operate at the 8,400–foot depth in which the *Thresher* was believed to have sunk. It was deployed in the Pacific and had to be shipped across the continent by rail. The *Trieste* was a diving tank with float controls; when seawater filled her tanks, her hull submerged. To return to the surface, BB-like shot was released by electromagnets. As the *Trieste* engaged in operations together with the *Fort Snelling* and *Preserver,* Russian tankers passed close by, ignoring signals to stand clear because of submarine rescue operations. Dive after dive was made, each one more tantalizing, until finally the *Trieste* began to track along a trail of debris which included scraps of metal, paper, and a yellow bootee worn by men in the reactor compartments of nuclear submarines to prevent radioactive dust from being picked up on their shoes. Eventually, enough debris was found to determine that the *Thresher* had sunk in the area. On August 24, 1963, the *Trieste* made photographs which were positively identified as *Thresher* bow markings, and the search was ended.

Meanwhile, a navy court of inquiry was convened to find out who or what might be responsible. The official reports indicated that there were indeed many problems with the equipment provided by the naval shipyard, and the court thrashed back and forth with testimony from a number of officers and enlisted men in an effort to obtain some clarification of the disaster. Rear Admiral Charles Joseph Palmer, the Portsmouth Naval Shipyard commander, was asked searching questions and was advised by the court that because of the nature of the *Thresher* loss, the construction and quality-control departments of the yard were suspect. Weeks of testimony followed, including statements by Vice Admiral Rickover, who appeared in mufti, read a prepared statement, and then briefed the court in camera concerning the possibility of radioactive contamination. In one of the last acts of the court, Lieutenant Hecker, the *Skylark* skipper, was exonerated after a plea by his navy attorney who told the court that while Hecker "doesn't for one minute hold that the court has branded him a scapegoat—a substantial segment of public opinion did, in fact, think very much along those lines." But there was to be no scapegoat, and in fact, although the hearings concluded on May 16, it was not until June 20, 1963, that the Department of Defense Public Affairs Office published a vague three-page document that summarized the findings as inconclusive. Perhaps this was the key statement: "The record states that it is impossible, with the information now available, to obtain a more precise determination of what actually happened."

And on that ambiguous note, the investigation into the worst submarine disaster in history closed.

As in most disasters of this kind—whether in space or under the sea—aside from the families of the victims who must carry the loss for a lifetime, a complacency about the disaster usually sets in very quickly. But the loss of the *Thresher* was different, perhaps because it involved the investigation of the hydrospace, the U.S. Navy's bid for supremacy in submarine warfare, and the natural association in the public mind with the romance and deadly business of submarining. The Navy Department studied the design of the *Thresher*, and several changes were made in submarine construction techniques. A program to improve the art of silver brazing for piping was pushed as a remedy to the suspect technical areas brought to light in the investigation. BuShips drew up a list of alterations which were to be made on deep diving submarines before they would be allowed to reach their maximum depth limitation. Thus, in the dramatic mystery of the *Thresher* disappearance, the public was abruptly introduced to the emerging new science of oceanography and our stake in the future of hydrospace development. A U.S. Navy Deep Submergence Systems Review Group was formed as a direct outgrowth of activities of oceanographers and research vessels in the *Thresher* search, and the press made a romantic denizen of the abyss of the *Trieste*—a marvelous vehicle on which to hang the story of life-and-death research activities at great depths. Hydrospace and oceanography became more familiar terms, like aerospace and Sputnik. And, like Sputnik, the *Thresher* loss set off a race for inner-space supremacy.

There were darker reasons suggested for the *Thresher* incident when the shipyard at Quincy, Massachusetts, reported that the nuclear-powered missile cruiser *Long Beach* was sabotaged. The submarine *Snook*, in dry dock in Pascagoula, Mississippi, also suffered damage that was laid to sabotage. Similar incidents in the two-year period prior to the *Thresher* disaster were reviewed by the FBI and Naval Intelligence. But it was difficult to determine whether these sabotage cases were the work of enemy agents, recalcitrant yard workers, naval personnel, or simple gross negligence.

Earlier, when the submarine *Triton* began her round-the-world submerged cruise in 1961, her ventilation valves would not close. Although there was a double valve in the ventilation system, the *Triton* skipper described the faulty valve as a critical component. Investigation eventually disclosed that a smashed and rusted flashlight had lodged in the valve seat—left there by a careless yard worker prior to sailing. Such incidents made naval designers more confirmed in their opinion that most of their problems were the result of poor quality-assurance at the yard facilities. Broad hints by Admiral Rickover and others that United States industry in general and shipyards in particular were guilty of poor workmanship and shoddy inspection procedures were aired in the press. Rickover had critized the improper use of materials in construction of deepsubmergence vehicles, and particularly submarines. He cited the problem of faulty welding, faulty radiographs, and defective castings—all deficiencies in basic, conventional processes of ordinary technology. Rickover had sounded this warning six months before the *Thresher* had gone to the bottom—six months after the navy had announced that all 31 nuclear-powered submarines then under construction were being delayed because of deficiencies in equipment and workmanship.

Enemy action was also cited as a possible cause of the *Thresher* loss. It was postulated that the *Thresher* was being trailed by a Soviet nuclear submarine for the purpose of observing the tests. An accidental collision could have occurred—possibly even one that would be difficult for the *Thresher*'s crew to detect. If her hull had been ruptured when she reached test depth, it could have given way. The Soviet submarine could have been fatally damaged also and sunk in great depths or could simply have gotten away.

Commander Wes Harvey and his crew of 128 Navy men and civilian personnel were lost because of some major defect that hung over the United States Navy submarine program for many years to come. The announced "most probable" cause of sinking was a casualty in the engine room, but the final reports were so ambiguous and indefinite that the exact cause of the submarine's loss was left open to the widest range of speculation. The *Thresher*'s crew became casualties in an instant, final moment when some event of mysterious origin caused her hull to buckle like an eggshell under the crushing pressures of the deep hydrospace.

16 Admiral William F. Raborn, Jr.: Management Genius

It is a matter of gratification to belong to a profession whose possession of a mind of some sort is a generally recognized attribute. Personally, I've never been overly exercised by the charge of possessing a military mind. We soldiers, sailors, and airmen regard a military mind as something to be sought and developed—an indispensable professional asset which can only be acquired after years of training in reflecting and acting on military and related problems. We hope that such a mind, when properly matured, will prove itself analytical, accurate, and decisive in time of crisis because history was shown that neither the battlefield nor the national council table is the place for conjecture, vagueness, or obscurity of thought.

—GENERAL MAXWELL TAYLOR, U.S.A.
Chairman of the Joint Chiefs of Staff

William Francis Raborn, Jr. fell in love with the navy as a farm boy in Marlow, Oklahoma. The prospect of sailing the oceans of the world in glamorous ships and wearing braid-crested uniforms was enough to recruit young Raborn from the dusty streets of Marlow to the Naval Academy in 1924. From the time he arrived at Annapolis, he was a dedicated flier. He spent weekends at the navy airfield at Anacostia, Maryland, flying or playing grease monkey whenever he was allowed. These were dangerous days for Raborn. There were close calls and brushes with death when a plane's engines quit or a takeoff had to be aborted. But Raborn loved flying and only regretted the two years mandatory sea time he would have to spend before he could apply for naval aviation.

But his tour lasted three years on the battleship *Texas*, and, when he applied for naval aviation, Raborn failed the eye test. Discouraged, he returned to the *Texas* for another tour of sea duty. A year later, he reapplied and passed the physical, only to find out that the class of 1932 was filled. Back he went to the fleet—this time to a destroyer—and it was only after a three-year tour of sea duty that he could apply for flight training again. On April 16, 1934, naval aviator's wings were pinned on his tunic, and his career in naval aviation began.

Raborn was spending his first holiday in months with his wife and young son and daughter near Kaneohe Bay, Hawaii, when the naval air station was bombed by the Japanese on December 7, 1941. As station gunnery and intelligence officer, he directed activities from the ground while the battle in the air went on between navy aircraft and the attacking Japanese.

As the bases on the island were rebuilt, Raborn opened a gunnery school. His methods were so effective and revolutionary that he was given a medal and transferred to Washington in mid-1943 to take charge of the navy's aviation and gunnery training program. It was not until the fall of 1944 that Raborn was released for sea duty and assigned aboard ship—the U.S.S. *Hancock,* a carrier on patrol in the Western Pacific.

Raborn was the executive officer of the "Fighting Hannah" in actions off Iwo Jima, and received a Silver Star for his action in restoring the carrier after it was hit by enemy bombers and given up for lost. The citation read: "For conspicuous gallantry and intrepidity"—a phrase that would be used many times again to describe his approach to an emergency.

When the war ended, Raborn was a full commander, assigned to senior staff positions with the operating forces in the Western Pacific for two years. When he was reassigned to Washington, he came to the Bureau of Ordnance as officer in charge of the guided-missile and air-weapons section, a job that gave him his first look at the missile-man's art. Then the war in Korea came along, and Raborn put back to sea in charge of an ASW task group that prowled the northern waters off the coast of China as a screen against the possibility of Russian submarine involvement.

When he was promoted to captain, Raborn was reassigned to the guided-missile detail in Washington, where he worked to develop the Navy Regulus and Sidewinder missiles. This was a time of stress for Raborn; in 1953 he divorced his wife of twenty-four years, the Academy sweetheart that he had married a year after graduation. With his personal life in turmoil, it was probably a relief to be assigned to sea duty again, as commanding officer of a large aircraft carrier, the *Bennington.* He needed a major command to qualify for flag rank, and Raborn was anxious to show what he could do with his first carrier command.

But two weeks after he came aboard, the *Bennington* was struck by one of the worst peacetime disasters ever to hit a navy ship— while cruising less than a hundred miles off the coast of Rhode Island, a giant pressure vessel containing hydraulic fluid for the airplane catapult exploded. During the early dawn hours, the fumes spewed into the carrier's ventilating system and gas entered berthing compartments throughout the ship, setting off more explosions—a disastrous string of bulkhead-shattering detonations which killed 103 officers and men—most of them as they lay sleeping in their bunks. Fire broke out throughout the ship, and there was a real danger that the bombs and high explosives on deck would detonate. But Raborn was equal to the challenge, just as he had been on the *Hancock* in a similar situation. He coolly directed the damage-control operations so that the raging fires were finally extinguished and brought the ship safely to berth at Quonset Point, Rhode Island. Raborn was credited with having saved the *Bennington.*

Admiral Arleigh Burke took Raborn's leadership ability into account when he selected him to head the Polaris program. Burke avoided choosing a technician, a scientist or a production expert; instead he chose a man who was a combat sailor—an officer accustomed to direct action and a man who could get people to work with him.

About the time Raborn was settling at the makeshift Special Projects Office in Washington, the Russians launched Sputnik I. The world in general came awake. Scientists pontificated concerning the Russian missile lead over the United States that six months before they had considered to be a five-year lag. There was frenzy in the White House and urgency at every level of the administration. Congressmen tried to explain to their constituencies why the Russians had been able to surprise and surpass our missile men. At the same time, they castigated our military for allowing such a thing to happen.

While the confusion reigned, Raborn put his staff together. He moved quickly. The Russians had done more on October 4, 1957, to expedite Polaris than any other single factor, and perhaps Raborn silently thanked them for the fireworks display. Short of a declaration of war, Sputnik was the kind of technological breakthrough that galvanizes the American production machine. When Polaris was approved by the Department of Defense in January 1957, the approval constituted not much more than an official blessing; Raborn was given a tentative go-ahead, but was still short of funds and under wraps. With the firing of Sputnik, the appropriations were made and the wraps came off.

17 The Fleet Ballistic Missile Program: Planning

We must insure that our nation survives, but we cannot be satisfied merely with survival. We are a global nation. Our well-being as a nation depends upon our freedom of action. We are not self-sufficient now, and we could not become self-sufficient in the lifetime of any one of us here. And even if we as a nation could arrange our lives and interests to survive by ourselves, what kind of nation would we be? A weakened, shriveled, and mean land at best. So we need to be concerned about our well-being around the globe. The major military challenge to our global interests is the Soviet Union. It is the only other truly global military power. And so we must gauge our ability to maintain freedom of action in terms of the Soviet Union, and in terms of the challenges that Soviet global interests and actions pose for us.

This is not saber rattling. This is not warmongering. This is not some kind of idle scare tactic. It is the most reasoned, responsible

*position I know for having our military
strength up to par.*

—GENERAL CREIGHTON ABRAMS, U.S.A.

United States Army, Chief of Staff

Polaris, the Fleet Ballistic Missile (FBM) program, is probably the outstanding twentieth-century example that bureaucracy can be successful—that the Pentagon works and that the laws which dictate that all large organizational efforts must be inefficient need not always apply. More typically, the Pentagon fails us; the Post Office is quietly inefficient; the State Department muddles our foreign policy; welfare programs are so confused that they alienate even the recipients. We are accustomed to news telling us that our politicians are corrupt, that police forces are partners with organized crime, that public programs are rife with cost overruns, and that the products of industry contain disastrous flaws. So, when a major program of the magnitude of Polaris—the development of a solid-fuel intermediate-range ballistic missile armed with a nuclear warhead and fired from a submerged submarine—when such an undertaking is completed ahead of schedule, under budget, and in projected technological excellence—well, that is more than news, it is a near miracle.

A shelf of books on the FBM program could be written and, indeed, some excellent technical studies have been released in unclassified form. To understand the Cold War at sea, it is important to consider the highlights of this program, both for its naval impact and because it resembles, to a greater or lesser extent, the type of effort necessary to develop the sophisticated weaponry required to master the hydrospace.

Strategic planners had been laying the ground work for the use of the ballistic-missile-firing submarine since before World War II. In the postwar period, when Russian aggression indicated that a major deterrent capability would be necessary to offset the threat of the Red Army, the research was pushed and liberally funded. Three weapons systems were considered as possibilities: long-range bombers, hardened ICBM sites, and missile-firing submarines. These weapons were to be designed not to strike at the enemy's military forces, but instead at the industrial and economic capability which was supporting the armies of the field. This was a new concept in warfare for Pentagon planners—and not one they were comfortable with in the beginning.

During the Second World War, American government-employed scientists and engineers working on weapons R&D programs gave priority to the development of the atomic bomb and the advancement of the aeronautical sciences. Germany, on the other hand, regarded the most important military weapon as the missile, and after that the submarine. German scientists spent most of their development time in these areas. In the summer of 1942 German Army technicians were experimenting at fitting out a U-boat with a short-range bombardment rocket. They succeeded well enough to achieve good accuracy at short ranges. Refinement of these techniques led to the construction of protoypes for launching the heavier V-2 rockets from submerged submarines. Fortunately for the Allies, the Germans were as bureaucratic as our own military; squabbles between the German Army weapons development team and the German Navy weapons department prevented the concept from ever becoming operational.

There are two types of strategic missiles: the ballistic missile and the cruise missile. The ballistic missile expends most of its energy early in its boost phase of flight and coasts the rest of the way to the target, much like a cannonball. The cruise missile flies parallel to the earth's surface and expends energy all the way to the target, in much the same way as an airplane. Ballistic missiles require guidance only during the boost phase, whereas cruise missiles require guidance all along the flight path. Because ballistic missiles leave the earth's atmosphere during the boost phase of their flight, they are uniformly powered by rocket motors which contain their own oxygen supply. The cruise missiles are powered by air-breathing jet-type engines. The ballistic missiles are capable of speeds in excess of 15,000 miles per hour; the cruise missiles fly at about the speed of jet aircraft, between 500 and 2,000 miles per hour.

Ballistic missiles are further subclassified by their range and type of fuel. Missiles with ranges over 5,000 miles are known as intercontinental ballistic missiles (ICBM); those with shorter ranges are known as intermediate-range ballistic missiles (IRBM). Ballistic-missile designs employ either solid or liquid fuel. Solid fuel is generally safer and easier to handle, but has less thrust and lift capacity per pound than liquid fuel. Because of its handling and storage capabilities, solid fuel is used for all of the new generations of submarines and shipboard missiles.

As the science of celestial navigation, radar, and other methods of guidance, surveillance, and detection became more sophisticated, the value of the land-based missile system employed at fixed sites was jeopardized. A first-strike attack could take out an ICBM system before it could retaliate; even in a hardened missile site, the ICBM was still a sitting duck. Thus, in concept, the submarine and the bomber became the preferred deterrent considerations, with the submarine ahead because of its ability to launch an ICBM from a mobile platform. This mobile-launching procedure is difficult to detect and makes it impossible to destroy great numbers of missiles at once. The survivability of the Polaris missile force would ensure its capability of delivering a devastating retaliatory blow and would thus provide the invulnerable deterrent—if it could be made to work.

After World War II, the submarine appeared to be the wave of the future. But until it was demonstrated that some other weapon was superior to it, the proven bomber would remain the Pentagon favorite—the preferred atomic-warhead-delivery scheme and primary threat. The U.S. Air Force was a politically potent force in Congress, and the bomber had long since proven its usefulness, while the submarine as an ICBM launching platform was in the planning stages. Even in the navy, it was far from a unanimous opinion that the atomic submarine and its nuclear capability would ever be developed or replace the supercarrier as the primary strike force of the future. So, as the navy vacillated, the long-range-bomber concept moved to the fore and won the major appropriations that were awarded the developer of the preferred deterrent concept.

It was only a matter of time until the Russians developed an ICBM—and with that capability, the United States Air Force's Strategic Air Command recognized that the bases from which their bombers were required to operate were in the same situation as hardened missile sites. Even in the era when the Minuteman missile system was still a drawing-board concept only sightly advanced from the nuclear submarine, it was clear to those military planners not tied to a particular service prejudice that a mobile deterrent was the ultimate weapon—and the more mobile, the better.

One of the difficulties of effective arms planning is the burden on the conscience of politicians. Some programs necessitate disregarding fiscal restraint. Others require recognizing the proposal of attacking large urban areas with dense populations in time of war. As a consequence, a sort of political Pontius Pilate attitude results. Many congressmen demur, so defense planning is left to the military and those few fearless politicians who either enjoy the military sport or have an ax to grind. When the first plans were made to create a strategic bombing force as the nation's deterrent scheme, Congress wavered. Then the Polaris missile system was born, and both programs were given leave to grow and prosper. Since Congress would not accept the responsibility of deciding between them, neither service forced a showdown.

The multiple-reentry and warhead concept for ICBM missiles was first given serious consideration when the Russians began constructing extensive antiballistic systems around their key cities and military bases. The design of the MRV warhead was a weapon that contained over a dozen separately guided reentry vehicles, each containing a hydrogen bomb. Such a missile would saturate a missile-defense system and render it ineffective against most of the warheads in any one shot. The development of this multiple-warhead program began in 1965, and the first missiles were deployed in

SLBM submarines in 1971. The new system was called Poseidon and was the forerunner of still another major missile redevelopment—the Trident system—which is projected to replace Poseidon in the early 1980s. The Trident will be more effective against Soviet submarine threats, and will also extend the range and capability of the present multiple-entry warhead missile to over 6,000 miles. To the strategic planners, Trident is a dream come true.

There is a mistaken assumption that because Vice Admiral Hyman G. Rickover was the father of the atomic submarine, he was also the naval officer who directed the FBM program. Not so —the officer responsible for the FBM program from its inception to the development of the Polaris was Vice Admiral William F. Raborn, Jr., who in many ways is the sailor's sailor behind the total FBM–nuclear-submarine success story. Raborn deliberately maintained a low profile while working tirelessly against schedules and deadlines which he regarded as a matter of national survival. Historians may pick up Red Raborn some time in the future, identify his contribution to the national defense, and elevate him to the rank of popular hero in the Billy Mitchell, Patton, Halsey, and Rickover image. But for the present, those who have worked in the FBM program over the years know his stature and the results of his leadership—and that is probably as much as Admiral Raborn wants or needs in the way of recognition. In the future, there certainly will be a Polaris submarine bearing the name of Raborn.

As important as any military program may seem to the strategists, it must do battle for official priorities and substantial slices of the budget and allocation of resources. These are the realities of life. Given the feasibility and the talent to accomplish their goals, program directors still see a definite correlation between the amount of money in and the amount of product out. They must scramble to stay high on the priority list in a military agenda crowded with programs competing for attention, their sponsors aware that in the final analysis, funding is necessary for success.

The manipulatory powers of project managers, generals, admirals, congressmen, senators, and the president often have more to do with the success of a governmental venture than its national utility, feasibility, or practicality. The success of the FBM program was largely dependent on the skills of its proponents in bureaucratic politics—and, happily, the program was gifted with some of the most talented, politically astute executives ever to sit in the Pentagon war councils. The naval officers who staffed the Special Projects Office were procurement veterans. They knew how to get things done and how to counter the skepticism of critics inside the naval establishment, in Congress, the administration, and wherever else opposition lurked.

The early objections to the FBM system centered around the possibility of effectively launching a missile from a seaborne moving platform, the safety of handling nuclear fissionable material aboard ship, and skepticism concerning the cost projections for the program. The navy had lost a major battle with the air force in 1949 over the B–36 bomber's strategic role. At that time, the navy's position was that a national policy centering on the destruction of cities and populations was immoral, if not unwise. Now, in 1955, the navy would have to counter this stand, at the same time re-entering the lists against now even more powerful air force opponents. And with a navy in disarray—even the submarine-force commanders had serious doubts about the FBM program. The senior submariners were not enthusiastic about the change in the basic role of the submarine. Other navy skeptics felt that designing a platform based on the navigational precision required to launch such a missile would take most of the navy's budget. And still it might fail.

Thus admirals and generals and armed-forces secretaries battled over the role of the services. When Admiral Arleigh Burke was promoted to Chief of Naval Operations in 1955, he examined the arguments and decided that there would be a navy FBM program— a big one, a successful one. He had wrestled with the air force in the B–36 controversy and, as a veteran of bureaucratic infighting, realized that the navy must present a united front in order to win. Burke asked his leading operational and technical commanders to formulate a single position. They did. Given a choice, the navy chose both: it would seek both ballistic-missile capability and a continued cruise-missile capability. But it was a consensus, and now the navy moved into the competition with the existing air force and army programs.

In response to the erroneously assumed and widely lamented Russian lead in space technology in the mid-fifties, there were three quick answers from the Pentagon: army, navy, and air force recommendations on how to right the strategic balance. The air force planners suggested burying ICBMs deeper underground, hardening their sites, and dispersing them over wide areas of the North American midcontinent. The army wanted to make the Jupiter IRBM mobile so that the missile could be transferred from point to point by truck or rail and quickly set up on portable launching pads for firing. The navy suggested developing a solid-fuel ballistic missile, marrying it to a nuclear submarine, and creating a platform that could hide under polar ice caps and on ocean bottoms off the Russian coast in the Atlantic and Pacific.

Actually, all three ideas were feasible, simple in conception, and would prove fantastically complex in their execution. The air force and army schemes suffered primarily from the delicacy of the instrumentation and missile-launching facilities available; at the time, no ICBM or IRBM site could survive a direct hit or a close near-miss by an atomic bomb. And there was no way to be sure that the army's Jupiter could be set up in time to provide a satisfactory counterblow or to adequately test the air force silo concept of building reinforced concrete structures buried deep in the ground to ensure that they would survive the earthquakelike shock following a nuclear blast.

Proponents of the navy submarine plan pointed out that their concept suffered from neither time nor tender-weapon limitations, and in spite of the proposed limited range of its SLBM, the missiles would in every sense be intercontinental, since the submarines would be stationed at points around the perimeter of the Soviet Union and could strike deep into the Soviet heartland, targeting the same areas as the land-based Jupiter and Atlas missiles. In addition, the large crews which were required to man the army and air force missile sites day in and day out, year round, were not only expensive but also could fall prey to assassins and saboteurs. Missiles of the mid-fifties could be disabled by a hit from a high-powered rifle bullet and were always vulnerable as they were being raised above the ground into firing position. Also, by relying on a primary deterrent force distributed across the United States, the military was ensuring that any first strike would concentrate on the United States alone—in hope of destroying a maximum number of missile sites and Strategic Air Command bomber bases.

As if these arguments were not enough, the navy pointed out that the Jupiter missile, with a 1,500–mile maximum range, required deployment on foreign soil, making it subject to the jurisdiction of other nations in the North Atlantic Treaty Organization and the United States allies in the Far East. Not only did the reluctance of these nations to accept the missiles come into play, but also the question of the control of the missile once it was on foreign soil.

To further credit the navy's case, at the time the navy was proposing a fleet ballistic missile, the nuclear-powered submarine was already operational. The *Nautilus* had been built and was on patrol—Admiral Rickover had long since silenced the critics. The navy was proposing a revolution in sea power—in a sense, the replacement of the aircraft carrier by the submarine. The carrier was beginning to lose its long-range-destruction capability as it became more vulnerable to bombers and missiles; the submarine was beginning to mount major weapons and look nearly invulnerable.

As was expected, the air force reacted negatively—not only because of the threat to its budget posed by the major new weapons system, but also because it was obvious that if a submarine could be designed and a missile produced to allow submerged firing even at IRBM ranges, that weapon could replace the strategic bomber. And if surface vessels were also equipped with IRBMs, as the navy was suggesting, then the traditional role of sea power would change. If the navy, with its new mobility, began to infringe in the area of strategic deterrence, a position the air force was most interested in carving out for itself would be breached. So the air force resisted.

But oddly enough, the navy was not completely unanimous.

The traditionalists were reluctant to propose such radical concepts as missile deployment aboard submarines without extensive tests. All through the 1954–1955 period, some of the navy's most senior officers displayed a timidity which was very un-navylike. They hesitated in advancing programs that would upset the "roles and missions" concepts of the three services. Perhaps they were still smarting under the air force victory in the bomber-vs.-carrier dispute, or perhaps the admirals were really not all that sure of what the SLBM program would produce. In any event, when DOD prodded the navy into providing projections on the capability of an SLBM submarine fleet, the forthcoming studies were both conservative and deferential to the air force position.

On the other hand, the air force and army missile-men were self-assured and condescending. They pointed out that there were serious problems in fueling and launching ICBMs, even with all the advantages of land sites. Aboard ship, such operations might be far too dangerous to attempt. And their major concern was guidance, they said. This problem alone would be more than any ship system could reasonably be expected to overcome. The solid-fuel missiles that were to be developed for a 1,500–mile shot would require years of research and production trials. Obviously, they said, it was foolish to base a program on something requiring such exhaustive laboratory investigations so remote from the present state of the art.

But always they came back to the guidance problem. In order to obtain reasonably accurate targeting for a missile, it was necessary to take a bearing on true north—and this was a difficult enough problem on land, where there was space available for sophisticated instrumentation. The slightest error in the determination of true north would throw off the guidance system; the missile men had found it difficult enough to eliminate errors from land-based fixed launching sites. They suggested that at sea, aboard a continually moving ship or submarine, the problem would be simply impossible to solve—not difficult or expensive, simply impossible.

Probably the one thing that kept the navy involved in the

192 THE SECRET WAR FOR THE OCEAN DEPTHS

arguments was the logic of the FBM–atomic-submarine weapons system. It was a natural—it had to be feasible. So, working in makeshift laboratories, navy scientists toiled long hours on the impossible problem and eventually made breakthroughs in the development of new and more powerful solid fuels. Finally the navy research team of Keith Rumbel and Charles Henders developed a fuel based on the addition of small amounts of aluminum powder which seemed to provide the needed compromise between stability and boost.

Secretary of Defense Charles "Engine" Wilson informed the navy that he had some good news and some bad news. If the navy wanted to proceed with the development of a solid-fuel missile, such a program would be approved. That was the good news. But funding must come out of the regular navy budget, which was the very grim bad news. There would be no extra money, no increased authorization—although there was a promise of the highest national priorities. When the navy's leaders examined the impact of this decision on their other critical programs, they were shocked; the navy might have to starve the fleet for years in order to support the ballistic-missile program even on a moderate basis. But the navy leadership accepted. The future of the mobile seagoing ballistic-missile-firing submarine was simply too important for them to accept any delay.

When the admirals bit the bullet and decided to proceed, the next step became the most important single decision to be made. The program had to have a boss of fantastic talents: a diplomat, a man who could supervise, a man who would be a consensus leader, a technical genius. Almost as impossible a task to locate such a naval officer as to develop the missile itself, Admiral Burke remarked.

In the face of mounting concern over a Russian arms buildup, President Eisenhower asked the National Security Council to form a select committee to assess the nation's strategic position. In 1954 the committee met and was given access to all top-secret government reports, war plans, technological summaries, and intelligence estimates of the Soviet military forces. The committee was headed by Dr. James R. Killian; and its report, although never made public, disclosed a serious situation: the Soviet Union was rapidly over-taking the United States in overall strategic weapons capability. The report has since been subject to searching questions concerning the validity of its assumptions, but essentially it was considered accurate based on the information available at the time.

The committee made three principal recommendations:

(a) that the air force accelerate its Atlas ICBM program;
(b) that the army develop a 1,500–mile IRBM;
(c) that the navy develop an IRBM that could be launched from ships at sea.

Still Eisenhower vacillated. The report was studied, read, and debated in Congress and at the Pentagon. But it was not until September 1955 that Eisenhower finally directed the Pentagon to implement the recommendations of the Killian report. With some reluctance, the Joint Chiefs of Staff gave the navy missile-men their go-ahead.

The signal to implement the Polaris program kicked off an inter-agency rivalry between the Bureau of Ordnance (BuOrd) and the Bureau of Aeronautics (BuAer). When CNO announced a task force for the development of the new weapon, jurisdiction and budget arguments between the two bureaus began. Finally it was decided to settle the matter by classifying the effort as a special project and creating the Special Projects Office. Commander William Hassler, chief of the BuOrd missiles-research branch, would set up a new organization which would be given extraordinary authority to cut across all organizational lines throughout the navy —in short, the ability to call upon any bureau or tap any technical resource to get the job done. And the Special Projects Office would be responsible to only one man: the Secretary of the Navy.

Thus the Special Projects Office organization came into being. Now the search was on for a messiah to head it. With the aid of his staff, Admiral Arleigh Burke, the Chief of Naval Operations, studied the possible contenders. When he asked for recommendations, the name that came up most often was that of a newly promoted rear admiral—William F. "Red" Raborn—a flier, a combat veteran, and a navy leader in the classic mold. Conferences were held; admirals were consulted; the Bureau of Personnel was asked for recommendations. All concurred. Raborn was the man to give the "hunting license" to—that extraordinary authority the navy had never before granted.

Burke assured Raborn that if he ran into any difficulty with which CNO could help, he was to report it at once, along with a recommended course of action. If Raborn needed people, he would get the best; if he needed resources, he would get whatever was at the navy's disposal. Raborn was told that the future of the navy— and perhaps the free world—was in his hands. However, Burke warned Raborn if at any time he was unsure of the future of the project to the degree that he felt the job was not technically feasible, he was to report the facts and Burke would "cut the project off dead."

The weapons-development liaison between U.S. military and industrial groups was changing; the classical way of doing business no longer applied in the postwar period. And yet some of the services clung to the theory that they could specify their requirements to the industrialists and research scientists and wait for the finished product. In turn, scientists and industrialists were supposed to embark on development programs, presenting prototypes for approval from time to time. Finally there would be agreement that the weapon met the needs and specifications of the military. Eventually, the weapon would be accepted and issued to the military operating forces. In the time of World War I, this pattern had worked well and with a relatively short cycle, since the numbers of new weapons developed over a decade were relatively few. It was more in innovation of manufacturing design than in the totally new concept of a weapons system where the research and development groups found most of their employment.

However, weapons grew more complicated, even to the point where medals were lavishly distributed to those involved in developing them, and military careers were wrapped up in the development of a single weapon. Enormous funds were made available for R&D. The time involved in each of the phases of weapons development grew longer, and the efforts required to deliver weapons to the troops in the field became prodigious undertakings. Often the cycles stretched to five years and longer—and sometimes the weapons received by the operating forces bordered on the obsolete. It was only after a number of military-procurement scandals in which major weapons were already obsolete and nearly useless by delivery time that congressional committees began to take a serious interest in weapons procurement.

Whether true or not, one of the great fears of the American leadership is that in Russia we face an opponent with autocratic power over industry that can appreciably shorten weapons-development cycles and can control the cost of production far more effectively than we can in a free society. Weapons are a function of availability, effectiveness, and cost, with one of the functions usually holding the highest priority. With Polaris it was availability, so the race with the Soviet missile-men was on. Time was a problem that Raborn faced squarely, from the day he was assigned the original delivery date of 1965 for his seaborne weapons system, which at the time involved Jupiter missiles. This delivery cycle would be progressively shortened by CNO—and perhaps Raborn anticipated the rush when he announced to his staff at the inception of the program that the schedule would not only be bettered, but be bettered by "a hell of a lot."

"Make your wife do her own shopping," he told his staff. "That demonstrates leadership. You stay at that desk."

Raborn put everyone connected with the Special Projects Office on what he called a wartime footing. A minimum five-and-a-half-day work week was inaugurated—which later stretched unofficially to six-, and sometimes seven-day weeks, plus nights. Fewer coffee breaks and no unnecessary meetings was the goal. Each day began promptly at 8:00 a.m. and ended when exhaustion precluded any more effective work being accomplished by anyone, anyhow, anywhere.

"None of this will get done after we have our golf game," Raborn told his staff, and proceeded to set the pace himself. "Put your hand on the back of your neck," he would tell them. "All right, you feel it? That's your neck. Well, that's what we are trying to save. That's what this program is all about."

Raborn disdained the Rickover stress-interview type of confrontation before selection for prospective SPO members. Instead, he chose the best men available and made it clear that Polaris was an all-consuming vocation: that the program was a labor of pure patriotism, that it was a love of service and country into which each man involved was expected to commit himself, completely and with little thought for anything else. If a man accepted the challenge, he joined the team—and forswore all the comforts and securities of a normal existence. Raborn searched the navy and civil service for the best—the best missile-men, the best accountants, the best planners, the best managers. And the people he ticked off on his requirements lists were immediately transferred to the program if they were within naval cognizance. Civil servants were another matter—a few refused, a few were not available—but most of Raborn's requirements were met.

To command this assembly of talent, Raborn had to be an extraordinary leader—and indeed he was. The staff watched him carefully. They observed that he was a man who showed a remarkable facility for absorbing large amounts of technical information and finding the single critical obstacle which had to be overcome. They marveled at his ability to ferret out the difficulties and then pinpoint where and how in the worldwide defense establishment the solution might be found. And they most admired his impressive ability to make up his mind quickly and decisively, then communicate his decisions to every level of the organization. Almost without reservation, these scientists and engineers accepted Raborn as their leader and the hard yoke of work and discipline he promised to lay on them.

While Raborn was successful in marshaling and organizing the technician's, from time to time the Project Office required people of special skills—contract negotiators, legal specialists, accountants, budget experts. Raborn noted that any time an outside consultant had to be called in, bottlenecks developed and time was lost. The other military branches in the Department of the Navy were not geared to his pace. The problem was solved in a direct way: job descriptions were written for all the experts who would be needed, and they were requested as permanent staff to be reassigned, physically removing them from their agencies and bringing them into the Special Projects Office. As the program pace quickened, the results were dramatic. The experts began to think like the rest of Raborn's people. Reports that would have taken weeks were released in days. The processing of plans for the construction of facilities such as test stands and laboratories which usually involved prolonged design cycles and extensive revisions were expedited to the point where time savings of several months were realized.

Senior managers in the SPO characterized Red Raborn as a master psychologist—the iron fist of a military leader inside the velvet glove of an industrial coordinator.

"He takes you apart, piece by piece. He doesn't yell. He doesn't snap at you. He just smiles and asks you one damn question after another about things you thought he knew nothing about," a senior scientist said.

"It's damn convincing," his associates agreed.

The technical experts began to realize that Raborn had that sine qua non of all great leaders. Napoleon characterized that quality in a question to one of his marshals who was praising the military skill of an officer he was recommending for promotion. Napoleon waved off the speech impatiently and said, "Never mind all that. Tell me one thing: is he lucky?"

Red Raborn was lucky. And somehow he managed to spread his special brand of luck throughout the Special Projects Office. "Every time we would get into a real tough spot, we would luck out. His program got hot right from the start and stayed hot," a Special Projects senior manager said. "And there was only one reason—it was Raborn. The man has incredible luck."

There was no other way to explain how Raborn would make so many correct decisions, particularly in the early days, when alternate approaches were considered daily and it was necessary to make decisions based on relatively inaccurate information-gathering systems. These decisions had to be made quickly, and they were critical; a wrong decision could have drastically affected the whole project and adversely affected the timing and the cost.

"Raborn was an old pilot—he must fly by the seat of his pants," an admiral remarked when asked to explain the Raborn phenomenon. His managers watched Raborn as he coolly passed judgment on technological approaches that they had been testing in conceptual design for many years, and yet were unsure about which alternative was the best approach. They were amazed because Raborn was invariably right. He picked the best approach, the best man, the best contractor unerringly. He was not an engineer, or a scientist, or a production specialist, but he was a superb administrator—and a born gambler, and a supersalesman, and a gentleman, and a fighter. But most of all, Raborn was a man who believed in the Polaris mission.

Raborn seemed physically gifted for a leadership role. He was a short, squarely built sailor with a roll to his gait, a warm smile, and a friendly and sincere manner. Everyone liked him, although he could be as tough, arbitrary, or ruthless as the situation dictated. He developed a trust among the major contractors who were so important to the success of the program. Raborn stayed in close touch with the presidents of the companies involved, but he also had time for the project managers and even the engineers on the line if they were working on something significant to the program. He quickly created a tapestry of relationships with the important men in industry. They trusted him implicitly and would take his word and act upon it, committing their companies to millions of dollars and hundreds of thousands of man-hours without a question or the need for quick confirmation.

During the period when military programs were bogging down right and left, where copious paper work was the order of the day and everything had to be justified, evaluated, and audited, Raborn's word was contract enough. The men he dealt with in industry knew he was honest and fair; the Polaris program was never delayed for want of an approval or official sanction. And, most important, somehow the word penetrated even to the boardrooms of the nation's largest military contractors. The presidents and directors began to think the way Raborn did about Polaris. He convinced many of them that this program was the most important thing that any of them had ever done or would ever do in their careers.

18 The Fleet Ballistic Missile Program: Background and Evolution

*Morale is the state of mind. It is steadfastness
and courage and hope. It is confidence and zeal
and loyalty. It is élan, esprit de corps, and
determination.*
—GENERAL GEORGE CATLETT MARSHALL, U.S.A.

Red Raborn described his approach to the FBM program in these words:

The management structure established for the direction of the
Fleet Ballistic Missiles Program is special and unique . . . the
decision to obtain a FBM capability was made in terms of a
complete program package. This total decision could only be
carried on by making an assignment of responsibility and a delegation of authority in the same complete terms. This means that
the buck stops at my desk for decisions made in carrying out this
program.

Raborn made it clear that he was designing a new and different
and totally integrated management system. Things would be done
the Raborn way. There would be no falling back on Pentagon
responsibility dodges or the old blame-the-contractor or blame-the-
Congress ploys. Either the program would succeed completely or
fail completely—there would be no excuses. Not before, not during,
and not after.

"I must be able to reach down to any level of the Special Projects Office activity and find a plan and performance report that logically and clearly can be related to the total job we have to do," Raborn told his staff. He was concerned that scientists could not outline for him the management techniques that they used in scheduling research and development activities. He was appalled when he spoke to the head of one leading laboratory and was told, "I got a group of people sitting over there thinking about a problem. If they come up with something this year, that's fine. If I have to wait until next year, well, I wait."

That was not Raborn's kind of talk; he could not take that approach. He had to schedule R&D and prototype testing in the same way that a production man schedules his manufacturing. The Special Projects Office had to build facilities and plants and set up manufacturing lines with equipment that had never before been built. But first the team needed a system to allow them to coordinate and follow the thousands of day-to-day steps required to schedule R&D, quality assurance, protection, and postdelivery checkout. Raborn laid down his requirements, and his staff began developing the new control system of management planning and communications.

Raborn demanded a simple system, and his administrative assistant, Gordon Pehrson, devised a multilayered pyramid which could be simply constructed, easily read, and used by all of the Polaris project leaders. He called it Program Evaluation Review Techniques—PERT. The top layer of the chart covered the entire system. The next layer was subdivided into 5 charts, one for each major component of the system. The next layer had 50 charts, and the next layer 100—each in the same format, each detailing a single activity or project and each tracing a direct relationship to the achievement cycle and timing of the overall program. Each of the charts showed all of the steps required to track a particular job and a timetable based on them. The charts showed who was responsible for seeing that each step was completed. Vertical black lines on the graph showed how the timing coincided with the flow of project activity. Colored markers were placed beside the steps to indicate where the project was with respect to schedule: a blue mark ahead, a red triangle behind, a green circle on schedule, an orange square an uncertainty—and so on.

The charts were updated frequently, and Raborn and his staff learned to pinpoint problems and anticipate difficulties by interpreting the schedules posted in the Polaris Management Center. Copies of the schedules were distributed to all program groups at a cost of a few pennies each—replacing an unbelievable amount of paper work. By developing communication techniques such as PERT and passing them on to contractors, Raborn made the problems of program control appear simple. Yet such control was the product of complex, detailed planning which was an improvement over anything that had been employed previously in military-system development.

An illustration of the scope of activity of the Special Projects Office involved three meetings which took place within a few days of each other:

Gordon Pehrson was lecturing his production staff and selected contractors. He walked back and forth in front of a view graph which showed a map of the United States projected on a screen with hundreds of black dots scattered across the map from coast to coast.

"Here are some of our more important contractors," he lectured. "Members of our industry team . . . this gives you an idea of what it takes to produce a weapons system. You must understand this. This is what we are dealing with: hundreds of companies throughout the country, every branch of the navy, millions of dollars. Our job is to keep in mind the parts in relation to the whole and in relation to the clock."

Pehrson was not an emotional man. He was a sophisticated top-grade civil servant: an expert accountant and a hard-eyed military planner. But when he surveyed the map and turned to speak to his audience, there was a catch in his voice. "And this is another thing: people will want to know what is expected of them. They will want to know their importance in relation to the whole. You must tell them what they are supposed to do and show them its overall importance. This is the subtle flavoring of our particular soup—getting them into the whole picture—getting them to understand our high purpose. Tell them we are helping save the country. As far as I am concerned, we are at war."

Two Polaris managers sat in a sound booth in a Hollywood studio, listening to the reading of a script prepared for a Polaris documentary film designed to keep contractors and government officials informed on the progress of the program. This was one of Pehrson's communications methods: the film would be distributed to all of the organizations represented by black dots on his map, together with a note from Raborn urging them on to greater effort.

George Fenneman, a radio and television personality best known for his emceeing on Groucho Marx's quiz program, had been the voice identified with Polaris in these films. But, as usual, Fenneman was having trouble with the technical terms.

"The G load on the missile at the time of ejection . . ." Fenneman began, then flubbed the next phrase and shrugged in disgust. "Aw, come on, what the hell is this? I don't know what I'm talking about."

Commander Bob Gardemal patted Fenneman on the shoulder. "Just read it, George. You don't have to know. You're just supposed to *sound* as if you know."

Fenneman composed himself and began dramatically, "Westinghouse engineers faced the problem of G load early. They also faced the problem of shoving a hydrodynamically unstable object." Fenneman looked up wryly. "What the hell is a hydrodynamically unstable object?"

Project manager Ed Mernone laughed and tapped his copy of the script. "Just read, George."

"You want me to sound intelligent, don't you?" Fenneman said. "How can I sound convincingly intelligent if I don't know what the hell I'm talking about?"

"Don't worry about it," Mernone said. "You sound wonderful. Read."

*   *   *

It was past dinnertime, and the engineers had worked all day at a Lockheed plant at Sunnyvale, California. Now they were still at it, in a conference at a nearby motel, discussing the Polaris missile shape. A bottle of bourbon was on the table. The men looked tired as they sat in shirtsleeves with clipboards on their laps, arguing, proposing, questioning, debating, sketching. The ashtrays were filled and the bourbon bottle was nearly empty. The leader of the group, Dr. W. H. "Butch" Brandt, believed that these nightly sessions should take place away from the office, so the motel-room meetings became a regular event.

"As I see the problem, we have to kid this bird and make it think it's in the air and not in the water," one of the engineers said. "That way it won't do any handsprings."

A junior engineer volunteered, "Maybe we could fool it by wetting it with detergent."

There were some questioning looks in his direction, but no one laughed.

"Maybe the best approach would be to let the missile go through the water in a big air bubble, or in a plastic bag filled with air," another engineer said.

"The trouble is, we don't know enough about air bubbles and we don't have enough time to find out," a designer said, not looking up from his slide rule.

"You know, the idea of putting some detergent on to create some kind of foam—to lighten the water around the missile—that just might do the trick," an engineer said.

There was silence around the room while they considered the idea, mentally picturing the Polaris missile rising from the submarine in a column of soapsuds. Finally Butch Brandt rose and walked to the center of the group.

"All right, gentlemen, what do we recommend—Dash or Rinso?"

The tension broke, everyone laughed, someone clapped the junior engineer on the back, and one of the complex problems in the Polaris launch system had been solved.

* * *

Pehrson's lecture to the contractors in the Management Center, Bob Gardemal's and Ed Mernone's coaching entertainment-personality George Fenneman in the art of technological discourse, and Butch Brandt's after-work sessions which led to the detergent decision—all were representative of the multifaceted effort that was the FBM program. As Pehrson had stated, it was like being at war.

19 The Fleet Ballistic Missile Program: Marshaling the Technologies

The Soviet Union can't begin to touch {us}
from the point of view of speed and develop-
ment of complicated weapons system.
—VICE-ADMIRAL WILLIAM F. RABORN, JR.,
U.S.N.

Navy missile-men approached the other services can-
didly and announced their sincere desire for independence—but
then offered to bargain in order to solidify their own position with
respect to the technology they would use. The army was told that
it was welcome to join the navy in developing a solid-fuel missile,
but that the navy's interest in the Jupiter missile was only transitory.
At the first opportunity, the navy would begin an independent program to develop a missile compatible with shipboard operations.
The army's opinion was voiced by Wernher Von Braun, one of the
early leaders of the Jupiter program: "The farthest east the navy
could hope to reach with a solid-fuel missile fired from the Atlantic
coastline of Europe would be the Simplon Railway Tunnel in
Switzerland." But the army and navy have always had a close accord, a relationship even more cordial now that the upstart air
force was claiming the lion's share of the budget. The navy began
its missile program under army sponsorship—a tolerable situation.
West Point had never treated Annapolis with less than a friendly,
cooperative disdain.

The navy had begun clandestine development programs in parallel with the Jupiter program to ensure that its real goals would be achieved. Such cloak-and-dagger activity is common in military development; it is considered almost a prank, even though it involves millions in appropriations and the possibility that the winners of the battle for funds will, in fact, prove to be the losers in technology and that the national defense will be jeopardized.

But there are senior officers in each service who feel they know what is best for the country, the armed forces, and their service— and quite often they decide to take matters into their own hands. So it was with the FBM program. Without obtaining approval of either the Department of Defense or the Secretary of the Navy, early in January 1956 a group of senior naval officers approached the Aerojet-General Corporation and the Lockheed Missile and Space Division for technical assistance in developing a solid-fuel ballistic-missile system. The navy wanted out of the Jupiter program, the contractors were told; and although committed to use Jupiter components in navy test rockets, they felt the time was close at hand for the navy to strike out on its own. The contractors were happy to assist, and in close collaboration with consultants of the Special Projects Office, quickly prepared missile designs under the disguise of the Jupiter program. A clever scheme was devised for carrying nuclear warheads; it involved clustering six solid-fuel rockets in the first stage and using a single rocket in the second stage. The air force was persuaded that the navy's program complemented rather than conflicted with its own, and a memorandum of agreement on solid-fuel data exchanges was prepared by the two services. The navy had gained an opportunity to build a solid-fuel ballistic missile by means of candor and stealth, politics and détente.

Then Jupiter foundered, and the standing joke around the navy wardrooms was: "What are we going to do with submarines with big holes in them?" The monstrous Jupiter design measured some 44 feet in height and 120 inches in diameter. It weighed 80 tons and required a submarine of 8,000 or 9,000 tons to carry four missiles. Clearly, this was not the answer. The navy had won the waiting game.

The National Academy of Sciences Committee on Undersea Warfare is one of the science advisory groups that has the ear of both Congress and the administration—particularly on appropriations for submarine and antisubmarine warfare. The group gathers at some watering hole every summer and calls together eminent scientists to work on important policy problems. The scientists and their families get a free vacation at government expense, but the results are well worth the largess. One of these meeting places was Nobska Point at Woods Hole, Massachusetts, close to the Oceanographic Institute and an ideal place for work and play. The resulting studies became known as Project Nobska, a continuing overview of underwater-warfare projects. The committee became the earliest proponent of the FBM and nuclear-submarine weapons. The Soviet response required to counter such a system would be so enormous that it would provide a substantial neutralizing of Russian capabilities in other areas, the group predicted, and therefore recommended that a fleet of nuclear submarines armed with long-range missiles would be one of the most effective deterrents this country could mount, as well as the most troublesome challenge the Russians would encounter in the 1960–1980 time frame.

Project Nobska studied the navy's most difficult production problems in acquiring a submarine fleet and determined that solution was contingent on progress in a number of technologies, particularly warhead development. The scientists recommended projecting dates for technological breakthroughs. They assumed that future development would result in the materials and techniques needed, and that the scientific community would develop them as needed. The watchword was to design ahead. Critical warheads were scheduled with materials which would be available in the mid–1960 time frame, but were unknown in the mid–1950s as the designs were being prepared. In some ways this was risky business. At the outset of the program, the Chief of Naval Operations was asked to risk the navy's budget based on the viability of a ballistic-missile system designed around future technological developments.

Many top navy officials strongly opposed this approach. They felt that the gamble was unnecessary, that the navy's stake in the deterrent scheme of defense was simply not all that important. But the CNO's support sustained Polaris.

In promoting Polaris, the navy tried to avoid the typical bureaucratic meddling that follows every major military effort. To do this, the Polaris builders realized that they had to present something other than a "business as usual" front. It would be necessary to define the FBM as a totally unique program with its own identity. To remain immune from the army and air force skepticism leveled at any navy technical program, it would have to be considered technically excellent and top priority.

And the navy achieved this in some very clever ways, both obvious and covert. Although military officers assigned to Washington billets normally wear civilian clothes during work hours, naval officers attached to Special Projects Office directing Polaris were urged to wear uniforms at all times. Overtime hours are discouraged in civil service, but Special Projects Office personnel worked extended hours. Even when the workloads did not require this kind of activity, they worked a six-day "must keep busy" schedule. FBM correspondence was stamped with red priority markings. Special devices, flags, and pennants were awarded to Polaris contractors to bring back some of the urgency and esprit de corps of the Second World War. Within the navy and the defense community, no one was allowed to think of the Polaris program as a conventional effort. The motto to all concerned was something on the order of "Think big or get out." The navy budget was presented to Congress with the FBM section separate, in an appropriations category all its own. Contractors were encouraged to carry on their own promotion programs concerning their part in the Polaris program—even to the extent of using Polaris in advertising campaigns.

And that was only the beginning. Fear of a Soviet missile attack was puffed up to substantiate the need for Polaris—the solid-fuel missile that could be launched from a submarine patrolling off the coast of Russia. "Bring the Cold War to the Russians shores" was the message—and it had national impact. Exaggerations concerning the program's promise and technological breakthroughs were encouraged. For example, during 1956, rumors mentioning substantial breakthroughs in warhead development and missile technology were circulated—when in fact there was little progress. Corporations were credited with dramatic advances in developing components for solid-fuel rockets, when in fact they were only at the beginning of their research programs. Fortunately for the propagandists, the technological breakthroughs did happen eventually, and the program's progress caught up with the advertising.

Managers in the Special Projects Office were instructed to be sure to include in their planning all of the navy research facilities and bureaus which might be useful at some time in the program. Keep everyone in the picture, recognize their contributions—this was the lesson they were preached. The air force chiefs owed much of their early success to first cooperating with and ultimately pre-empting the role of the other services in some program or mission. First joint venture—then in one way or another obtain a "piece of the action"—then slowly take over. The air force had prospered with this strategy. The navy had watched the performance carefully. Now it was time for the admirals to put on the same kind of act.

Praise was spread around, and joint venturing became a watchword. If something would help the program, the Special Projects Office would be sure that everyone involved received credit. No military agency need feel threatened by the FBM program or its mission. Cooperating with the SPO was in the best interest of the navy as a whole, and the other party in particular. Thus were BuShips, BuOrd, and other highly independent groups brought into the fold by the Polaris planners.

The first steps in the Polaris program were different from other major military programs only in the way the Polaris Special Projects Office took them. Actually, for every missile system, new aircraft design, ship, or space vehicle, there is the same gantlet to be run at the Pentagon, in Congress, and with the contractors. Polaris moved ahead while facing senior submarine commander opposition on one side and air force meddling on the other.

But with Raborn at the helm, Polaris prospered. Admiral Raborn was a man who could push hard and yet go slowly. He knew that senior submarine officers were advising junior officers that their naval careers might be advanced more quickly by avoiding the FBM program. This hurt, but he held his peace, and where it was reasonably possible, he catered to the whims and traditions of the submarine service. He weighed in the balance the effects of long-term vs. short-term gains and used the considerable clout of the Special Projects Office only sparingly.

When SPO was riding high in Congress, it would have been possible to gallop roughshod over the navy opponents of the program. But Raborn recognized that the larger battles for survival of the Polaris concept would be fought within the navy, with navy operational staffs and the navy top brass at the Pentagon before any battling with the other services took place. The big guns of Congress were at the ready and occasionally brought to bear, but seldom used. Raborn was moderate and careful to identify himself with the "good old days" of the submarine navy. There were no white helmets with lightning bolts painted on them or bright-colored scarves, sidearms, or any of the other badges or marks that would set the FBM crews apart from their fellow navy men. No green berets or aiguillettes or jumpsuits. And whenever it was possible, the FBM program delegated the authority for a particular function; for example, in most cases, R&D was left with the Chief of Naval Communications and legal responsibility was left with the Chief of Ordnance and Ships. Only those elements that were absolutely necessary for control were held with the SPO.

Senior admirals and generals grumbled that Raborn had taken a leaf out of Teddy Roosevelt's book and was walking softly and carrying a big stick. He was not fighting fair; this was not the no-holds-barred mud-wallow that the navy, air force, and army were used to when they were competing for appropriations. The Special Projects Office was lavish in its praise, quiet in its reproofs, and took its lumps in silence, even in the face of attacks on the feasibility of a sea-based ballistic-missile system. The morality of establishing a second major-deterrent system after land-based missiles was debated in the press; and the massive total of expenditures was published by opponents, often distorted or in error. But Raborn kept the peace and preached that there was only one enemy to be recognized: the

Soviet Union. He told his senior project managers that today's opposition might well be tomorrow's support, and to act accordingly. He asked for the FBM program's fair share—no more or less—and thereby was able to tread his way past the obstacles that had sunk many another well-conceived but poorly organized weapons program.

20 The Fleet Ballistic Missile Program: The Failures Leading to Success

. . . changes of tactics have only taken place after changes in weapons, which necessarily is the case, but . . . the interval between such changes has been unduly long. This doubtless arises from the fact that an improvement of weapons is due to the energy of one or two men, while changes in tactics have to overcome the inertia of a conservative class. . . . It can be remedied only by a candid recognition of each change. . . . History shows that it is vain to hope that military men generally will be at pains to do this, but that the one who does will go into battle with a great advantage.

—ALFRED THAYER MAHAN

Problems and progress followed each other in quick succession, one after another—from disasters to brilliant scientific breakthroughs, from simple bottlenecks that defied problem solution to quantum jumps in the state of the art in missile technology. Solid-fuel mixing plants blew up, but Raborn reassured his superiors that the fuel would be satisfactory for use aboard submarines. Scientists packed to leave the strange land of California and return to their native Germany; but Raborn convinced them that they were the best in the world and needed, so they stayed. Brilliant engineering manager Butch Brandt died suddenly at the age of forty-seven. Raborn shored up his technical group and pushed them on. Contractors balked at the accelerated schedules, engineers refused to be committed, scientists wanted more time to work on basic research. Somehow Raborn persuaded them all to fall in line with the program's time requirements. He pushed and pleaded and persuaded —and finally it all began to happen just as he said it would.

Then the Polaris was ready to go to sea. Raborn sent emissaries to meet with Admiral Rickover, the Atomic Energy Commission, BuShips, and other interested parties to determine whether a partially completed submarine under construction at the Electric Boat Company in Groton, Connecticut could be modified to become the first SLBM submarine. There was no time to start from scratch. Raborn needed a boat now. He felt that the *Scorpion,* sister ship of the *Skipjack,* could be used if she could be bisected and missile tubes installed. He intruded into the sacrosanct field of submarine construction without hesitation and was persuasive enough to win the new construction. The welders unceremoniously began to disassemble the *Scorpion's* 250–foot keel with torches, slicing the hull away at midships to make room for the Polaris launching tubes. It was something on the order of slicing a cigar in two and replacing it on either side of a matchbox—the missile section gave the submarine a rectangular midsection which was covered by a humped back of steel. But even with the jury-rigged design, the *Scorpion* would provide a satisfactory platform for the new weapon. Special Projects insisted on rechristening the *Scorpion* the *George Washington,* and the navy agreed to go one step further and designate it as a ship. This meant the name of a hero instead of a sea creature, the traditional navy nomenclature for submarines.

Since the *George Washington* was the first vessel of its kind, the shipbuilding crews were particularly interested in making sure that it was built with care and precision. There was room for everything in the *George Washington,* they said, but a mistake; and the Groton workmen did not intend to make that single fatal mistake.

But first-of-a-kind submarines are plagued with construction errors, and as careful as the builders were, unfortunate things happened. A pipefitter cut a hole in the bulkhead and ran a pipe where it didn't belong. A vendor supplied a piece of machinery with a valve placed opposite where it should have been. Entire sections had to be ripped out and redone four or five times because of faulty welds. The skilled shipbuilders of the Electric Boat Company had turned out a 1,500–ton submarine every two weeks during World War II. They were proud of their achievements and were working hard to do all they could to keep their record intact in constructing the *George Washington*. But construction slowed down and Raborn worried.

On May 27, 1958 a second Polaris submarine hull was laid down for the *Patrick Henry*. It was to be an exact duplicate of the *George Washington*—hopefully without the pains of first design and construction. And it did prove an easier task; with most of the problems associated with the design and construction of the *George Washington* now worked out, building the *Patrick Henry* was a smooth, fast operation.

Raborn had insinuated one of the navy's master expediters into the FBM program; with the two nuclear subs under construction, Admiral Hyman Rickover was now completely involved. The Electric Boat Company's management had few moments of peace —they complained that Rickover called at any time of the night and asked for immediate answers to complex problems.

"Rickover's idea of a long time is an hour," the shipyard general manager complained. But he worked to Rickover's schedule and finally admitted that he found it was easier to do things twice as fast rather than incur Rickover's wrath.

By November 1958 there were three yards involved in the construction of Polaris submarines. The *Theodore Roosevelt* was being constructed on the ways of the Mare Island government yard at San Francisco, the *Robert E. Lee* was being built at Newport News Shipbuilding and Dry Dock Company at Norfolk, and the *Abraham Lincoln* was started at the government yard at Portsmouth, New Hampshire. The job of coordinating construction of the three submarines between yard was taxing the combined efforts of Rickover and Raborn and their staffs. But the team was equal to the program; in one fortunate situation after another, schedules were shortened, breakthroughs were made, and building was kept to the SPO timetable. The Raborn charm continued to shine on all their efforts. Crews of construction workers labored long hours of overtime, technical specialists worked seven days a week, and subcontractors rushed their own production schedules.

Perhaps the best illustration of the Raborn push was the story of Charley Kraus, an electrical engineer so absorbed in running fire-control tests one evening that he completely forgot about his expectant wife. Without calling him, she took a taxi to the hospital. At 9:00 P.M. a nurse phoned the plant, finally reached Kraus, and told him that his wife had just given birth to twins. There was a long pause on the line, he thanked the nurse politely, and went back to the tests. It was not until he stopped for his coffee break at midnight that the full impact of what he had been told registered —then he went wild with joy and relief.

Raborn's problems in the navy were probably best put by Representative Clarence Cannon of Missouri, Chairman of the House Appropriations Committee, who remarked, "The navy's not of one mind. The carrier admirals just don't like the idea of going to sea in pigboats." As many a submarine and ship admiral has remarked, the navy is run by the aviators. The prospect of seeing the cherished carrier replaced by a missile-firing submarine horrified the naval aviation admirals almost as much as it did the air force generals who saw the submarine as a threat to the bomber.

Finally Raborn received his first setback: the program was evicted from its testing facility. Lockheed had successfully fired the Polaris missile from a test site at Point Mugu, California. This was satisfactory in the first stages of the program, but now that the Polaris was nearing completion, it was necessary to use conventional test facilities. This meant moving from Point Mugu on the Pacific to the Atlantic Missile Test Range at Cape Canaveral, Florida. At this time, the Cape's greatest days were still ahead. The barren strip of Eastern Florida beach was just in process of being converted to America's leading spaceport for the great missile race of the sixties. The Cape was being used to test the huge Atlas ICBM and the Vanguard missile which was being readied to put the first satellite into orbit around the earth. The Polaris was a novelty, and the air force generals who operated the Atlantic Missile Test Range were wary of this new design. They had never before dealt with a large solid-fuel-propelled ballistic missile. All of the launch missiles were just hardware standing on their pads until the highly explosive propellants were pumped into them just before launch time. A solid fuel sounded dangerous and would require special precaution.

Missile facilities were divided into two areas for safety purposes: the industrial area and the launching area. The industrial area was composed of administrative offices, machine shops, storage buildings, hangars, and other support facilities. The launching area contained pads, steel gantries, work towers and equipment which surrounded the missiles, all located in thick-walled concrete blockhouses at remote beach areas. If a missile filled with propellant exploded, the damage was confined to the launching area.

This arrangement was satisfactory for liquid-fuel-propelled missiles, but obviously not for Polaris. When Polaris missiles were transported to Cape Canaveral, they were loaded with thousands of pounds of propellant—a danger all the way enroute. The air force questioned the stability of this propellant, and although the navy gave assurances, the air force was not convinced. Major General Donald Yates, air force commander of the test range, was a man who made safety a part of his religion; his record at the Cape was outstanding. After studying the Polaris design, he informed Raborn that the Polaris facilities would have to be completely isolated—regardless of the cost. To Raborn this meant time and money—but there was no appeal, so the Special Projects Office accepted the grant of a wild piece of beach a few miles south of the Cape and went to work. The land was seventy acres of sand with a few palm trees, inhabited by hordes of mosquitoes and reptiles. On this lonely, barren site, a complex of hangars, laboratories, machine shops, and launching pads grew up over a six-month period. The first engineers were Lockheed representatives who were quartered in a sheet-metal shack close to the site and who worked under the baking Florida sun in the most primitive circumstances. But they were optimists; they informed Raborn that if Polaris misfired, nobody but project people and snakes would know about it.

A year after the air force granted the Special Projects Office their piece of real estate, the first Polaris launching was ready. On September 24, 1958, a full-scale test was set up. A 28–foot missile sat on the launching pad, and Admiral Raborn and staff sweltered in the Florida heat watching the huge missile readied for firing. This test was the culmination of 21 months of constant activity—thousands of laboratory tests, over 20 hot-test launchings, and dozens of static firings. If all went well, the missile would lift skyward for several miles, gently tilt toward Africa, and soar over the Atlantic 10 miles before the first stage dropped away. Then, 20 miles farther in flight, the second stage would drop away and the reentry body would fall into the sea 700 miles from the launching site. If all went well.

Admiral Raborn smiled and made small talk and waited while the technicians made final adjustments and the range safety officer conducted checks with the coordinators. Finally the test conductor pushed the button in front of him and the countdown needle in the blockhouse dial went to zero. The Polaris missile emitted a shattering roar and left the pad. Clouds of white smoke shrouded the launcher; flames came from the nozzles; the missile roared up and began climbing straight up into the blue sky. There were cheers around the launching site. But then, suddenly, 40,000 feet over the launching area, the missile shuddered and exploded. Observers dashed into the buildings to avoid parts of the missile that showered over the area, some of them in flames. Several struck the launching pad and caused minor explosions. Later it would be learned that an inexpensive electronic timer failed, so the missile's turn to sea had not been accomplished and the safety officer had ordered the missile destroyed.

The SPO crew was devastated. The engineers were frustrated and furious over the minor flaw that caused the missile's destruction. But Raborn was busy—he had no time for tears or sympathy. He hopped the first plane to Washington with key members of the staff. He knew that the morning newspapers would carry the story of the first Polaris disaster, and he had to be at the Pentagon to do a lot of explaining.

Admiral Rickover delivered several tirades to the managers of the Polaris program on the malfeasance of contractors and their continuing shoddy performance. But the warning did not shake Raborn's confidence in his Polaris team. He listened to the discussions concerning the test failure—then made the decision to get back to the pad and try again.

The second test was as bad as the first. This time the explosion was on the pad, the first stage spouting flames and erupting like a Fourth of July firework. When the second stage ripped away and began ascending, the range safety officer pushed the destruct button again and the missile exploded—raining burning debris for miles across the Cape. Brush fires started and poured smoke into the sky to make an even bigger show of the misfiring missile. Finally firemen extinguished the fire erupting from the missile, put out the brush fire, and bagged the hundreds of snakes that crawled into the highways to avoid the smoldering palmettos. It was quite a show.

Raborn's team pressed for him to blame the contractors—something Raborn had always been reluctant to do. Finally it fell to budget expert Gordon Pehrson to deliver a lecture to the admiral. As Raborn watched from a front-row seat, Pehrson stood in front of his PERT charts at the Polaris Management Center and talked to a group of industrial representatives from across the country who were assembled to discuss Polaris problems.

"This is difficult to put into words—so let me try with a little story. When I left college, I went to work for the government as a bank examiner—the very lowest grade bank examiner—and part of my job was to go around with a team and count money. Of course, as the lowest-grade bank examiner, I was assigned to count the change. In the first bank I went to, I was taken to a vault by a bank official and he kicked a pile of money bags and they jingled. 'There they are,' he said. 'You can count them if you want, but we usually just kick 'em and if they jingle that means they are okay.' Well, I decided I didn't like that idea too much, so I opened them, and do you know what I found? I found the shiniest washers you've ever seen. And this is what is happening in the Polaris program now. We've stopped kicking these bags that contractors with high reputations have handed us, and we've started looking inside, and unfortunately we are finding plenty of washers."

Everyone got the message, including Red Raborn. Tighter controls were ordered—and contractors were alerted that failures due to poor quality would not be tolerated. The navy was paying for quality and it had better be getting quality. Finally, some of Rickover's philosophy began to rub off on Raborn—and just in time, because the next problem was beyond the quality-control-type failure. It involved a major mistake in the missile's design.

Raborn had always been a man to carry the message of Polaris to the factory floor, to stop to tell a man on a machine about the program, to call presidents of large corporations and personally thank them for their help, to take aside a small group of junior engineers and explain the mission of a Polaris fleet in detail. He felt that all of the people associated with Polaris were one large team and had to be told and told often how important the program was to the navy and the country. He recognized that the missile was really the work of thousands of men and women in industry who would never be recognized in any way. He was a contractor's man, from start to finish—and contractors found working with him to be both enormously satisfying and roundly educational. Now they had their opportunity to rally around him in the most serious problem the program would face—a design limitation severe enough for Raborn to consider telling CNO Burke that he faced a stone wall.

With continuing test disasters and the inability of the engineers to decide what was wrong, the program looked as though it might be coming to an end. At this point Raborn was called to Washington and his superiors strongly suggested that he might be trying to go too fast. He was advised that the program should be allowed a cooling-off period and that he should stop testing. When Raborn refused, the senior admirals took their objections to Admiral Arleigh Burke, and the Chief of Naval Operations considered them carefully. But Burke supported Raborn—and sent him back to find a cure for his problems.

Basically the Polaris had been designed with what missile men call a "hot bottom": the materials in the missile could not stand the heat from the burning propellant, and the tail was simply falling apart in flight. Because solid fuel was new, there was not a solution immediately available. Nor did anyone know where to begin to find one. And if one was not found, and found in a hurry, Raborn knew that the FBM program was finished. He also knew that not only was it necessary to be successful, but successful within a brief time frame. But he decided to push on.

"I don't care if we have five more blowups," he told the staff. "I want to lick this, and I want to stay on schedule. Now let's do it."

And the Polaris scientists tried and failed, and tried and failed. The air force technologists were patronizing. It was too bad, they said, but everybody knew that a big solid-fuel-propelled missile was a weird idea to begin with. Not that the engineers on the Polaris program were not good ol' boys and a fine and dedicated lot—but it was too bad they had chosen to attempt the impossible—a case of too much too soon. Solicitous air force generals regretted that the navy had eaten up so much of its budget on the project. Raborn listened to the criticism and patronizing, gritted his teeth, smiled, and pushed his staff harder.

Then on April 20, 1959, with engineering changes made to correct the "hot bottom" and other design problems, a resumption in the firing program was scheduled. There was grave concern at the Navy Building and the Pentagon, and serious doubts at the Polaris complex at the Cape. But, in anticlimactical fashion, the missile took off smoothly, turned slowly toward Africa, and a few minutes later the nose cone dived gracefully into the Atlantic 300 miles downrange.

Raborn waited in Washington for the news of the launch. As his senior staff men described the firing on the phone, Raborn could hear the uproar in the background—the shouting and cheering and whooping of the Special Projects team members who were celebrating with the air of the newly delivered.

After the successful launching, the program moved from the R&D to the production phases. Launching followed successful launching. The *George Washington* went to sea, and in the summer of 1960, underwater tests of the Polaris system were completed off Cape Canaveral. After one false start, the submarine fired missiles downrange over 1,000 miles—"right down the pickle barrel," in the jargon of the range spotters.

The making of Polaris was completed—what had been a dream of a few farsighted naval officers in the mid–1950s was now, in the early 1960s, a reality—a force in being, the most potent weapon system in the world. Raborn spent most of his time now politicking for a larger Polaris fleet. He watched his once-scorned brainchild become the darling of the Congress, his management techniques become the standards taught by business schools and used throughout industry. Even the air force finally paid him homage when the bomber generals moved to a tentative support of the Polaris mission—while suggesting to the Congress that the Polaris fleet be placed under the control of the Joint Strategic Air Command.

Eventually Red Raborn joined the CIA as the agency's director and after a brief tour left to become a successful senior executive of a large aerospace corporation. The story of Raborn's success is stimulating—a folktale in the American tradition—but the story of how he managed it is more significant. In an atmosphere which predicted catastrophe when the United States fell behind Soviet Russia in military power, the phenomenal abilities of Red Raborn and his staff catapulted the country into a five-year lead over the Soviets in the most critical weapon in the strategic arms inventory.

21 The Fleet Ballistic Missile Program: The Why and How of Winning the Arms Race

The portion of the missile force at sea is still the least vulnerable element of our strategic triad, and as far as we can see ahead, it is likely to remain so.

—JAMES R. SCHLESINGER
Secretary of Defense

The dynamics of how the Polaris program was initiated, went ahead as a fledgling, and finally took wing and soared is the story of the greatest single weapons program in the underseas war arsenal, and perhaps in the world arsenal. It has emerged as the nation's chief deterrent, a devastating retaliatory force of hydrogen missiles, poised and invulnerable.

The success of this massive technological effort was a function of a revolutionary new management system—developed by the navy to make Polaris possible. It was a totally new concept; perhaps not as effective as the Special Projects Office portrayed it, but what mattered was that the military, Congress, and those most involved in military appropriations matters thought it was. The Secretary of Defense, key members of Congress, and even Presidents Eisenhower and Kennedy were finally convinced that the managers of the Polaris program could work wonders. When they missed scheduled commitments, the fact was overlooked. When they failed to prevent large, significant design errors, the results were minimized. When they needed more money, it was provided quickly. The Navy Special Projects Office won most of the skirmishes and all the battles for funds and priorities and manpower within the navy, and with the army and air force. It was a program insulated from bureaucratic interference and the jaundiced supervision of government controllers and auditors and meddlesome congressional investigation committees.

The religion of the Polaris team was to build a missile and integrate it with the submarine. It was a crusade—nothing less. If the advantages of the Special Projects Office type of management had to be sold, puffed, and in some cases downright lied about—then that's what its members would do. But the management breakthroughs outnumbered the fabrications; the philosophy of achievement at any personal sacrifice instilled an esprit de corps in the program personnel and a confidence in Congress and the Defense Department which saw the program through. What more was necessary? What more could be expected of any management system?

There is a dark side in any successful manipulative atmosphere. The program's scientists and managers had a refreshing independence of activity—but there was also a fierce spirit of competition and a *Darkness at Noon* atmosphere of being of the "correct" technical persuasion. The penalties for failure were severe—from both a career and employment standpoint. The officers and scientists were made fully aware that they were expendable, that only excellent performance would be tolerated. No matter the long hours, exhausting travel, or sad separations from their families they had endured. If they failed in even a small way, there was the real prospect of being summarily released from the program and reassigned. And the example was clear to all in several cases when branch heads and senior managers were chopped with devastating personal consequences in terms of their civil service or military careers.

These conflicts and tensions were well understood by the program's top management; they could not avoid the carrot-and-stick that every management system incorporates. And it worked: in the near-religious atmosphere of Polaris, the stigma of failure was so great that less than total commitment was unthinkable.

Admiral Raborn carried the program first class; no cost was spared to accommodate the contractors and officers in their travel, living, or entertainment. Promotions for navy men associated with the program were advanced, civil servants were upgraded, and contractor personnel were highly paid. There was a continual round of personal commendations, awards, and medals. Raborn himself was the kind of charismatic leader the program needed—a man convinced that personal motivation was the most important element in getting an impossible job done. He subscribed to all that he taught.

The psychological orchestration of Raborn's program was a work of genius; it brought a degree of commitment and a willingness to make personal sacrifices far beyond anything that a military hardware program had ever engendered in the past. There was an urgency communicated to everyone—the officers, the contractors, the workers, their wives, even their children. Polaris could not fail because the country depended on it. The potential national consequences of a failure to produce a nuclear submarine capable of launching ICBM missiles was something that all the Polaris managers lived with, day in and day out. This was not just another military system—this was the system that was going to stop the Russian threat. Perhaps only Raborn could have succeeded in this cleverest postwar manipulation of management—an adventure of reward, fear, pride, and patriotism that goaded and coaxed the managers and made true believers out of everyone who came within the sphere of the Polaris program activities.

The United States is a country that expects very little from government in peacetime. There is skepticism at the announcement of any great national commitment. Citizens are jaded to the disclosures of inefficiency in public services, budget overruns, and gross waste in military spending. Thus Raborn's achievement stands out as even more extraordinary. He pushed patriotism and devotion to duty and total dedication to a point which was almost alien to the national mood—to a patriotic pitch which was unknown in this country in any peacetime period.

Only after the decade of Polaris passed could it be recognized as such an extraordinary period—perhaps the last time a contracting group within the services will have the organizational independence and political support to perform the feats that the FBM program team managed. The Poseidon project was later built by the same government and contractor team that built Polaris, but it was a radically different situation in terms of management effectiveness, meeting schedule deadlines, and performing within budgets. The Poseidon program was basically Polaris extended—the same technology and the same mission. Yet it has faced an unfriendly Congress and continual harassment and audit. And Trident, a similar effort, seems headed for an even harder road now that the ground rules have changed and Trident managers deal with a more centralized authority in the Department of Defense. In the beginning, the FBM program managers were political entrepreneurs as well as technological innovators and military strategists. Now that game is well known and played by many other groups, and the Trident program faces the kind of competition engendered by the FBM success. Imitation is the highest form of flattery—and the groups competitive with the FBM program were clever enough to learn from it.

With this change in the organization of the Pentagon came a slowdown and lack of religious zeal, so something has been lost to the Poseidon and Trident programs. In theory, they should have carried the full head of steam of Polaris to greater heights of technology and weapons production. Instead, the opposite seems to be true. This red tape and apathy has begun to adversely affect Trident, a program massive, novel, and complex enough to require the Raborn touch once again.

What are the lessons of the FBM program? First, the refusal to accept failure—any failure. Goal attainment was the only standard by which the program's success was measured. A "go–no-go" evaluation. Either the job was done—the program was implemented as planned—or if it was not, severe measures were taken. No excuses, no technical nonsense, no Monday-morning quarterbacking. From the outset, Admiral Raborn and his managers decided that they would do the job or they would consider themselves failures. They would make the highest and best use of the funds and manpower allotted to them, and they would not let anything stand in their way. Their concentration would be on the performance of their own program and the success of their own organization. Everyone connected with Polaris was convinced that the military security of the United States turned on the successful completion of their program—nothing short of that. And that conviction was probably the most significant reason that they succeeded so well.

Next in importance was Raborn's insistence that they establish two well-defined goals very early in the program: a solid-fuel ballistic missile and a fleet of missile-launching submarines to act as the platforms for those missiles. This was their mission: building the major deterrent in the Cold War. Candid, clear, perhaps impossible—but something around which a man could wrap his life and career.

From the outset, the FBM managers expected to achieve a success that was greater than any other weapons-development effort. They were given resources and talent and responsibility without parallel by the United States Government. But time was short; therefore they had to innovate.

The FBM program has been compared to the Manhattan Project, which operated under wartime secrecy and in many ways was similar in its independence and isolation from critics. Admiral Raborn was determined that there should be a favorable environment for the FBM program—an esprit de corps and public acceptance. He managed this by a variety of public relations and morale-directed policies. Their success in forging a political and military consensus of opinion that the FBM program was the single most significant weapons program of its age was amazing. This was a lesson in public relations not lost on the program management teams that came after—but apparently it was not capable of duplication.

Using their allies, the FBM planners learned to tap the almost unlimited resources available from government funding. A program which was basking in the sunshine of congressional and administration approval had a real advantage in competing with the other armed services for the role of strategic offensive missile deterrent. It was obvious early that one of the services—and possibly two—would have to be denied a primary function. Starting from a last-place position behind the front-running army and air force, the navy very quickly managed to gather an amazing array of support for the Polaris program. Once Polaris had taken a front position, the FBM managers did not relax; they continued to project Polaris while assisting one after another of the competing systems into the stretches of elimination and oblivion. They charmed reviewing agencies, consorted with the right congressmen, pleased the Joint Chiefs of Staff, included influential newspapermen as insiders, and provided liberal fringe benefits and intellectual stimulation for their friends in the academic community. At all points, they marshaled their contractors, who were often the key to congressional support for the SPO and had generous slush funds to subsidize political campaigns and entertainments.

But all of this planning and manipulating would have been for naught if the FBM group had not learned how to manage an advanced technology program. In the 1950s and 1960s technology burgeoned in all the sciences, but few groups were able to successfully channel this technology into a single weapons system. FBM introduced PERT (Program Evaluation and Review Technique), CMP (Critical Path Method), and other advanced management concepts to do this, stressed decentralization, and fostered fierce competition, total dedication, and religious fervor. As the near-messiah preaching the cause of national survival to the already baptized, Admiral Raborn unnerved the old sea dogs who ran the navy. But they went along and watched the United States vault ahead of the Soviet Union in one of the most startling coups in modern military history.

22 The Cold Warriors: The Legacy of Rickover and Raborn

Nearly all the military people running the Navy are not experienced in what is required to carry out a major engineering development successfully, and are not experienced in the training required to operate complex equipment using modern technology. We have a situation in the Navy today where there are basically three groups of officers. There are the aviators, the surface ship officers, and the submariners. The aviators have the greatest influence. Next are the surface ship officers, and lowest on the totem pole are the submarine officers. This is largely because the submariners are so few in number.

—ADMIRAL HYMAN RICKOVER, U.S.N.

The engineering development and production in both the nuclear-submarine and fleet ballistic missile programs represent some of the most significant accomplishments in military technology made in this century. Both marshaled industry on a broad scale, polarized the navy as a whole, revolutionized R&D management, and created new project-organizational systems. Producing a fleet of submarines driven by a completely new type of propulsion and armed with a completely new type of ballistic missile was certainly equal to anything that was done in the science of aerospace in the postwar period. While the success of technological innovation must be judged over a long term, the military tactical and strategic impact of these developments can be assessed on a current basis—and when judged by any yardstick, the accomplishments of Rickover and Raborn are outstanding.

Whatever other influences may advance or retard the development of an all-nuclear navy, its beginnings were very impressive. The factors that account for Raborn's success are straightforward; it is much more difficult to determine the reasons for the exceptional accomplishment of Rickover. But by any professional management standards, they were both brilliant, resourceful, and visionary.

Rickover fought many battles on many fronts. He changed his tactics so frequently that to have brought off the program in the fashion he did showed him to be a genius. He used a curmudgeon's sometimes devious approach, and it worked for him. He needed luck far beyond Raborn's, a managerial skill far beyond what he found in industry, and a sixth sense that told him where the real problems were lurking. And he had them all—and used them all. If we define genius as an infinite capacity for taking pains, then Rickover is indeed a genius. He worked most of his waking hours, six or seven days a week. He exercised an extraordinary degree of control over all facets of his many complex projects. He challenged institutions and seemingly powerful personalities and watched them eventually crumble and kowtow. He had an intuitive skill which served him well both as a manager and an engineer. But most of all, he seemed to adhere strictly to his own principles that people —not organizations—get a job done, and that nothing is impossible to the leader willing to pay the price in work and personal sacrifice.

Rickover's methods alienated him in the navy but endeared him to Congress; after all, Congress is a collection of individuals, and its committees usually reflect the personality of their chairmen. The legislative process depends as much upon relationships between individuals as on formal procedures. So Rickover deserted the navy after twenty-five years of operating within its structures and boundaries and began an informal liaison with politicians. He moved his responsibilities and prime relationships to the halls of Congress—and with that move he won great rewards for this new loyalty.

There is a natural comparison between Rickover and Raborn —perhaps an unavoidable comparison. Both men were outstanding successes. Both created a new management style. Both inspired technological crusades. Both created a cult of loyal followers. Both respected the role of personality in leadership. Raborn was a naval officer in every sense, he was a man of the system; Rickover was a naval officer in almost no sense; he fought the system throughout his career. Raborn was an administrator but not a technical specialist; Rickover was a technical specialist but not an administrator. Raborn was selected because he knew how to lead men; Rickover was selected because he knew how to marshal a technology. Raborn built a superb organization which survived him; Rickover scorned administrative activities not associated with technical problems and built an organization around himself. Raborn was a master of psychological techniques and public relations; Rickover was a master of overcoming technical obstacles, and his public relations talents had a manipulative image. Raborn was the friend and the inspiration of his subordinates; Rickover their scourge and challenge. Raborn treated his contractors as members of the team and encouraged his staff to establish personal ties with them; Rickover demanded personal responsibility from his contractors and forbade his staff to have any social contacts with them.

Thus the two men seem to compare directly only in one aspect: they both were successful. Does this lead to the conclusion that there is no single path to technological innovation? Perhaps Rickover's legacy is most dramatic; in blazing the way for all iconoclastic genius, he demonstrated that it is possible to be effective in technical innovation through a highly personalized approach. He refused to be intimidated by highly sophisticated technology, by tradition, by rank, by prestige, or by seniority. Rickover had served as the only head of the naval propulsion project through dozens of Secretaries of Defense, Secretaries of the Navy, Chiefs of Naval Operations,

Chiefs of Bureau of Ships, Chiefs of Naval Personnel, Chairmen of the Atomic Energy Commission, and Chairmen of the Joint Chiefs of Staff. They came, they went, and Rickover stayed. So, whether it can be defined or measured, Admiral Hyman G. Rickover has taught a great lesson concerning technology and its organization, and about how much one man can influence its course. In his generation he was the great individual creator of the military weapon. In every sense, he is the superwarrior of the atomic age.

What Americans have done, Americans can do again. There will be another time, perhaps soon, when we will need such great steps forward—and the leadership of extraordinary, skillful, and committed people like those who made *Nautilus* and Polaris possible. The military-industrial complex can take great satisfaction in the achievements of the Special Projects Office and the Nuclear Propulsion Program.

When Americans learn to marshal and control the nation's bureaucracy, we are up to any job. Still, it would be comforting to see the likes of a young Red Raborn or Hyman Rickover emerge as Trident moves along. For all of their organizational skills and new management expertise, the military now seems to be sorely lacking in charismatic leadership.

23 The Wet Cold War Accelerates– Phase Three

What, do you think that Great Britain and the United States—the United States, the most powerful state in the world—will permit you to break their line of communication in the Mediterranean? Nonsense. And we have no navy.

—STALIN to the Yugoslav vice-president, discussing intervention in the Greek civil war

With the condition called "overkill" came the neutralization of armed forces called "nuclear parity." With the acceptance of this philosophy it was agreed that although the Soviet forces were clearly inferior to those of the United States in all deterrent capabilities, they were nevertheless adequate to provide a devastating blow in any large war. In theory, no nation would pay the price of self-annihilation—so to engage in warfare, it was necessary to step down to a level where combat on land, sea, and air was feasible without the danger that one or the other of the superpowers would resort to unleashing a nuclear holocaust. A difficult arrangement to imagine—but the planners had only the most unthinkable alternatives to deal with. At some of these plateaus, a tactical nuclear capacity would exist, and conventional weapons—torpedoes, missiles, and depth charges—might conceivably be employed. Graduated deterrent thresholds were postulated; but finally the whole matter of speculating on degrees of Armageddon seemed silly, and the Pentagon became more reserved on public information concerning the stages of escalation leading to holocaust.

With the overkill capacity of ICBM systems—land, submarine-based, and bomber-transported—the strategic role of the carrier came under question. In 1963 the carrier strike fleets were relieved of their primary strategic mission and were assigned to close ground support and interdiction. The A–5 Vigilante supersonic bomber was discontinued in production and replaced by the squadrons of strike aircraft. The carrier aircraft were primarily equipped with conventional weapons and operated in tactical troop support and forward bombing during the Vietnam War. They retained a capacity to deliver tactical nuclear weapons if the situation demanded, but emphasis was now on their role in conventional warfare.

Amphibious-warfare methods were devised for sea transport and landing of troops in such a way that they would not be completely vulnerable to tactical nuclear weapons. Maneuvers showed these tactics to be reasonably effective.

The buildup of the Soviet submarine fleet was closely followed by the United States Navy planners. They recommended the development of weapons systems which would allow the detection and destruction of submarines at maximum distances, so the navy's long-range sonar surveillance network received a top priority. Radar and sonar instruments had their ranges substantially extended, and magnetic and infrared weapons were developed. The ASROC anti-submarine missile was put into service, and submarine homing torpedoes were upgraded. Target-seeking wire-guidance devices and the SUBROC missile were installed aboard ship. These devices were incorporated into the Thresher class hunter-killer submarine and the Farragut and Belknap class frigates. The Charles F. Adams class missile destroyer and a number of old destroyers in the Gearing and Sumner classes were upgraded with new ASW weapons. The older destroyers were given large-scale FRAM I and FRAM II conversions, which included arming them with ASROC launchers and in some cases installing landing decks for the un-

manned or manned DASH and LAMPS submarine-warfare helicopters.

Military planners were delighted with Soviet Chairman Khrushchev's saber rattling; the propaganda image of a decisive Russian
technology lead woke up the American people with a shock. The
missile gap was largely a figment of the fertile imagination of the
media who had news to sell and of political office-seekers with
much to gain from frightening the voter. Their cause was helped
by the Soviet propaganda machine on one side and the Pentagon
gloom purveyors on the other. Happily, it galvanized a vast program of technology in the United States, so that by 1962 the
American scientists were widening the lead in both the deterrent
and strategic-weapons race. The Soviets dropped behind and that
strange phenomenon occurred: the paranoia that afflicts Soviet
leaders began finally to catch up with Khrushchev. He saw American technology threatening Mother Russia at all her borders, and
he decided to threaten our shores by arming his Cuban ally.

In 1961 the Soviet leadership acknowledged that their own
submarine-launched, ballistics missile program was falling drastically behind. The United States lead in both submarine-launched
missiles and ICBMs was increasing at too fast a pace to provide
continued Russian security. The Cuban gamble in October 1962
was an attempt to threaten the United States at its exposed southern
flank in much the same way that Russians were threatened by
United States nuclear submarines operating from the Arctic. The
Cuban crisis led directly to Khrushchev's downfall; the modern
reconnaissance methods available to the United States military at
the time had little trouble in detecting the presence of missiles in
Cuba, and United States sea power was strong enough to make any
Soviet threat meaningless. Khrushchev's government survived for
two years, but it was a transitional period.

Party Chairman Brezhnev and Prime Minister Kosygin eventually succeeded as party chiefs with the commitment of balancing
the Soviet arsenal. Meanwhile the Soviets worked frantically on
their solid-fuel propulsion design of an ICBM, while at the same
time continuing development of the large liquid-fuel SS–9–SCARP
missile.

The Russians tried to increase production to catch up with the United States in the number and payload capability of the ICBM force. They pushed their shipyard capacities in Severodvinsk and Komsomolsk to produce a class of nuclear submarine designed very closely on the model of the U.S. Navy's *George Washington.* It was the prototype of the Y class submarine fitted out behind the conning tower with sixteen paired launch tubes for the newly designed SS–N–6 missile, a solid-fuel version resembling the Polaris A–1.

Successors to the N class submarines were designed as torpedo-armed V class boats. The Soviets were still concerned with striking at the enemy's surface forces, and particularly their old nemesis, the aircraft carrier. The nuclear-propelled E class missile-carrying submarines were assigned to an anticarrier program. Since they were required to fire their missiles near the surface, they were vulnerable and largely discounted by military observers. The Soviets designed a replacement of the Shaddock type missile which could be fired from a submerged position and installed on the new nuclear C class submarines; but even working the full shipyard capacity in a crash program, they still fell behind in submarine construction, and the increased mobility of the American carriers began to minimize the submarine role in the Soviet anticarrier operation plans.

In 1964 the fully-nuclear-powered United States Navy's Task Force I was formed, which included the carrier *Enterprise,* the cruiser *Long Beach,* and the frigate *Bainbridge.* The task force cruised around the world without refueling or replenishing, and the lesson was not lost on the Soviets. They began pushing their anti-carrier strategy and evolving new tactics which would put their missile-carrying ships in direct contact with American carrier strike forces. It was another kamikaze role for the Russian destroyers— ships that would operate in a major battle at sea with the hope of surviving long enough to fire their weapons and eliminate at least a part of the carrier force before being destroyed themselves. The Soviets were serious enough about this plan to redesign ship missile systems after 1967. They replaced the longer-range missiles with shorter-range systems to operate within radar range of the enemy and allow the missiles to be guided from their launching ships—

thus doing away with relay stations. This missile system—the SS–N–10—was installed on the Kresta II class of missile cruisers; a similar launching system was installed on the Krivak class multi-purpose destroyers.

The Soviet naval high command seemed confused between the carrier threat and submarine threat. Russian shipyard schedules were shuffled and strained with the requirements for both missile frigates and destroyers. The construction of the Kotlin and Krupny class destroyers was interrupted by modifications which included sonar domes in the bow, a variable-depth sonar, and a helicopter landing deck.

This was a hectic time for Soviet planners. The first United States Navy nuclear submarines carrying the Polaris A–1 missile were now patrolling off the Russian coastline. An agreement with Spain allowed the United States to build a second European base at Rota. Then the longer-range missiles were available; the nuclear submarines were carrying the Polaris A–3 missile capable of hitting any target on the European continent and well into Asia. A major Polaris base was established on Guam, and in 1963 an American intelligence relay station was located on Australia's Northwest Cape. Polaris submarines patrolled the Pacific, the Gulf of Bengal, and the Arabian Sea—the Soviets had yet to mount a competitive system.

In 1964 Soviet naval formations began a forward deployment program. They sailed farther away from home bases than they had previously ventured—into the Mediterranean and into the Atlantic. They had built submarine bases in Albania at the port of Valona; but in 1961, when Albania enlisted in the Chinese camp, the Soviets abandoned their only Mediterranean foothold. By 1966, however, the Russians were maintaining a regular Mediterranean force, usually consisting of one cruiser with a three- to five-destroyer escort and a dozen submarines. The main mission of the formation seemed to be spying on the United States Sixth Fleet, although they did make ports of call in Egypt and Algeria. In the north the Russians conducted navy maneuvers off Murmansk and war games as far away as Iceland.

By 1967 United States weapons superiority was growing; a force of 1,000 solid-fueled ICBM Minuteman missiles had been installed and augmented by 54 liquid-fueled Titan II missiles. There were 40 Polaris submarines operating on station with a total capability of 656 missile launchers. A force of 600 B–52 bombers formed the third leg of the deterrent triangle. The United States was clearly superior to the Soviet Union in each deterrent class.

The Minuteman I design was replaced by Minuteman II in 1968 at a rate of 150 missiles per year, and in 1971 both series were replaced by a substantially improved version—the Minuteman III—which significantly increased the range of the missile. In 1970 the changeover had begun for nuclear submarines. The A–3 missile was replaced by the Poseidon missile, which not only increased the range but also included multiple warheads which allowed the choice of a megaton warhead or 3 warheads of 200 kilotons each in the MRV design. Poseidon also had the warhead capability to accommodate 10 of the 50–kiloton MRV warheads, selectively equipped with electronic penetration aids.

The Soviet ICBM potential grew far more slowly than was reported in the press in the United States. More credit and significance was attached to the buildup by the new media than by military strategists. The Soviets increased their ICBM arsenal to 1,500 missiles by the end of 1971—primarily the SS–11 missile, a rough copy of the Minuteman I in range and explosive force. The Russians also began commissioning the Y class nuclear submarines in 1968; by 1973 these submarines were fast closing the gap in total numbers, but were inferior in performance to the United States designs.

In the 1960s the Soviet antiballistic missile program threatened the ICBM potential of the United States. The Russians developed the Galosh missile; much larger and more sophisticated than the only United States antimissile weapon, the Nike. In 1965 the United States had developed a short-range antimissile system called Sprint and was well along in developing a long-range Spartan missile, having test-flown initial models in 1968. The overall systems for antimissile defense would require a network of long-range radar surveillance in order to provide a sufficiently reliable early-warning system to detect the launching of any enemy missiles. Work on a national surveillance grid was begun. In 1972 the system was far enough along to become a major threat to the Soviet's strategic-missile capability.

The Soviets began work on a new class of missile to be placed aboard the SS–N–8 submarine projected to an extended range and greater accuracy which would be installed in the second-generation Y class submarines to upgrade their threat to Polaris potential.

When the Soviets announced plans for a blue-water fleet, the Kara class cruisers was put on the ways, and it was rumored that aircraft carriers of more than 30,000 tons were scheduled to be built. In order to put a deep-water fleet to sea for long ocean cruises, the Soviets would have to develop sophisticated replenishing methods at sea or obtain large and complete forward bases. They tried both approaches, but their efforts were only marginally successful. They were active in the Mediterranean and Indian oceans and the Arabian Sea with a force of nuclear submarines accompanied by tenders and surface flotillas of cruisers and destroyer escorts. Russian warships began to make port in friendly countries, and maneuvers were conducted in the Baltic Sea, Arctic Ocean, the Black Sea, and the Mediterranean. Recently there has been activity in the Pacific Ocean and the South China Sea, but the Soviet maneuvers are impressive primarily as firsts. Soviet Navy watchers have reservations as to their capability of commanding and co-ordinating fleets of ships around the world. Most Western military planners feel that the forward deployment policy of the Soviet Navy is principally a political development. Simply showing the flag in a trouble spot with even a relatively weak naval force can go a long way toward neutralizing a strong naval force that is trying to avoid combat. Any fleet presence is impressive, particularly in developing countries; ships with modern weapons systems present a dramatic appearance when supported by a clever Russian propaganda program.

On the advice of Admiral Gorshkov, the Soviet high command had finally freed the Russian Navy from the Red Army's dominance and a primarily defensive mentality. Beginning with Khrushchev, all important Soviet leaders have agreed that the first priority should be given to both the strategic rocket forces and nuclear-missile launching submarines—weapons which they felt would not only deter the United States, but in the event of war, would result in a Soviet victory. In the Soviet Union all major decisions are based on and subsequently dominated by politics, so now the Soviet admirals have their place in the sun.

The massive naval move by the Soviet Union was not based on careful planning or the attainment of objectives which were at once consistent with Soviet expansionary policy and within the realm of capability. The Russians decided to build a surface fleet which would, if not challenge the fleet of the United States, at least show the flag around the world. Clearly this was entering a race with the West which they could not win—in a theater of battle they could afford to ignore. They did, however, concentrate on the ultimate weapon; the submarine-launched ballistic missile, and also on a force of attack submarines that would become offensive weapons against fleets and merchant shipping in time of war. The Russian trawler fleets organized on military lines to work the fishing grounds of the world while the Soviet merchant fleet bargained to attract more commerce and eventually hoped to break the United States stranglehold on worldwide commerce.

24 Trident: The Supersubmarine

*The king of the sea, with his whiskers of weed
and his trident and dolphins, truly represents
the main and gives it character.*

—FELIX RIESENBERG

As a young engineer fresh out of the Naval Academy, President Jimmy Carter once served as one of Admiral Hyman G. Rickover's spear carriers. He credits Rickover with being one of the most influential people in his life, and Rickover was quick to re-establish his influence at the White House after a period of decline during the Nixon-Ford administrations. But then stories leaked that although Rickover had indeed tried to sell Carter on nuclear power and done his very effective job as a flogger of supercarriers and submarines, still Carter expressed questions about the advisability of building the submarine Trident rather than a number of smaller submarines to do the same job. Stung again, the program moves along slowly, at this point bearing very little resemblance to the massive and magnificent effort that Admiral Raborn put together to push the FBM program and Rickover himself mounted for the first nuclear submarine.

Trident is no simple continuation of the Polaris/Poseidon program—it is a new form of superdreadnought, bearing little relation to the Polaris/Poseidon missile-carrying submarines except as an extension of their mission. The Trident will be about twice the size of anything that has come before—a submarine that displaces more than 18,000 tons, is 5 times larger than the *Nautilus,* the first nuclear submarine, and has three-quarters the tonnage of a World War II aircraft carrier. Her sail stands a majestic two stories high.

The 24 vertical firing tubes are each capable of sending a MIRV intercontinental ballistic missile over 4,000 miles with pinpoint accuracy, and that range will be gradually increased until sometime in the 1980s the missiles will carry 6,000 miles, and farther. To some people, Trident is the Minuteman program put to sea—a massive mobile ICBM platform that will be able to strike at the Soviet heartland while on patrol close to the coast of the United States, within the continental limits, and under the secure protection of the navy ASW forces and air force air cover.

Initially, ten Tridents are planned, and East Coast and West Coast base facilities. The first base to be constructed will be at Bangor, Washington on the Straits of Juan de Fuca, where a submarine can proceed through the Hood Canal to sea to be screened by protective ASW destroyers and submarines until she leaves the exit area and moves quickly to take her patrol station well into international waters.

The development of the Trident has been assigned to the Director, Strategic Submarine Division and Trident Program, an office created within the complex of the Office of the Chief of Naval Operations to keep it under the top management's wing. It is, quite obviously, the pet navy project and one that the navy has been beating the drum for in Congress for over ten years. Unfortunately, it is also where critics of the Polaris/Poseidon program, in particular, and the sea-base deterrent in general, have decided to make what must be their last stand. After Trident, anything goes. So the controversy rages much as it did in the air force and the navy during the bomber vs. aircraft carrier argument in the 1950s.

The navy's case rests heavily on survivability, on providing a deterrent that will assure a major second-strike capability and one that will not be vulnerable based on any technological advances projected between now and the middle of the twenty-first century. But the detractors point to the billion-dollar-a-copy price tag and wonder if an extension of the present surveillance capabilities will not be adequate to track the Trident at some time in the future and make it a prime first-strike target. The navy replies that the ocean will be the Trident's friend and create such ambient noise conditions and bottom protection in shadow areas as to make her detection highly unlikely. The admirals point out that there are 60 million square miles of ocean in which the superquiet, deep-diving Trident can hide and still target all significant installations in the Soviet Union and People's Republic of China. The critics say sonar ranges are increasing. And so the debate continues.

Project Trident is the product of the military think tanks—the Department of Defense study teams that project Soviet moves and countermoves and plan weapons systems years in advance in order to take advantage of anticipated weakness in the Russian defense posture. In the early 1970s a problem was posed to our long-range planners: could Soviets develop and deploy an ICBM force sufficiently large to directly contest the United States' capability from both a first-strike and retaliatory standpoint? It was a period when the Vietnam war was winding down. There were military spending cutbacks in prospect; and budgetary ceilings imposed by Congress seemed sure to curtail the growth of the military establishment. The think-tank planners and systems analysts and technology specialists were being asked to decide between the alternatives of larger and more sophisticated aircraft, missiles, and at-sea systems. When the brain trusters made their report, the navy and Trident wound up the winners. Most studies suggested that the sea was the likely place to go; that future replacements for even mobile Minuteman systems would be far less secure than missiles aboard ship; that submarines were the preferred vehicle over any surface ship in design stages, with the possible exception of some sophisticated surface-effect configurations which were not capable of analysis.

In 1970 the navy began spending money to develop the Trident, at the time called ULMS (Underseas Long Range Missiles System), and although not commanding the consensus that the Raborn-Rickover team had in early Polaris days, the Trident continued to forge ahead slowly, with spending at a $2 billion annual rate and rising.

By now the navy thought it had learned how to sell large submarine systems by charming congressional committees and feeding them "supersecret" information in closed sessions which surely would be leaked to their colleagues, and then to other influential Washingtonians who might offer support. One Trident was compared to three Polaris/Poseidon submarines in terms of its effectiveness—which took some of the sting out of the billion-dollar price tag. Navy hucksters used dramatic photographs and maps and charts to depict the coverage of Trident missiles which commanded critical areas that the Polaris/Poseidon systems could not reach. It was pointed out that the Trident operated in deep waters—in the Atlantic, the Pacific, and Indian oceans, and would provide an almost invulnerable platform which, beginning sometime in the early 1980s, would be capable of firing 24 MIRV rockets over 6,000 miles. These MIRV hydrogen-bomb-tipped missiles could cover all targets on the Eurasian land mass from several positions in the Pacific and Indian oceans. It was an impressive, dramatic, and well-told story.

In 1970 a group of senators and representatives formed a club called Members of Congress for Peace Through Law (MCPTL), and provided an even stronger backing for Trident by promptly issuing a statement stoutly supporting the sea-based nuclear missile system as the country's first-line deterrent. They compared it to the potential of the fixed land-based systems and pointed out that regardless of future ABM systems, the sea-based deterrent would not be adversely affected. Overall, its cost-effectiveness would be greater. What more could be said? The MCPTL had been critical of the Pentagon in many other areas; here was a warm and cordial support of one of the navy's programs by unbiased experts.

Because reliable contractors (particularly General Dynamics and General Electric) had been developed during the Polaris/Poseidon programs, the navy timetable for the Trident was relatively short; the deployment of the first submarine was scheduled for 1980. Lockheed Missile and Space Company, a subsidiary of Lockheed Aircraft Company, was the contractor for the two new missiles, Trident I and Trident II. Trident I would be a 4,000–mile missile roughly comparable to the Poseidon and interchangeable with Poseidon for increased capability of present submarine systems.

But as the program moved along, it became obvious that Trident II, the 6,000–mile missile, would not be compatible with the Poseidon tubes and, indeed, the navy was even against deploying any Trident I missiles in Poseidon submarines. In fact, the navy was so opposed that it delayed the development of the Trident I missile to coincide with the program for the Trident hull, in effect denying the availability of the missile to any Poseidon submarines. This ploy cost the navy some support. The argument for employing the extended-range missile in existing submarine launchers was so attractive that it caused a congressional storm at the shift in schedule, and even members of the MCPTL denounced the proposed delays.

The Trident critics—that ever-present and vocal lobby—pointed out that many advantages of the program, including the extended-range missile and the quiet-running features of the Trident submarine, could be incorporated in the present Polaris/Poseidon fleet. They revived the argument that Trident—as proposed by the navy—did not offer any significant advantages over the four or five Poseidon submarines (their figures) that could be constructed for the same price. And to further confuse the issue, they pointed out that the Trident paralleled the flaws in the ICBM program by concentrating more missiles in fewer platforms, consequently making these platforms more vulnerable as potential prime targets. Why help an enemy's ASW forces by offering them a smaller number of larger targets, they argued.

To aid these skeptics, the air force brought its big guns into play. Zeroing in on arguments concerning the reduction in the number of submarines, they pointed out that with the state-of-the-art sonar surveillance detection methods—ignoring technological breakthroughs which were bound to be a part of the technology of the 1980s—even now with conventional sonar, it might be possible to locate Trident submarines accurately enough so that Soviet missiles (the SS-II was used as one example) could be set for an underwater blast which would be lethal for a 3–5 mile range and probably badly damage a Trident submarine at something up to 10 miles, even if it did not sink it. Simple arithmetic would establish that firing of four SS-II at any Trident position was all that was required to have a very disruptive effect on its performance. Knocking out 24 missiles—a very favorable trade ratio whether or not the Trident submarine was sunk—made the numbers all in favor of the SS-II—by air force calculation.

But Trident weathered the storm and survived the heated debates in the Senate Armed Services Committee. The navy was using its most effective campaigner, Admiral Hyman G. Rickover, to blitz and dazzle and amaze the representatives and senators in one of the most successful campaigns ever staged in Congress in behalf of a Pentagon program. In 1973 Secretary of Defense Elliot Richardson had requested a $1.7 billion continuance of the Trident program, doubling the budget request of the year before and putting Congress on notice that the sky was the limit, apparently, as far as future Trident budgets were concerned. The unlikely team of admirals Elmo T. Zumwalt and supersalesman Hyman G. Rickover were simply too much for the few frugal opponents in Congress. The two admirals proselytized and threatened and made it perfectly clear that an anti-Trident vote was a vote for the Russians— there was no other interpretation possible. Secretary of Defense James R. Schlesinger was appointed at midcontest; he quietly took a seat in the galleries to watch the end of the fight.

It was a close vote: the Senate approved the Trident program 49–47. The Senate's champion arms supporter, Senator Henry M. Jackson, had warmed to the battle when the navy promised that Trident's home port would be located in his backyard near Bangor, Washington. So the Trident survived, but barely. The House Appropriations Committee nicked about $250 million from the $2 billion authorization—then, spurred by the House's action, Secretary of Defense Schlesinger forced the navy into the modest compromise of extending submarine construction schedules, in time and number.

It was rumored that Schlesinger was playing Trident as a buildup to the SALT II discussions—and the Trident program would be a large bargaining chip, indeed. Since there was reason to believe that the Russians were more concerned about their fiscal problems than in attempting to match an enormously expensive system, Schlesinger reasoned that they would make broad concessions in exchange for a slowdown in Trident. Obviously, this was not a popular stand with the navy, and when Schlesinger was summarily fired a short time later, it was not without some jubilation in the ranks of the Trident supporters.

Now the navy has come away with over $1 billion committed in Trident R&D funds by Congress, and the program has reached that stage of development where it seems as invulnerable to the attacks of its opponents in Congress and the administration as someday it may be to enemy ASW forces. But there are still rough seas ahead, and the funding battle will continue to bounce back and forth in budget debates. It will suffer the same continual examination and reexamination as the B–1 bomber and other military systems huge enough to be an easy target for those budget-minded members of Congress. However, Trident will push on with deliveries in 1979 or 1980, with 10 or 12 ships patrolling by 1984 or 1986.

With the B–1 bomber gone, Congress is more friendly toward Trident. The missile force at sea is the least vulnerable element of the strategic forces, and gradually, as the DOD budget shifts increasingly to programs like Trident, it becomes obvious that the future of the navy will be under the seas. The supersubmarine is the only credible deterrent upon which the forces of the Pentagon, Congress, and the administration can reasonably come together.

Military thinkers debated for years on what new SLBM should follow Polaris. Because of the cost of such a system, its technical complexity, and the disproportionate amount of the military budget required to implement such a program, the debate at the Pentagon went on for over a decade. Congress was concerned with costs; operational commanders were concerned with the performance of the larger design of missile-launching submarines and the more powerful generation of missiles. Finally, the front runner was accepted—the Trident program was funded. But still the debate continues concerning its advantages and disadvantages, its cost trade-off and employment.

The most significant aspect of the Trident is its program budget.

All military programs are becoming increasingly expensive, with a tendency to overrun original estimates. So when the initial figure for 10 submarines was set at $20 billion—and each additional submarine was scheduled to cost $1 billion—Congress was taken aback. Serious doubts were expressed about the need for such a weapon and the requirement to fund its development. But the navy finally won the support of Congress, and the program was given a go-ahead, although such approval is always subject to modification or withdrawal. The proponents of the program argue its need and the efficiency of submarine production in the past; its opponents counter with arguments of redundancy and indicate that cost considerations will make the entire program prohibitive far before its completion. One point both sides agree on: the Trident is technically feasible—and that is no small concession, to acknowledge that the military can design and industry produce such a system. This admission seems amazing in its own right; such miracles of technology are now taken almost for granted.

From its inception, the Trident program has been a combination of three separate development and production programs: two based on the development of ballistic missiles, and one for the overall submarine. In order to keep costs within bounds, the navy initially began to develop an Underseas Long Range Missile System (ULMS) which would be accommodated by the Polaris submarines modified to use the Poseidon missile. However, with Admiral Rickover leading the charge, the decision was reversed. A new submarine was designed for a large missile known as the ULMS-2, D-5 design—eventually, the Trident II missile system.

On the military belief that idle hands are the devil's tools, since its inception in the 1950s, the Polaris system has been subject to a succession of redesigns of the basic ballistic missile. First the A-1, then the A-2, then the A-3, then the C-3—each one costing millions and increasing the range, payload, and sophistication of the basic missile design. The C-3 is called the Poseidon missile and is now installed on the majority of Polaris submarines. This missile has a range of approximately 2,500 nautical miles and a payload of 10 MIRV weapons, each with a yield of approximately

50 kilotons. The successor to the Poseidon—the C–4/Trident I design—will have a similar payload but will increase its range to approximately 4,000 nautical miles. The deployment date for these missiles is presently 1980. Meanwhile Rickover and his planners are hoping to divert some of the budget projected for the future arming of the submarine fleet to the Trident submarine, passing over the Trident I missile and the C–4 design to go directly to the Trident II missile in the D–5 design.

The new Trident submarine is projected as an amazing feat of naval engineering. It will displace approximately 18,000 tons, or twice as much as the Polaris submarines. It will carry 24 missiles, rather than the 16 carried by Polaris. It will be quieter, faster, and more maneuverable and have improved sonar capabilities. It will also be simpler to maintain and overhaul, able to spend far more time at sea. The Trident II missile is designed for the Trident submarine alone and will not fit into the "old design"—the Polaris submarine. This D–5 design will not increase payload over the C–3 or C–4 missile, but will have an extended range up to about 6,000 nautical miles. Like both the C–3 and C–4 designs, the C–5 will be able to trade off its range against the number of warheads carried. The Trident planners envision the completely new base to be built at Bangor, Washington as the forerunner of a network of logistic sites suited for covert operations, since the Trident is seen as a two-ocean warship. Bases on the east and west coasts and perhaps around the world will be built so that there is approximately one base for each 10 submarines in operation.

There is no question that somehow the navy will redesign and upgrade most of the Polaris system. Admiral Rickover has mustered his supporters in Congress to this rehabilitation project and, lately guaranteed the sympathetic support of the Carter administration, will surely win a full and final approval. Like all military programs, submarines vie with other concepts and with the practicality of how much can be done with the resources available. Military budget proposals are put forth based primarily on two justifications: the need to maintain momentum in a particular strategic area and the need to develop a weapons system superior to the related systems or antisystems. The Trident is a response to the development of the Russian submarine fleet and the development of their antisubmarine capability. But in Trident there is an additional consideration now that the SLBM has taken the place of the fixed ICBM as the primary deterrent force. The submarine has assumed that image in Congress and will be funded accordingly.

Other than the military need for the Trident, there is the consideration of our deterrent philosophy and the ploy that as we increase our momentum in military systems, we produce "bargaining chips" that put the United States in a stronger position with respect to the SALT decisions on arms limitations. But the military need is paramount: Trident would certainly put the United States in a superior position for an all-out nuclear war. This is critical within the Pentagon, but a much fuzzier consideration in Congress and therefore is not expressed publicly by either the admirals or politicians, and certainly not by any responsible representative of the military-industrial complex. The "bargaining chip" position is used instead, and it is much more convenient, since it avoids the concept of a nuclear holocaust which seems to boggle the imagination of all but the most intrepid.

Sea-based deterrents are offered because of their relative invulnerability, compared to land-based systems. Mobile land-based systems are in the design stages; in fact, the B–1 bomber was considered a mobile land-based system. But the Minuteman missile system has long been considered vulnerable to enemy first-strike attack, and bomber systems are now considered as a backup strategic force rather than a primary deterrent. Barring some fantastic breakthrough in antisubmarine warfare, the submarine can claim priority both in terms of deterrent and offensive capabilities that are the real factors of our military planning, if not the part that is openly discussed. Thus Trident moves on ahead of other weapons systems that the air force and army cannot fully justify based on either their deterrent or "bargaining chip" value.

Besides the military arguments that favor Trident, there are strong endorsements from the aerospace/hydrospace industries, big labor, Congress, and the technical community in general—all who have much to gain from a major new military program on the Polaris model. Although they have excellent arguments and in some cases a stronger rationale, the pressure groups opposing Trident are more muted voices—primarily arguing against fiscal irresponsibility and the failure on the part of Trident proponents to prove their arguments. But lack of hard evidence seldom prevails if the public is properly prepared and Congress is willing.

The Trident submarine is still being studied by the ASW community to determine possible responses. In the past, the military has been embarrassed by designing and constructing systems with outstanding performance characteristics, in every way superior to any weapons system in the world—but obsolete before the first units were put into operation. Either weapons have missed the mark with respect to the enemy threat and therefore become unnecessary, or some newer technological advance has provided an effective counter. Before this supersubmarine underwent construction, some searching ASW analyses were made—and their results were far from conclusive.

Can the Soviets develop an ASW capability which would give them the ability to surprise and destroy the United States SLBM force in a very short period of time? Such an antisubmarine-warfare capability would discount the Trident's deterrent threat and again give the Russians an unrestricted first-strike capability. Second, can the Trident submarine be destroyed over a protracted period of time in a prolonged war—a war which would continue after a thermonuclear exchange. Destroying Trident submarines would mean Russian victory at sea in a war of attrition after the United States responded to a Russian first-strike. If a system could be designed and developed to make either prospect worthy of consideration, then those who control the nation's purse strings must be cautious. The United States cannot afford to be wrong about Trident from a financial point of view, particularly now that the B–1 bomber is defunct.

Probably the most bothersome concept to Trident supporters involves the constant-tracking theory—Russian attack submarines continuously trailing Trident submarines with the aid of long-range sonar surveillance networks. If pounced on prior to the outbreak of hostilities by submarines capable of trailing them closely enough to take effective action before a declaration of war, our SLBM submarines might be hit before they began firing at their targets. Such a scenario involves employing both active and passive sonar and continuous submarine trailing and targeting missiles from both land-based and sea-based missile launchers. There is also a concept of trailing vehicles being airborne, operating in conjunction with ships or attack submarines and fast surface-effect ships or hydrofoils.

The counterargument runs that the Trident's increased missile range will allow these submarines to operate relatively close to United States ports and therefore enjoy more covert operation and complete air cover. Any ASW forces or attack submarine trailers will be required to operate at great distances from their own bases and under the threat of United States air and sea power. The Russians have only a few advance bases available and a poor forward logistic-support system. As Trident submarines would be programmed to pass through "scrubber" situations—either mine fields or relatively shallow areas—the trailing forces would be periodically identified, harassed, and driven off.

But trailing is a problem. Although the Trident is being designed to be faster, more maneuverable, and quieter than Polaris, its great physical size will always make it more easily detectable by acoustic means. Smaller attack submarines will be capable of keeping pace with the Trident in trailing operations. The inherent simplicity of the trailers precludes the need for size or sophistication; they are designed to be fast, maneuverable, deadly, and expendable.

The Trident concept of a larger, faster, more sophisticated submarine is consistent with the progression of the Rickover philosophy over the years, but critics of the program argue that a serious mistake could be made simply by continuing to increase submarine size and performance; a large number of smaller submarines might be a better concept. If trailing is the major threat to the future SLBM force, then it is much more difficult to trail a larger number of smaller submarines than a smaller number of Trident submarines. The loss of a small submarine would be much less significant than the loss of a billion-dollar Trident. Strategists point out that the Soviet Union has apparently adopted the smaller and more numerous theory, thus significantly complicating our own ASW problems.

Concerning the second threat to Trident—the gradual attrition of the Trident in a prolonged war—based on the experience of previous wars, the most effective counter to Trident would be an attack on the submarine bases. But the navy has a number of well-located bases which could be converted to Trident support and overhaul. Considering the wide dispersal of SLBM fleets, the advantages of speed, quiet, and long operating time come into play as an advantage of the Trident design. The subs would be away from their bases for longer periods of time with a reduced exposure during the vulnerable transit time to station. Furthermore, it is not logical to imagine any long period of attrition time or a war in which the SLBM force was attacked on a gradual basis. Such a war would certainly be a thermonuclear conflict—not a limited war when SLBMs would be at sea as a deterrent but not employed in an offensive action. The improbable conflict that reverts to "half and half" strategy of a Cold War beneath the sea and a hot war above is a complex consideration in which the danger of escalation and brinksmanship makes any practical strategic or tactical considerations difficult.

The problem facing the Trident deployment is twofold. One has to do with geography—the dispersion of the fleet around the world; the second is the high cost of constructing facilities for Trident submarines. Probably Bangor, Washington and New London, Connecticut will be satisfactory as the first two base sites; but as the fleet expands beyond the initial ten submarines, additional facilities will be very expensive. New bases must be built in secure areas, hardened against missile attacks and located to make ASW operations most difficult.

Critics compare Trident to the B–70 bomber mistake—the plane designed to fly at great altitudes and fantastic speeds, which by the time it was developed in prototype became obsolete in the face of the threat of thermonuclear missiles. The missile sites were vulnerable to low-altitude penetration by conventional B–52 bombers; the B–70 required enormous expenditures to operate in an environment which no longer existed. In the absence of any serious threat to the present SLBM fleet of Polaris submarines or any significant change in Russian military strategy, critics argue, the navy is requesting a mind-boggling budget to create a technically superb weapons system for which there may be no long-range requirement. Modification in present tactics and operational procedures could counter any threat that the Soviets might mount to our present SLBM fleet, so why simply put more eggs into the same basket? Their logic is difficult to counter.

These questions have been posed for many years in the councils of the Pentagon and in the halls of the Congress. But now a go-ahead for the Trident program has been given. The reasons for the decision are still not clear, and the intended beneficiaries—the American people—will probably never know on what basis the military planners decided to spend their tax money on submarines with the unbelievable price tag of $1 billion dollars per copy, plus extras.

25 The Sanguine/ Seafarer Fable: The Search for Reliable Submarine Communication

The effective command and control of our SLBM [submarine-launched ballistic missile] force, the element of our strategic offensive forces which is the least vulnerable to sudden nuclear attack, is of major importance. At the present time, the communications links from the National Command Authority to the individual ballistic submarines are much less survivable than the submarines themselves. Reliable and survivable communications links must be maintained with these forces.

—MALCOLM R. CURRIE
Director of Defense Research and Engineering,
Department of Defense

As the story goes, the Soviet Navy developed a unique system of communicating with its atomic submarines at sea. This was a long step ahead of the United States in sophisticated and unjammable communications, and the Kremlin was delighted. The Soviet Chief of Staff congratulated the scientists responsible for the

254

project. Medals were distributed and vodka toasts drunk. The project had taken many years and cost billions of rubles. It had taxed the navy's R&D budget sorely; but now it was ready for installation, and the fleet would be profoundly strengthened. A site was selected based on optimum radio transmission capabilities, and after some minor skirmishing at a party conference, a committee in secret meeting made plans for the construction to begin. The ideal spot was located near a small Ukrainian city, and the navy prepared to go to work.

But wait. As the announcement of the impending construction of the system was made, the mayor and his townspeople gathered in the city square, denounced the government, and stated unequivocably that there would be no such lethal radio system put within a day's crow-fly of the city, so long as they had their say. The ecologists among the citizens said that the radio transmissions would render them and their cattle infertile, would make the drinking water appear milky, and prolong the winter snows by at least two months. They presented proof in the form of current astrological charts and data gathered by the local dairymen's association.

The Soviet Chief of Staff fussed and fumed, but what could he do? The citizens would not have it. So an alternative secondary site was chosen much farther to the north—near a small town on the Moscow-Leningrad turnpike. But the natives there had been warned by their fellow citizens from the Caucasus. They rose up and replied with the same arguments and added new ones that had to do with the adverse effect of radio transmission on the habits of the elk herds and the well-known phenomenon of the low-frequency radio waves curdling fresh goat's milk. Once again there it was; a vote of no-support from the citizens. The navy was now complaining it was losing much of the technological lead over the United States that this breakthrough had given them. The United States Navy was following these procedures and arguments very closely in the Soviet press and quietly launching a catch-up program. In vain the Soviet Naval Chief pleaded. Still the citizens said no go—take your radio waves elsewhere. Sadly, the Soviet scientists moved on.

Now the navy discovered a hamlet near the western shores of a remote lake that was an acceptable site—a place where nothing much had happened for a thousand years, and the inhabitants were living crudely on meager fare only a step from starvation. The navy sent representatives to the area—and they promised the natives jobs and new homes and the local constabulary new uniforms with fur shakos and leather boots and the elders a rest home—anything to ensure their friendly cooperation. And for a time it worked. But as the citizens of the hamlet learned exactly what the navy was trying to do, they staged a general strike and took up a collection to fly representatives to Moscow to protest. Finally, as the navy watched its technological lead slip completely away, they became desperate, and—

The story may not be exactly fact—that is, not for Russia. It is not so far from what has happened to a United States Navy project now called Seafarer—once called Sanguine—and always called the best and the worst of names depending on which side of the technical-social equation the description came from. Most recently, the U.S. Navy communicators have tried desperately to find a peaceful home for this extremely-low-frequency (ELF) radio communications network in the barren reaches of the Upper Peninsula of Michigan. But once again, as had happened with the citizens of Wisconsin and Texas, there was a hue and cry against the installation of the system. It was called a rape of Michigan by the ecologists, as well as a danger to the trappers, fur traders, and rock farmers who inhabit the Upper Peninsula, that remote and picturesque area of the northern wilds.

The navy's Sanguine project has been under development for seventeen years. It remains a floating pool of technology which has not been employed to any useful purpose, while systems of the same generation have performed for years. CAESAR, AUTEC (Atlantic Underwater Tactical Evaluation Center), Minuteman, and a host of other programs have gone through design, development, production, installation, and several stages of redesign. But Sanguine continues to look for a home—and after seventeen years and a research budget of about $100 million, it seems no more permanent now than it was in the late 1950s.

As originally proposed two decades ago, Project Sanguine was to be a 6,000–mile antenna cable buried in Northern Wisconsin in a gridlike pattern which would cover some 22,500 square miles in total, or over 40 percent of the state. The Wisconsin area was chosen because of an underlying rock formation—the Laurentian Shield—which does not conduct electricity easily and greatly adds to the efficiency of the antennas. The transmitters were to be buried on the same site in order to make the entire system relatively immune to nuclear attack.

The ELF system's radio transmissions would communicate with submerged submarines at sea. Because of the characteristic frequency and power involved, the signals would be virtually unjammable and would penetrate many hundreds of feet below the surface of the ocean, making it the ideal doomsday machine. No preemptive nuclear attack could prevent retaliation. The Sanguine communications network would reach its SLBM submarines under the high seas regardless—and in a clear, unjammable command would order them to fire in retaliation. Thus, any concept of a surprise attack by Russia would be ruled out— at least until some unforeseen technological advance threatened the jamming of Sanguine—a most remote possibility. Here was a system whose chief goal was deterrence—an assurance that in the event of a nuclear war, the order to retaliate would get through to submarines without fail. Conventional submarine communications systems required them to come to the surface to monitor radio traffic—and in the process of hoisting an antenna made them easy targets, capable of quick identification by long-range surveillance. Now they could remain safely submerged and still be in communications with their fleet commanders at all times.

With the technology completed, the navy went ahead to plan the site construction, but political opposition grew in Wisconsin, and so much flak was generated that the navy withdrew and went to its secondary site in Texas.

Where the Wisconsin natives were more concerned about their ecology and the effect on their dairy herds, the Texans were concerned about attracting enemy hydrogen bombs in the event of a war and driving down property values. So the Texans balked, and by shouting the arguments that electromagnetic radiation would shrivel up Texas, the ecologists won again. While arguments raged, Congress detected a crippled-duck program and quietly directed that planned capabilities be lowered and the funding reduced by budget cuts. Sanguine became Project Seafarer, a less secure and effective system now covering 4,000 square miles instead of the original 22,500 planned. The antenna cables would be buried 3 to 6 feet below the surface, and the signal strength reduced. Far fewer transmitters would be employed than the original system had called for, and they would be housed on the surface, where they could not survive enemy attack. No more doomsday machine at the ready. Nevertheless, the navy still lobbied for the funding of some system, saying they felt that even a Seafarer capability would be important.

Now three new sites were under consideration: the Upper Peninsula in Michigan, a Nevada atomic test range, and an army base in New Mexico. The Michigan site was preferred; it would cost $300 million less to build Seafarer there because its underlying geology would enhance signal transmission strength. But alas, Michigan political leaders began begging off and the navy was directed not to push too hard. The Joint Chiefs of Staff were now publicity-sensitive to Sanguine.

After two rebuffs, even a sailor might become discouraged. But no—the navy took another tack. The National Academy of Sciences was asked to form a committee to review information on biological and ecological effects of the kind of electromagnetic radiation that occurs at Sanguine/Seafarer frequencies. In a last-ditch effort to save the Michigan site, the navy hoped that a favorable report concerning the health and safety of animals, plants, and other organisms would let them get out of the public relations business and into the antenna-building business at some early date. But the locals in Michigan would not bite; they contended the navy had already loaded the academy committee with scientists who held a brief for the navy program. It seems useless to point out that in Sanguine/Seafarer very little electricity flows to the ground. The concept involves an entirely different phenomenon from ordinary transmission lines, and there was no evidence that the system would damage any organisms. But no matter, if a single moose miscarriage were reported, the Michigan citizenry would know who and what to blame.

It seems that the opponents of this system have backed it into the last possible corner. With politicians arguing and the National Academy of Sciences in an internal conflict concerning the bias of the members proposed for the committee, it is unlikely that very much of significance will happen in the near future. The navy's academy committee ploy may checkmate Seafarer more effectively than the ecologists and trappers. Appropriations will be withdrawn, and that will be the end of the long, hard road from concept to oblivion.

While a victory for the ecologists always seems to be a case of chalking one up for the good guys, it is hard to justify the treatment of a system like Sanguine/Seafarer by the loyal Americans of three states. It is a flippant disregard for American's military capability and the communications involved in supporting the country's number-one deterrent, the SLBM submarine fleet.

Sanguine/Seafarer is not incidental in the story of the buildup of the Trident fleet. Communications is the heart of the problem. Without adequate command and control, the Trident program becomes an uncertain and risky next step. The air force has been quick to point out that without such a command and control system, the SLBM force becomes less effective—perhaps more vulnerable to nuclear attack than it is reasonably safe for the military to accept. Director of Defense Research and Engineering, Dr. Malcom R. Currie stated:

The effective command and control of our SLBM force, the element of our strategic offensive forces which is least vulnerable to nuclear attack, is of major importance. At the present time, the major communication links from the National Command Authority to the individual ballistics submarines are much less survivable than the submarines themselves. Reliable and survivable communication links must be maintained with these forces.

The citizens in Llano, Texas—the county seat of the area where Sanguine/Seafarer was to be erected—stood on their individual rights. They compared the program to Watergate and simply refused to have it. The navy gave up and quietly moved north in the hope that somewhere in this great land someone is concerned enough about the nation's defense to let them start digging. Only in America could such a farce be played out.

But what about the Russians and their program—how did they fare? After that little hamlet on the lake refused the Soviet version of Sanguine/Seafarer, where in heaven's name did the poor Russian admirals find to locate their system? Well, at least that fable has a happy ending. The admirals finally decided that it would be simpler to relocate the citizens, you see, and put the system in where they damned well pleased. So the people were packed off to a faraway place and kept so occupied that never again did they concern themselves with the effects of ELF radio waves on people or plants or elk herds or goat cheese.

26 The Antiballistic Missile Program: Threat to the Sea-Base Deterrent

We are here to make a choice between the quick and the dead. That is our business.

—BERNARD BARUCH
Address to the United Nations Atomic
Energy Commission, 1946

The decision not to employ ABM technology or expand the ABM systems is discussed elsewhere. It was the most significant disarmament decision arrived at since the end of the Second World War. However, despite SALT agreements which limited each superpower to two ABM sites, the United States and Russia continued research and development work on ABM systems —and today these updated versions wait only for approval to be quickly installed. The Site Defense Minuteman (SDM) system is being tested at the Kwajalein range, run through the same program previously conducted to prove out the Safeguard system in the mid–1960s. The AEC is working with the Defense Nuclear Agency on this and other ABM approaches, analyzing the overall field of military nuclear weapons and developing countermissiles. These antiballistic missile systems pose the most serious limitation on the future SLBM submarine fleet and are far more significant than the ASW ships that the Soviets display so prominently or even the long-range sonar surveillance systems that are being implanted to monitor the oceans. And yet they are the bargaining chip the United States gambles away most readily at SALT time in negotiations with the Soviets, who trail badly in both SLBM and ABM technology.

Even with the best guidance control, it would be almost impossible to intercept an ICBM—in the sense that the ABM missile would collide with the attacking nose cone. It would be like trying to hit a bullet with a bullet, although the ICBM is going at about ten times the speed of a rifle bullet. Instead, what makes ABM feasible is the same force which makes the ICBM worth developing; the destructive power of nuclear energy. The warhead is vulnerable to the effects of a nuclear explosion that generates X rays, neutrons, and shock waves. Potentially more destructive systems involve laser-beam guidance and control, and neutron particle converters. Both the United States and the Russians are close to developing practical models of ABM systems based on these technologies.

When a nuclear explosion occurs at high altitude, that part of the energy which would be transmitted as a shock wave in the atmosphere appears instead as X rays. In the absence of any absorbing material, these X rays are transmitted away from the explosion until they encounter another form of matter—a missile warhead, for example. When they strike this other matter, the X rays are absorbed in the outer surface and the energy is transmitted into the interior in the form of shock waves which vaporize the material through intense radiation. When used in an ABM system, this phenomenon is referred to as an "X-ray kill," and is extremely effective at high altitudes where a high-energy-yield blast will not cause ground damage.

The neutrons generated by the defensive bomb blast are more penetrating than X rays and will enter the fissionable material that is the heart of the approaching nuclear weapon, located inside the nose cone. A sustained chain reaction will not develop, but there will be energy released by fission reactions following the absorption of the neutrons. The resulting heat will melt or badly distort the blocks of fissionable material so that a nuclear explosion will not occur. This is referred to as "neutron kill" and can be effected at much lower altitudes than "X-ray kill," since the energy yield for this type of weapon has sufficient radiation to effect a "neutron kill" and yet not cause extensive ground damage.

The effects of the shock of an ABM missile blast are similar to those resulting from a near-ground detonation. If the approaching warhead is severely shocked, its heat shield may not be sufficient to protect it, and its mechanisms may be seriously damaged. Shock blasts are much more effective at lower altitudes where the air medium is denser and the shock energy is better transmitted.

Laser beams, particle generators, and other ABM systems in the laboratory stage of development are not yet sufficiently evaluated to project their effectiveness or costs. The present ABM science rests on the X-ray, neutron, and blast methods of "killing" a nuclear warhead.

The United States began developing antimissile systems in 1956 and learned to develop counters for single missiles, but because of inadequate radar coverage could not cope with multiple targets or targets that threw off decoys. It was not until the development of phased-array radar that the antimissile concept became effective. This radar has no moving parts and is independent of the mechanical rotation scanning that limited radars of the 1940s and 1950s. In phased-array radar, a beam of energy is directed away from a large fixed array of many small antennae by controlling the phase of energy pulse which is sent to each beam. The radar can be focused in any direction for very brief intervals and therefore gives a frequency many times greater than the rotating antenna radars.

Air Force missile-men realized that the solution to the antimissile problem might lie in the design of a missile which would ignore the decoys and direct itself to the interception of the warhead. The Spartan missile was designed to intercept at long range and high altitude. With a range of 4,000 miles and tipped with a family of warheads with higher and lower megaton yields, this missile has proven versatile, controllable, and effective. The long range means that X rays will completely destroy light decoys and probably the warhead far enough away to avoid confusion and danger from the blast and minimize the degree of electromagnetic blackout close to home base. For those few nose cones or heavy decoys which might survive a Spartan shot, a second interceptor was designed; the Sprint "follow-up" missile for use within the atmosphere, at a range of approximately 25 miles. The Sprint nuclear warhead is in the lower kiloton class, but its blast effect at lower altitudes produces an effective "mop-up." The Sprint had the advantage of being fired late at targets, as there would be survivors after the initial Spartan blast. The Safeguard System consists of both Spartan and Sprint emplacements, together with two phased-array radars known as the Perimeter Acquisition Radar (PAR) and the Missile Site Radar (MSR). All system components are joined by communications and computer networks.

The PAR detects the approaching warheads at long range, tracks them, and provides the information needed to evaluate the threat and calculate a means of interception. Information from the BMEWS and other early-warning radar systems is helpful, but PAR was designed as a self-contained total tracking concept. The MSR is used to discriminate between warheads and decoys, and controls the missile interceptions by tracking not only Spartan and Sprint missiles, but also enemy warheads.

In the Safeguard systems concepts, the PAR initially acquires and tracks the target and determines the threat; then, in sequence, the MSR acquires the missiles and carries out its discrimination and interception functions. Launched under the control of MSR, the Spartan missile is detonated above the atmosphere, with a high probability of destroying the reentry vehicle. Even if it fails, it most probably will dispose of the decoys; and, as the MSR continues to track the warhead and discriminates between the warhead and decoys, a Sprint missile will be then launched under the control of the MSR to intercept the attacking warhead in the atmosphere, now at a relatively low altitude.

The area which can be protected from tracking missiles is called the "protected footprint." The footprint for the Spartan is large;

for the Sprint it is much smaller. The Spartan's footprint is a wide-area defense, with a coverage of between 800 and 1,200 miles; the Sprint has a footprint area between 50 and 75 miles.

Prior to discontinuing deployment of ABM systems based on the 1972 SALT agreements, the Pentagon was considering both systems; the Sentinel and Safeguard. Safeguard was to give priority to the defense of the strategic weapons systems in the continental United States, while Sentinel was designed for a thin protection of the entire country. The national plan for this combined ABM system was generally along the following lines:

(a) *Phase One* would have installed two ABM complexes: one at Grand Forks, North Dakota, and the other at Maelstrom Air Force Base, Montana. These systems would protect the Minuteman missile silos at these locations. The systems would comprise a PAR, MSR, Spartan battery, Sprint battery, and the computer and communication complexes required.

(b) *Phase Two* would have extended Phase One by installing an MSR, Spartan, and Sprint complex at Warren, Wyoming; Whiteman, Missouri; and Washington, D.C., to protect Minuteman complexes and the National Command Authority.

(c) *Phase Three* would have involved installing variations of these components if it appeared that there was an increased threat to the SAC bases. Additional MSR, Spartan, and Sprint complexes would have been installed and a network of PARs located to eventually cover all of the likely directions of attack.

(d) *Phase Four* would have further modified and extended the system if a threat to cities was projected from Chinese missiles.

Although the eventual number of sites varied, the preliminary plan discussed was for twelve sites which would have offered a thin protection for the entire continental United States, Alaska and Hawaii. Priority was given to the components of the Minuteman system, next the threat of a limited nuclear attack from Communist China, then protection against accidental attacks.

In May 1972, at the time the SALT accord was reached in Moscow, Phase One of the Safeguard system was under construction. Since the SALT agreement limited both Russia and the United States to two ABM complexes—one for retaliatory weapons and one for the national capital—it was necessary to abandon the Maelstrom site completely. The Grand Forks site was completed, and included an MSR, PAR, and a 100 missiles ready on their launchers. The site was linked with BMEWS and other radar complexes in a communications network supported by satellites, phased-array coastal radar and other detection devices.

The counterdevelopment of deceptive warheads called Multiple Independent Reentry Vehicles (MIRV and MAV) and the newly incorporated "penetration aids" was also pushed. The Soviets' limited ABM capability suggested the development of a "smart" system to counter it; a terminal guidance capability wherein the bomb itself contains a miniaturized navigation and control system. These re-entry vehicles navigate themselves by stellar or terrain-guidance methods; in effect, using a built-in map as a part of the missile guidance system. As a superaccurate homing device, these "smart" bombs are almost ABM-proof.

The Russians ABM system is a scaled-down version of the Spartan-Sprint network. The Galosh system around Moscow has a comprehensive target acquisition and tracking radar network, including a phased array of the PAR type and 60 missiles on their launchers. This system is estimated to have an effective range of 200 miles, and the missiles' warhead ratings are in the several-megaton range. The Russians have been slow to build Galosh, but still will be allowed 6 ABM-type radars and 100 missiles in accordance with the SALT treaty. Thus, eventually their network would be equal in numbers to the United States systems, but far inferior in overall capability.

One of the factors that will most influence the development of the SLBM submarine fleet will be the progress in ABM technology. As the Wet Cold War continues, the submarine will become the key strategic weapon—and a powerful tactical weapon as well. It will launch both strategic and cruise missiles and will become an antiship, anticity, and also antimissile system. But its effectiveness will be governed most by the efficiency of the enemy's antimissile defenses, particularly those deployed at sea.

Following the submarines will be the sea implantments and eventually the sea fortresses in the form of ICBM and ABM platforms. Already the navy has proposed the relocation of ABM forces to sea, as a bottom-mounted, or submarine- or ship-mounted system. Eventually, a submarine-launched ABM system will be installed. In fact, work toward this application of the Spartan technology is now going on in research laboratories and will result in a major system ready for employment within the next few years.

Since the end of the Second World War, the military confrontation between the United States and the Soviet Union has been misstated and always exaggerated. There has never been a threat of conventional war between the two countries; the threat has always been depicted as a nuclear holocaust. And the relationship has been subject to many shifts and moods—miscalculations, alarms, mutual accommodations, hostilities, stabilization—and continuing uncertainty. The Russians always claim a military superiority that is bogus, and the United States usually supports this fraud. There are widely publicized bomber gaps, missile gaps, and security gaps—but no one in the White House or Kremlin has seriously considered the possibility of a nuclear war between the two countries.

Even the Kennedy-Khrushchev confrontation over Cuba was never cast in that context. National leaders realized the consequences of a holocaust—the death of millions, the slim survival possibility for their nations. This kind of situation was not in prospect when the president of the United States and the premier of the Soviet Union squared off over the missiles headed for Cuba. When U.S. Navy ships were sent to intercept the Russians, both sides were in close communication with each other; each side knew every tactical move that would be made. By reading compromised (broken) codes, by evaluating sonar and radar surveillance position plots, and by espionage, both sides knew what was happening. No precipitous decision on the part of the Russians to press on, or on the part of the United States to launch a counteraction was imminent. So, by covert agreement between the leaders of the two states, the power balance was maintained.

And it continues to be. It is now popularly called deterrence —more accurately, scientists and military planners call it "the anticipation of assured destruction." Theoretically, both the United States and Russia possess a second-strike capability that could retaliate and inflict what is termed unacceptable damage on the other, even after receiving the first strike. The premise that rational leaders will not attack in the face of a certain suicidal nuclear exchange is the thread by which the survival of the two superpowers is suspended.

Even with sufficient thermonuclear weapons for either side to devastate most of the populated area of the world many times over, the United States and Russia continue to build their missile stockpiles. Each country is pledged to maintain an equivalent number of deliverable warheads and continues to improve its position with the development of multiple, independently targetable, reentry vehicles. But there is an ongoing argument over what is merely numerical superiority and what is total nuclear superiority—the presumption being that one does not necessarily relate to the other. Numerical superiority is obvious, a count of the number of different types of weapons.

Nuclear superiority also includes an appraisal of their sophistication and the total power concept—the ability of a nation to inflict on another a first strike of such force that the other is not able to sufficiently retaliate to inflict unacceptable damage on the attacker. Presumably, neither the United States nor Russia possesses such power at this time, and both hold a belief that neither can hope to obtain a nuclear superiority in the foreseeable future.

As a consequence of this offensive-weapons stalemate, both countries have invested heavily in ABM development. And in the kind of insane momentum that develops in the weaponry field, once a concept is feasible, there is a push to have it deployed. But, early in the ABM research phase, both countries recognized that the deployment of an extensive ABM system would severely imbalance the deterrent equation and result in a new arms race. So, although there was pressure to move ahead, the Russians deployed only a few systems (called Tallinn, after the Estonian city first protected by it, and later named Galosh, when it was installed around Moscow). They waited for a U.S. counter. The United States had developed the Nike X, a successor to the Nike Zeus missile, and went on to build the Sentinel system around key military and industrial facilities. Both countries watched each other and China, which entered the nuclear club in 1964. It was only after the Chinese threat was deemed trivial that the SALT conferences were held and both countries agreed largely to abandon their ABM efforts.

After SALT, the research of ABM techniques continued in both the United States and the Soviet Union—but the military was relieved of the responsibility for developing a working, deployable system. This was satisfactory to the Joint Chiefs of Staff in the United States and their opposite numbers in the Kremlin. Military men are primarily offensive in outlook; they would much rather build fleets of supercarriers and bombers than be assigned to defending cities by deploying an antimissile defense and deal with the civilian involvement that would go with such a project.

Beginning in 1975, intelligence reports began to mention work by the Soviets on a new beam weapon designed to intercept and destroy the ICBM and SLBM weapons. The system employed a charged-particle beam which could quickly be deployed to many sites, in effect setting up an instant ABM defense around critical military areas. The technology was based on an ability to direct and focus atomic particles into a coherent pattern to intercept and destroy reentry vehicles at great distances. Since a similar project had been pursued by the Defense Department's Advanced Research Projects Agency (ARPA) through several subcontractors, the news came as no great surprise. But the information leaked to the press, and one after another high-level official was quizzed on the Russian progress. Naturally, the senior military spokesmen would offer little in the way of insight. The Pentagon position was one of high skepticism, and reports of Russian successes were branded as gross exaggerations. On the eve of the SALT talks scheduled to begin in the spring of 1977, Dr. David E. Mann, Assistant Secretary of the Navy for R&D stated, "There is no solid basis, either inside or outside of the government, nor solid body of technical and scientific evidence that such a weapon exists or has been tested."

However, the continuing specter of a successful Soviet super-ABM is the most significant threat to the United States' strategic weapon arsenal, and Dr. Mann's statement was not enough to satisfy the Pentagon. A vocal anti-SALT minority exists, and unless there is a truly amazing accord generated at SALT, the armed forces will certainly push a development program to establish a nationwide ABM defense system, wider and more sophisticated than any planned by the Soviet Union.

The basic decision concerning a national ABM system includes system limits and the technological and engineering development, as related to a mind-boggling budget. The system would include some combination of the following detection schemes:

(a) Radar detection of the nose cone in ballistic flight. The United States Ballistic Missile Early Warning System (BMEWS) has giant radar installations in Alaska, Greenland, and England, and is capable of ballistic-missile detection as soon as the nose cone rises above the horizon. The warning from BMEWS would probably be on the order of 15 to 20 minutes ahead of missile impact.

(b) Radar detection reflected from the ionized gas of the rocket exhaust during the propulsion phase. Over-the-Horizon Backscatter Radar (OTHB) uses the ionosphere that extends from 40 to 300 miles above the earth as a reflector to scatter radar beams and project these beams beyond the horizon. Such radars would detect not only the missile but also the ionization produced by hot gases of the rocket exhaust.

(c) Disturbance of radio signals reflected by the ionosphere which are disturbed by the passage of the rocket. Over-the-Horizon-Forward Scatter Radar (OTHF) makes use of the reflection from ionosphere to ground. The bounce or mirror properties of such systems would detect a large rocket's penetrating the ionosphere, and, in effect, altering its reflecting properties.

(d) Detection of infrared energy radiated by the rocket's exhaust. Infrared energy detection is accomplished primarily by orbiting satellites which read infrared signals and relay them to ABM ground stations.

Each of the four methods has limitations. In order to receive a highly reliable warning, it is necessary to combine the information from all the systems together with statistical information concerning the characteristics of enemy weapons, weapon tests, space vehicles, and other air and sea activity based on intelligence. Obviously, there is very little room for error; the decision to fire or not fire the nation's arsenal of ballistic weapons must come from the information generated.

The warning that a missile attack is imminent must be supported by detailed information. The system must be able to discriminate between real warheads and decoys, and, in the case of MIRV and MAV weapons, be able to compensate for both a multiple reentry and steerable reentry bombs. Fast, critical decisions are necessary to determine which missiles are most dangerous, and even which missiles to leave unopposed if the capacity of the defense system is overtaxed. Here the concept of "real time" is important, as distinguished from the time which includes the delay caused by the transitional processing of information. Real-time communication is necessary to track the missiles and operate the system at the high capacity required so that there is no delay in terms of decisions or options. The interception of missiles moving at over 4 miles per second is a complex and highly technical matter that requires quick and decisive action; the interceptor missile must be initially targeted and subsequently corrected in trajectory to intercept the attacking vehicle as far from the American targets as detection and destruction means allow.

In a touch of legislative madness that mystified the military pundits and the world, late in 1976, the United States Congress directed that the ABM system which had taken twenty years to design, develop, and install be dismantled and the program "terminated." When pressed for a reason for this unilateral removal of all Spartan and Sprint warheads and the dismantling of ABM equipments, a spokesman for the Office of Defense Research and Engineering, Deputy Director John Walsh replied: "In the area of ballistic missile defense we have, by treaty, agreed not to deploy anything except the limited system which we have now decided to phase down, so the question is: why are we in the ballistic-missile defense business at all?"

With the Russians accelerating both their ABM and civilian defense programs, with air-raid shelters building at a brisk pace and new rapidly deployable ABM systems in design, it would seem the Soviet leadership has no intention of being pressured to lay down their arms. In fact, by our apparent willingness to make significant arms reductions unilaterally, we may be persuading the Soviets that the risks involved in a nuclear war are now more acceptable.

27 Strategic Arms Limitations: SALT I and Sea Power

You may either win your peace or buy it—win it by resistance to evil; buy it by compromise with evil.

—RUSKIN

Since 1972 and the initial SALT agreements, the United States and the Soviet Union have been specifically prohibited from the deployment of national antiballistic defenses against strategic missile forces. These agreements were intended to remove one threat to the effectiveness of strategic offensive forces. So far, the submarine-based deterrent forces have escaped limitation—but now they threaten the effectiveness of land-based missile systems and so will probably be a major issue in future arms-limitation negotiations.

Just as the ICBM weapons system is threatened by the ABM, the SLBM effectiveness is jeopardized by aggressive ASW forces of the type presently being built up in both the United States and Russia. Given the importance of the submarine-based deterrent and the gradual acceptance of the land ICBM limitations, it is only a matter of time until a major commitment will be made to increase the submarine forces and negotiate to limit the ASW threat to the SLBM deterrent forces. Certainly SALT negotiators are faced with determining the feasibility of some arms-control limitation on antisubmarine warfare which threatens the SLBM submarines, since only if both the United States and Russia accept

273

the invulnerability of the ballistic missile submarines does a true deterrent force continue to exist. Unless both nations have a high degree of confidence in their SLBM systems regardless of the situation relative to the other strategic forces, one leg of the deterrent triad is destroyed. This deterrent force has the advantage of requiring only a part of the submarine force to be in firing position. The submarine's survivability for any long period after the outbreak of a strategic world war is certainly desirable, but not necessary. If most of the submarines are close to their firing stations and the submarine force could survive for a few hours, their deterrent capability would be sufficient to satisfy the military planners of both nations.

The submarine will operate in one of the three conditions: Cold War, nuclear war, or protracted conventional war. In the nuclear age, a protracted war of attrition—a conventional war—may be so unrealistic that it does not warrant serious consideration. But fleet tactics to fight such wars are very seriously considered, despite the fact that a nuclear war at sea would certainly spell the end of capital surface ships in a very short period of time. Debating the question of survival for any type of ship seems ridiculous, and yet the carrier survival argument has been debated in Congress for over thirty years. The carrier remains an important part of our military planning, and World War III scenarios still assign it a major role in sea-power projection.

The gradual attrition of the SLBM submarines by ASW forces in a protracted war is an extremely unlikely prospect; neither superpower would allow this to happen. Any realistic negotiations concerned with arms limitations must consider a hot war against SLBM forces without nuclear retaliation a dim prospect. Instead, acceptable levels of ASW activity will probably be defined in the same fashion as the antimissile program, with controls that will provide insurance against the development by either power of a capability which might seriously threaten the SLBM fleet of the other. Another proposal for reducing the threat to the SLBM force would be a direct reduction in the total numbers of attack submarines. But any concept which tries to guard against attrition of

SLBM submarine forces during a conventional war in which tactical antisubmarine warfare would be practiced against attack submarines should be regarded as unrealistic. Such artificial constraints are too risky for any SALT-type agreements.

Active trailing of the SLBM submarines by attack submarines, aircraft, or high-speed surface ships is the one area which concerns both sides most—and this seems an area in which some control agreement is possible. Proposals recommend either completely eliminating active trailing or putting a distance limitation which would govern the approach to an SLBM submarine by any means. Another proposal involves defining sanctuary operating areas which would provide freedom for the submarines of both sides. Limitation might also be placed on any kind of clandestine warfare tactics, including long-range surveillance sonars—perhaps in the form of a bilateral agreement to assure that one nation would not covertly develop systems which could be used to monitor the other's sanctuaries.

Somehow guaranteeing safe passage to SLBM submarines seems a workable plan; in effect, exempting them from the type of antisubmarine warfare measures which may be used against conventional submarines by specifically identifying areas which would always be safe. However, if an all-out war should develop between Russia and the United States, it is difficult to imagine that either side could guarantee to the other its conduct with regard to the SLBM fleet (or anything else). While aggressively pursuing the war, tactical nuclear weapons would be employed, and any agreement would simply not be a feasible or logical condition on which to allow the safety of a deterrent force to rest.

ASW is a total problem. The consideration of a capability related to both attack submarines and the SLBM fleet is like comparing a pinpoint-bombing program using tactical nuclear weapons and the Minuteman ICBMs. The two are related in purpose, but not necessarily in effect. But one weapon would never be employed without the other; and in the same manner, in war, neither side could provide a strong enough proof to assure the other that the war at sea would be fought so as to exempt the submarine deterrent forces. Somewhere an opportunity would present itself, and the first tactical nuclear weapons would be used against an SLBM submarine. Then escalation would proceed very rapidly.

Thus the employment of the strategic missile-carrying submarine changes the basic role of the submarine and requires a rethinking of the ASW situation in terms of totally new problems. Based on the mission of the SLBM fleets, each SLBM represents a substantial percentage of the country's deterrent force, and at present these submarines have no role other than acting as platforms for ballistic missiles. So there is no requirement to construct a point defense against them; in fact, they will avoid confrontation with any force since their mission is covert and not antiship. SLBM submarines will carry standoff missiles to fight off attackers. Some of the Polaris submarines are presently armed with conventional cruise missiles, but the primary mission of the SLBM fleet is deterrence—and any effort to attack one must be assumed as a threat to the country's sea-based deterrent force. The consequences of this kind of attack are far different from conventional ASW operations. Such an attack represents one of three situations:

(a) An attempt at a preemptive first strike which would be interpreted as a move to destroy the enemy's SLBM fleet. Assumption: Nuclear attack.

(b) A damage-limiting attack on the SLBM fleet in order to limit the retaliatory damage the SLBMs would cause. Assumption: Nuclear attack.

(c) An attack on SLBM submarines individually, over an extended period of time during peacetime or in limited war, when these encounters might be mistaken for accidents. Assumption: Inconclusive.

The alternatives run the gamut of credibility. The difference between damage-limiting and preemptive first strike is really no difference in intent, or in assumption. Any strike against the enemy's SLBM force will probably be considered damage-limiting; the effect would be the same as a preemptive strike since it would be nearly impossible to destroy the entire fleet at one time. However, there is a secondary consideration: if a substantial part of the enemy's SLBM force can be destroyed, he may or may not choose to retaliate. The accidental destruction alternative and result is not credible unless we assume that a series of "deliberately accidental incidents" spaced over a period of time would not be interpreted as an act of war or as a reason to escalate to a nuclear war with the concept of "extended deterrence" coming into play. For example, in a limited nuclear war, the Soviet Union might refrain from antiship attacks in order to avoid an aggressive ASW program by the United States which might, presumably by accident, destroy a substantial part of the Soviet SLBM fleet. In one of those improbable scenarios where the two superpowers confront each other with conventional or tactical nuclear weapons with serious reservations concerning an ICBM exchange, almost any assumptions with respect to the safety or peril of the SLBM fleets may be made.

Consider the first of the alternatives: it is highly improbable that one of the superpowers would unleash a first strike against the other unless it were sure that the location of every SLBM submarine was known in real time, and could be projected continuously for a period long enough to assure their effective annihilation. In addition, the weapons system selected for kill would require a very high degree of accuracy since it would be necessary to destroy all of the submarines within a very short period of time to avoid retaliation. Even by such location techniques as continuous trailing and very accurate long-range sonar, it would be extraordinary to find all submarines vulnerable to destruction at any one time. For the entire SLBM fleet to be in position for an enemy's preemptive strike, such a massive attack would have to be made in peacetime, since in war the antagonists would be on guard against trailing activities and would use jamming and submarine decoys against any type of sonar tracking.

The damage-limiting strike is more realistic in terms of actual warfare conditions; it is more likely regardless of the intent, since even a first-strike attack would not take out all of the SLBM force. And since a strike of any type against the SLBM force would certainly trigger the bomber and missile forces, it is difficult to imagine anything less than a holocaust as a result.

The use of satellites as ASW monitors has been limited because of treaties concerning the use of outer space for military purposes. But eventually the satellites will become a most formidable tracking system when they are combined with a CAESAR-type sonar network. This system, coupled with trailing by some combination of submarine, surface craft, and aircraft, will be the preferred high-confidence ASW system. Hunter-killer submarines are the most effective at this mission—but with the development of the Surface Effect Ship (SES), a more lethal trailing platform will be available. Used in conjunction with submarines and aircraft, the combination of long-range sonar surveillance with SES ships will gradually threaten a substantial part of the SLBM fleet —perhaps enough to require military planners to reassess their deterrent position. For the United States, the problem is relatively simple, since the Russians have no carrier task forces on the high seas. The Soviets must counter both an SLBM fleet and a carrier fleet, essentially with the same tracking and trailing tactics. Some division of their sea forces must be made, and this may tip the balance drastically.

The arguments for and against the Trident submarine are based largely on its potential vulnerability to trailing and long-range sonar surveillance developments. The SALT II negotiators will consider proposals for limitations on ASW in the same spirit that limitations on ABM systems were negotiated at SALT I, but their effectiveness will depend on the systems of monitoring that can be devised and agreed upon to ensure compliance. With the Russians lagging so far behind in both sonar surveillance and supersubmarine construction, they may be unwilling to negotiate any long-term agreements that favor the security of the Trident fleet.

Much has been made of the conduct of damage-limiting operations since they represent something close to actual nuclear warfare. If we accept that damage-limiting operations, depending on their degree of success, would be answered by damage-limiting operations, it would result in a situation similar to conventional war with tactical nuclear weapons. The problem of policing this "response in kind" type of retaliation is just too complex to have any confidence in controlling. Such a war would escalate by degrees, neither country sure of when a counterattack would come against its urban centers or other strategic weapons. In fact, damage-limiting tactics would reduce the hedge against an all-out thermonuclear war by degrees, since they would represent a type of increasing threat to the strategic forces. Both powers would be deprived of the advantage of maintaining a strategic strike force. At some point, the threat would be unacceptable to one or the other, and a total nuclear strike would be initiated.

In the SALT II negotiations, several measures have been considered in the attempt to reduce the danger of a preemptive or damage-limiting attack to the SLBM fleets. These measures include:

(a) Negotiating the number of implantments of large ocean-surveillance arrays, particularly at remote points around the world far from the country's own shoreline.

(b) Limiting or carefully controlling the development and deployment of Surface Effect Ships and other surface ships and submarines and aircraft—ASW forces able to track submarines on an uninterrupted basis for a long period of time—either singly or in some type of task-force cooperation.

(c) Restricting the frequencies and power of ocean-surveillances arrays to limit their capacity for monitoring.

(d) Limiting the number of hunter-killer submarines a country may operate in relation to the SLBM fleet of the other.

There will be other limitations devised with respect to the employment of ASW weapons or the operation of ASW forces, but it is difficult to see how any of these restrictions benefit the United States. All limits on ASW are heavily weighted in favor of the Soviet Union—and unless our negotiators are manipulated once again, it would appear that the only concessions the Soviets could make would be in areas of technology related to the other legs of the deterrent triangle: the bomber and ICBM systems.

The philosophy of the arms race under the seas reflects the confusing and conflicting images of the Cold War. Since the American military are presumably prohibited from a first-strike consideration, the United States insists that it should always hold a lead, and in most areas a marked weapons superiority over the Soviet Union. The Soviet Union insists on a parity of arms with the United States and has set its goal to achieve weapons superiority in at least some weapons systems—particularly the ICBM and underseas warfare. Neither side has been willing to accept the other's minimum conditions. Although from time to time agreements have been reached—the ABM systems eliminations, for example—these are usually in the form of unilateral concessions by the United States in areas of her own substantial strength.

Since both countries now have surplus weapons, the arms race has turned from quantitative to qualitative due to the inability of the antagonists to use military power effectively. The Cold War victories come to those who can make the "big bang" technological breakthroughs. In an age of overkill, both countries are now caught up in a momentum of technological grouping. In the oceans, for example, an oceanographic research program on the part of the Soviets has elicited the mind-boggling budget involved in designing and developing the Trident class submarine by the United States.

On the bright side, both Russia and the United States have handled direct confrontation at sea with restraint. The periodic stupidities of adventurous ship and submarine captains playing games of "chicken" and "chase" have resulted in collisions, near-catastrophes, and square-offs—but no serious arguments between the two powers. So perhaps there is hope that a sea-base deterrent and satisfactory parity can be maintained.

There is the possibility that a third country—one of the thirty nations of the world that presently have the capability to build an SLBM submarine—will become a factor in producing a type of fleet which must be considered in a deterrent policy. Countries other than the two superpowers possess combined submarine fleets that are as large as that of the Soviet Union and almost double that of the United States. Over 300 submarines have been supplied to other countries by the United States and Soviet Union, and although these are older craft—nonnuclear and obsolete compared to those operated by the United States and Russia—still they do constitute a substantial force and should not be ignored. The eleven NATO nations have approximately 160 submarines, either in operation or under construction. If we accept a scenario for a nonnuclear war, then the number of these submarines becomes very important—in fact, they could wage a very satisfactory nonnuclear war against the Soviet Union without the assistance of the United States. The People's Republic of China has about 40 diesel-powered attack submarines—most of them obsolete Soviet types delivered to the Chinese years ago and capable only of ocean action in the Western Pacific. This fleet is too old and obsolete to be considered seriously—but China is constructing new underseas craft, on the model of recent Russian submarine designs. If an SLBM submarine fleet were built by China, it would certainly disturb the two-nation deterrent status.

Australia and Japan have excellent submarine fleets. Australia operates the modern British Oberon class, and Japan has more than 15 new attack submarines. The Australians and Japanese have also concentrated heavily on developing sophisticated antisubmarine warfare forces to operate in conjunction with the United States naval units in the Pacific. So the advantage held by the United States and its allies in submarine forces is much greater than the Soviets in both numbers and quality. From Latin America to the Indian Ocean, the United States has conducted joint programs with many friendly nations and so is able to accurately measure the performance of their submarine and ASW forces and naval aviation capabilities and how to most effectively use them.

In the Mediterranean, Turkey has 10 submarines, Italy has 12, and France more than 23. This combined force would hold a balance of power which would not only dominate the total Mediterranean area, but also bottle up the Soviet Black Sea Fleet and prevent the exit of Soviet naval units, including missile-carrying and attack submarines. The Russian Pacific Fleet is effectively countered by the Japanese control from Ceylon to the Kamchatka Peninsula. The Baltic Fleet is dominated by NATO powers, including Denmark with 6 submarines, Germany with 23, Norway with 15, the Netherlands with 7, and the United Kingdom with 33. Besides these 84 submarines, the NATO forces have a modern ASW force trained and equipped to conduct an aggressive campaign against the Russians in northern European waters.

By using Murmansk and White Sea bases, the Russians might have the best opportunity to avoid the NATO ASW forces, but this would largely limit Soviet operations and make the global surveillance problems much simpler for the United States. For all their brave pronouncements, the Soviet Navy would be firmly penned up close to their own shores in any future war—and they know it and we know it.

In a conventional war with or without tactical nuclear arms but short of the type of holocaust involved in ICBM exchanges, the submarine forces of the United States and Russia could be the most significant factors of the sea war. However, since any accidental attack against Soviet SLBM submarines could result in nuclear escalation, it is doubtful that the attack submarines of the Allies would operate to their fullest potential. With the possibility of such an escalatory action, a United States military commander might be reluctant to pursue an aggressive ASW campaign which would necessitate relying on foreign commanders.

The British and French SLBM fleets and the forces of the Republic of China will have an effect on the world balance of sea power—but it will be a complex matter to factor in. As the strength of the world's maritime powers continues to grow, their submarine and ASW warfare capability will also expand—and this seems to increase United States power. Japan and Australia will dominate the Pacific; Canada and West Germany are leading NATO in building strong ASW forces. In the Communist world, only the People's Republic of China seems to have the capability of building a major submarine or ASW force—but probably not before the year 2000, and then there remains the question of how it would interface with the Soviet fleet, if at all.

In the future, the United States, France, Great Britain, Japan and West Germany will probably deliver their obsolete submarines to other powers, but will retain their SLBM capability. If this happens, the United States will maintain a substantial edge in both numbers and technology over the Soviet Union to the year 2000 and beyond, based on present fleet construction and weapons development programs.

The Russians are not a peace-loving people. From 1480, when the Tartar rule ended, to the beginning of the First World War in 1914, Russia had been involved in at least 50 wars, an average of more than 10 per century; 5 against Lithuania and the Livonian Order, 9 against Sweden, one against Poland and Sweden, 5 against Poland, the Seven Years' War against Prussia, the Napoleonic Wars, 4 against the Khanate of Kazan, 7 against the Khanate of the Crimea, one against Astrakhan, 9 against Turkey and her allies, 2 against China, one against Japan, one against Khiva, 4 wars against Persia, over 42 years of continual warfare in Central Asia (1842–1884), and 48 years of cruel and bloody war in the Caucasus (1816–1864). All this besides the 1917 Revolution, and World War II, and postwar campaigns against Polish and Hungarian insurrections. This excludes the internal wars of the Time of the Troubles (1600–1612), and the fighting involved in the risings of Stenka Razin (1667–1674) and Pugachev (1772–1774).

This is a truly remarkable record. Before 1480, political units were different, but the picture was substantially the same. The Russians have been engaged in some type of fighting since they appeared in historical record. Though they sometimes have submitted to foreign rulers—for example, the Arangians and the Golden Horde—they have supported only rulers that have led them into battle. So much for the Russian national disposition to disarmament and abiding peace.

The Soviet leadership often talks of peace and disarmament. Russian representative Valerian Zorin, head of the Soviet delegation at the Ten Powers Disarmament Conference in April 1960, laid down the principles for disarmament in a plea for peace that has become a classic of its kind. Zorin put forth his country's position in five main points:

(a) That the ultimate aim of the superpowers should be to disband all armed forces, liquidate all weapons of mass destruction, eliminate all foreign bases and to abolish all military organizations.

(b) A program of disarmament should be carried out by agreed stages with a time limit of four years for total disarmament.

(c) An international control organization should be set up to supervise measures appropriate to each stage of disarmament.

(d) Each state should retain an internal security militia designed exclusively to maintain public order.

(e) The disarmament program should not be interrupted and would be made independent of the fulfillment of any condition not provided for in a treaty which the Ten Powers had agreed upon.

Clearly this was the most ambitious program ever supported by a Soviet national leadership. And earlier, Premier Nikita Khrushchev's speech at the United Nations had set the same tone. On September 18, 1959 he suggested a new phase of East-West negotiation by offering a proposal for complete disarmament, on which Mr. Zorin's statements were based: "It goes without saying, that if at present, due to certain reasons, the Western Powers do not manifest their readiness to embark on general and complete disarmament, the Soviet government is ready to come to agreement with other states for appropriate partial steps for disarmament and the strengthening of security."

This was in part propaganda, cajolery, threat, and genuine purpose—all intended to lull the West into the proper frame of mind to accept the arming of Cuba with nuclear weapons. Khrushchev's fine words and subsequent actions typified the continuing Soviet policy: talk of arms limitation abroad while emphasizing an arms buildup at home. A very old strategy—but one that often works on a naïve or timid adversary in a confused political situation.

Since the end of the Second World War, the Cold War between the Communist empires and the free world has gone on, but so far the two sides have been able to avoid a major clash of arms. Yet the two irreconcilable ideologies continue to coexist as armed camps despite all negotiations, meetings, and summit conferences. No gesture on the part of the free world has created goodwill; no concession in hope of reducing international tensions has persuaded the Communists to abandon their plan for world conquest. The Communist leaders aim at total domination and the destruction of the Western way of life. Just as Hitler spoke plainly about what he intended, so do the Communists. To do them justice, they have never concealed their aims or purposes from the West. It is strange that the people of the free world generally do not appear to believe these pronouncements. The nations of Europe and the United States ignored what Hitler said until it was too late to prevent a war; the same situation is repeating itself as the Cold War spreads to Africa, the Mideast, and South America.

There is no room for doubt about Communist intentions, any more than there should have been about the Nazi intentions. Their purpose is plain. The Communists have warned the West that they intend to bury them, and nothing in their behavior would leave Western diplomats any grounds to suppose that they do not mean what they say. Their hostility toward the United States is the mainspring of their foreign policy; it influences all of their actions and will not be appeased except by surrender and retreat in one after another area of conflict. In short, the antagonism is absolute. The differences are irreconcilable. The end should be war.

In the past, such a deep and abiding hostility between two great national groups having diametrically opposite interests in every corner of the globe would have signaled that war was imminent. Combine these circumstances with a temporary imbalance in military power in favor of one side or the other, and it would have created a situation of instability that would have precipitated a great international war. But that is not the military situation today. A "hot" war is not imminent. Further, the military power of the two countries is unbalanced on occasion, when conventional forces or weapons technology is taken into account and one side or the other holds a superior position. So why are we still at peace?

The answer is simple. In addition to conventional forces, each side has a nuclear capacity which is more than sufficient to annihilate the other. A military balance has been created in which neither side dares to resort to full-scale "hot" warfare because of the appalling and irrevocable consequences of such a step. Clearly, if nuclear weapons were abolished, the two countries would go to war on a global scale in a very short time. So why do they discuss disarmament? They don't, really. They talk in vague generalities about disarmament but really discuss arms limitation, which is the rate of acceleration of the weapons buildup and the areas of emphasis in their military strategies.

The idea of open, high-level talks with those who are bent on each other's destruction is relatively new. But lately it has been put forth as an effective substitute for military defense, despite the past evidence of futility and even danger of such high-level conferences conducted in the full glare of publicity. Mutual distrust continues—in fact, it grows—and the absence of any real success so far would seem to be proof that honest negotiations are impossible. However, the United States Congress seems to feel that there has not been enough of it. They forget that the Russians have an Oriental patience and indifference to the passage of time and are prepared to talk for years—probably even decades—rather than to give way on any point of substance, while the United States leadership may be influenced by impatience and popular pressure to achieve results. So the Soviets wait and the United States is pushed into making unwise, unnecessary, and sometimes disastrous concessions.

The West persists in fearing the more formal, structured secret diplomacy in which a genuine settlement might be achieved. Open negotiations are pursued even though the records show there are few treaties which the Soviets have not broken, either in letter or in spirit. Except between free and friendly nations, the process of diplomacy has always proven unfruitful, but the naïve and timid continue to try. They seek accommodations with the Nazis in one generation and with the Soviets in the next. They ignore history and thus are fated to repeat it.

Therefore SALT II is under way, and will probably substantially reduce the United States position relating to both submarine and antisubmarine warfare. If the history of the American negotiations with the Russians bears any precedent, we will emerge from these meetings sadder but not wiser, with fewer guarantees of peace—but perhaps finally convinced that our real security lies in American strength and unity.

28 Maintaining Naval Supremacy

*The Pentagon likes to have Congress play
these comparison [of weapons and forces]
games, even though such comparisons are
usually irrelevant. The Russians often have
different types of forces just because they have
different geographical and strategic needs.
Congress listens to briefings about how many
more submarines the Russians have without
once hearing the briefer explain that the
Russians are building a large submarine fleet
to interdict the U.S. naval supply lines in a
time of war, and that the United States does
not need so many submarines because the
Russians do not have long naval supply lines.
But the Pentagon does not explain comparisons, it only makes them. The Navy is probably
better at this than anybody else in the
Pentagon: when necessary, the Navy can
come up with a whole new set of statistics to
reinforce an otherwise questionable argument. . . .*

—U.S. SENATOR LES ASPIN
(D.–Wisc.)

The budget foe of the balanced navy is the supercarrier—and lately Congress has been alerted to the costs of the

proposed nuclear carrier fleet. The House and Senate have both expressed grave concern, but on the whole seem unequal to the carrier supporters in the House Armed Services Committee and the contractors' lobby. Led by the indefatigable Admiral Rickover, this coalition of "brown-shoe" admirals and nuclear proponents has used every ruse and wile to make a case for building more Nimitz class carriers—from the rumored Soviet ABM "shields" to the fuel shortage.

Three of the conventional carriers would be equal in cost to one of the Nimitz class. And the new carriers would not be of different capability; the primary difference would be size. The next Nimitz class carrier would be approximately the same size as those in service: 93,400 tons, compared to the conventional-powered carriers, which displace 40,000 to 50,000 tons. According to critics, three conventional carriers would have a lower operating budget than a single Nimitz class and would be less vulnerable.

Unable to ram the fourth Nimitz through Congress, the lobby has taken the tack of drawing up specifications for larger conventionally powered carriers and pushing their displacement up to 78,000 tons in order to make a better cost comparison with the Nimitz supercarriers. And to stall any action short of a favorable decision, they have arranged to defeat the proposal for a multimillion-dollar VSTOL aircraft study on the theory that if you kill the VSTOL aircraft, you at least severely wound and delay the VSTOL carrier program.

The question of building more aircraft carriers of any class is no longer debated in spite of the warning about the carrier's vulnerability. Congress is determined to build a large seagoing aircraft platform. But regardless of the carrier's mission and vulnerability, building only supercarriers, refusing to accept anything smaller than a 93,000–ton behemoth as inadequate to the navy's mission, is bordering on strategic insanity and a technical subversion of the national defense posture.

The navy relies on the aircraft carrier for two missions: power projection and sea control. But lately both roles have come into question; in a major war, we would have to look to the air force to support ground-combat operations. It seems disastrous to rely on carriers operating in areas where they would be threatened by Soviet nuclear weapons, even for the close troop support required in amphibious operations. For sea-control missions, the carrier becomes a more suitable weapon platform; but, with its increased vulnerability and the 3–to–1 cost ratio between the conventional and supercarriers, the trend in carrier design should be to smaller, independent ships that can operate without large escorts to protect them.

Every time there is a major shift in strategy, there must be a resultant shift in tactics—and, just as surely, every time a major weapons system is replaced, there will be painful experiences for those military men wedded to the obsolete concept. From sail to steam, from battleship to carrier, from carrier to submarine—the situation would not seem to be so very different. But the most distressing situation is always that the old concept will simply not die; it is usually kept alive by powerful men in high places who are not convinced, or simply oppose the change because of self-interest or prejudice. Even the most enlightened naval leaders and military experts continue to speak of naval balance and weapons superiority and ship numbers and creative new tactics—not for the atomic confrontation that will happen if the United States and the Soviet Union ever go to war, but for some improbable situation, some extraordinary happening, wherein the two superpowers confront each other in total war but decide to fight along the lines of World War II or Korean-type actions.

It must be granted that the military man badly needs the kind of support that he is not getting from the people he is being paid to protect in Western society. But civilians have been soured over the past twenty years by exactly the kind of duplicity, misleading statistics, and outright lies that are offered them year in and year out by the military-industrial complex in its never-ending fight for larger budgets and assured appropriations. The military has damaged itself by these tactics far more than it has been by an unpopular war in Vietnam or any intellectual preference for a more socialist form of government.

To come to a realistic appraisal of our naval force and its requirements, we can probably base our judgment on the following:

(a) The size and capability of the naval component of our deterrence forces. This can be done quite accurately—if we accept the premise that the next war will be a nuclear holocaust. We can relate the factors of survivability, countermeasures, hard target-kill capabilities, and industrial performance—all over the short period of a tactical or strategic nuclear war.

(b) A comparison of the U.S. and NATO forces with Soviet forces trying to achieve a like objective of sea control or power projection. In those areas where our lead is substantial, as it is today in most areas, admit the relative superiority and redirect our military expenditures to areas where we have a less commanding posture. Discard the outworn concepts of matching carrier against carrier, submarine against submarine, cruiser against cruiser, in anticipation of the Pacific fleet-type battles of World War II. Look to the missions required of our forces and the conditions of a future conflict—Russian naval base limitations, for example—or the vulnerability of U.S. surface units to nuclear-tipped missiles. Decide on a reasonable economic basis what our long- and short-term goals will be and tailor our naval forces around them, rather than simply engaging in continual comparison involving periscope counts, aircraft carrier numbers, and other misleading indicators.

(c) An assessment of our overseas interest and commitments and the support we can expect from our allies. Make a strong budget stand in areas where overseas bases are necessary, where surveillance installations are critical, where new technologies must be advanced—not only by our scientific community, but in cooperation with our allies. Far better to hang tough on a Sanguine program and insist on reliable command and control communications in the face of the irate citizenry of a few states than to spend billions on supercarriers of questionable value simply because everyone loves a pork-barrel project.

There is no reason why the navy's role and capabilities should be confused and surrounded by such controversy. By focusing on the truth rather than clouding the issues with misleading statistics, by entering into a dialogue with the American people that is candid and straightforward about the role the navy intends to play in the national strategy, by answering questions honestly concerning the future of the navy, the service will ensure a willingness on the part of the country to support it to the fullest. The perception of our allies, neutrals, and even our opponents concerning our naval strength is very often far more accurate than our own—at least based on Pentagon pronouncements.

There is no question in the minds of the Soviet military about who has the command of all the world's oceans—and who could effectively exercise that command in time of war. However, while no one expects the U.S. Navy to adopt an uncharacteristic, chest-thumping posture, it is also unnecessary to engage in the annual wolf-crying, prebudget exercises wherein former CNOs moan that our navy would be defeated in conflict with a far inferior fleet in the Mediterranean—and that the navy is only marginally capable of carrying out the national strategy.

The American public not only discounts such grossly misleading statements, but tends to doubt all else from the same sources. And this further estrangement of the citizenry from the professional military in the United States only serves to damage the respectability of the military profession and, in the end, adversely affect the national defense far more than the reduction in military appropriations that eliminate weapons of questionable value.

When a major industrial power like the Soviet Union begins to build a navy, after a careful analysis it should be possible to ascertain most of the reasons for the program, and which are most significant. On one hand, there is the prospect that the Soviets are reacting to the perception of a threat; on the other, the prospect that they are contemplating an offensive military action that they had not considered before. Or there may be economic, social, or diplomatic reasons—showing the flag, trying to convince the world of growing strength, or creating a bargaining chip for an armament-limitation forum. Perhaps some reasons seem small justification based on such a mammoth expenditure of money and manpower—but the Soviets do strange things at times.

If we assume that the Russians are building a navy to combat the naval strength of the United States, primarily, and of NATO and our other allies, to a lesser extent, then we must decide what is the balance between the present and projcted naval power of the United States and that of the Soviet Union. We must recognize that in the United States and the NATO countries, any movement of the Soviet Union is interpreted as hostile and their weapons numbers and sophistication are subject to gross exaggerations by Western military men. And often politicians and the press as well. To assess the present situation in the Wet Cold War, it is necessary to make some realistic judgments of how the East and West stand with respect to sea power.

As we have seen, the Soviet Navy came to the Cold War as an insignificant force after World War II—and its expansion has always moved to counter the threats posed by United States military forces. When the Russians began to build a submarine and coastal-defense force, they were lacking experience in blue-water warfare. To compensate, an accelerated shipbuilding program was begun after the war by Stalin, slowed down by Khrushchev, then resumed with ever greater emphasis by Brezhnev and aggressively pursued for the last decade. Since the Russians have faced first a defensive, and later a "catch-up" offensive situation, their weapons tend to be less sophisticated, more quickly and crudely developed than those of the United States Navy—and their missions blurred with respect to overall sea control and interdiction. They put great store on the submarine and have accumulated over 400 submarines of various types in the mid-seventies—a polymorphous collection of conventional and nuclear designs, many of which are badly obsolete and some which date back to the fifties. The nuclear submarines mounted crude cruise missiles and guided missiles and the SLBM submarines—both diesel and nuclear—were more a defensive weapon deployed to counter air strikes from U.S. carriers than a strategic threat.

Although it is commonly misinterpreted in the West, the Russian fleet is still primarily a submarine navy, supported by a growing ASW force and "show" navy of larger surface ships which are largely non-mission-oriented. They are building more and larger ships, but fewer than the United States and of different designs. Their small carriers embark VTOL aircraft and missile-carrying helicopters and will be used primarily for ASW and in close anti-ship defense operations. The destroyers and cruisers are also ASW oriented. The Russians are sophisticated enough naval strategists to know that larger surface ships were nearly useless to the Germans in World War II and would be even more vulnerable in future conflicts when tactical nuclear weapons would be employed. Those who insist that Russian fleet building programs must, of necessity, represent an overall challenge to American control of the seas are simply not looking beyond the obvious. The Russians are building a defensive navy. Period!

The United States has built its navy along different lines, relying on sophistication in weapons systems and placing far more emphasis on the quality, firepower, and performance of ships at sea than the total number of ships in commission. During World War II, the U.S. Navy fought a brilliant two-ocean war and won; the Russian Navy did very little and what they did consistently resulted in defeat. Since World War II, the United States Navy has fought two major wars and participated in a number of military operations while the Soviet Navy has been completely inactive.

Most recently, the role of both navies is progressing toward that of strategic deterrence and naval presence more than preparing for any future confrontation in which one or the other would try to control or block a sea area. In fact, even the ability of a navy to project sea power ashore, either in the form of attacking aircraft or amphibious operations, is now more important than fleet confrontations. And the United States is far and away superior in both respects, based on its large carrier fleet and more advanced amphibious forces. So, in all the significant areas which can be measured—from the ability to control the seas to the ability to project power ashore—the United States Navy is clearly superior to the Soviet Navy and shows every indication of widening the gap. Laments of the United States Navy brass at budget time notwithstanding, it would certainly be heartening to the military if they could be sure that a future conflict between the two nations would result in a meeting of the United States and Russian fleets in direct sea confrontations to determine the outcome.

But, of course, this will never happen; the World War II high-seas fleet confrontations between carriers, cruisers, and battleships is now as remote as the man-of-war duels of the days of fighting sail. Any war between the United States and Soviet Union would certainly involve nuclear weapons at sea—and recognizing these new weapons, the tactics employed by both sides would be radically different from any previously pursued in sea warfare. But, unfortunately, this logic does not very often creep into the debates in Congress over naval budgets; the rhetoric there tends to deceive and distort the issues of sea power and naval supremacy. The Pentagon points out that the Soviet Navy is now growing faster, by more major ships and an increased ability in technology. Then Congress—believing that the number of Russian ships in service somehow equates to sea power, and discounting the ability and mission to those ships—appropriates more money. By counting every single ship, including obsolete submarines and the smallest shorebound mine layer, Congress adds up the tab of growing Russian sea power and funds supercarriers.

The United States Navy redeploys and contracts; it eliminates forces in some traditional deployment areas, scraps obsolete ships and realigns its numbers, and there is little public notice. But let the Soviet Navy demonstrate any increased activity, and the budget masters in Congress point out the change in pattern as a new threat —whether or not the genuine naval strength is changed or the balance of forces is altered. This conception of strength in the mind of the citizens of the United States and her allies is all-important because it influences the legislators who must vote for military appropriations. The illusion has become more important than the substance.

Is this approach correct, or should informed, subjective judgments be presented, accurately and sincerely, even if they prejudice some budget considerations or undermine some pet weapons program? As military systems become more complex and budgets more huge, the U.S. and Soviet citizen alike are ever more at the mercy of their military establishments. Some threats and capabilities and new weapons systems and relative strengths and weaknesses are clear and visible—but by and large, the American public must believe what the military discloses to Congress and the administration; and from this information assess any increase in vulnerability or the extension of capability. Unfortunately, as military budgeteering has become a game with as little responsibility for the truth as liar's dice, the layman who is not privy to the rules of the game is badly confused, often to the point where he cannot take a reasonable approach or make sound judgment concerning the problems of the defense of his country. And this is a dangerous condition.

There is no more striking illustration of this national confusion and its results than the clouded controversy over the supersubmarine Trident and supercarrier *Nimitz*. These costly construction programs, symptoms of the navy's predilection to bigger, better, and more expensive weapons, are simply beyond any reasonable man's ability to comprehend in terms of initial and operating costs. The navy has now passed the air force in its ability to command the military budget; the navy's share of the defense dollar is larger than the other services' and increases every year. Now the admirals are so well versed in carrying their message to Congress that they are proposing construction of a carrier fleet, based on the Nimitz design of a 94,000–ton floating airfield that carries 90 aircraft, 5,300 men and operates on 2 nuclear reactors; and a submarine fleet based on the Trident design of a nuclear submarine, at a current cost of over $1 billion for each. All this in the face of findings by evaluation committees at all levels—including the prestigious National Security Council—that the carrier's prospective vulnerability in any future war makes it a very non-cost-effective weapons system and the Trident is a much more attractive target than several smaller submarines—and perhaps more vulnerable.

The navy is in process of building two Nimitz carriers, is trying to convince Congress to authorize one more, and has future plans for others. Each of these carriers together with its complement of aircraft costs somewhere in the vicinity of $18 billion to purchase and operate over its useful life. Such an expenditure can be based only on the absolute certainty that the carrier is the superweapon of the future. But unless the naval leadership plans to fight another conventional general war at sea, there is simply no rational basis to expend such funds on a major surface ship. These supercarriers with their staggering price tags are analogous to the battleship at the beginning of World War II. The United States Navy went into the war stoutly maintaining that battleships were the backbone of naval power and that battleships would be the main elements of the fleet—this against all indications that the battleship was vulnerable to air attack. Pearl Harbor proved the point. The naval leadership quickly did an about-face. The aircraft carrier became the capital ship of the fleet, and the battleship faded into obsolescence until today there is not one in commission in any navy in the world. Now we have come full circle again: the same navy thinking wants to build a fleet of Nimitz carriers, ignoring the threat of nuclear-powered submarines and cruise missiles.

In a weak defense, the navy points out that the Russians are at long last building aircraft carriers—but these are special purpose 40,000–ton Kiev types, roughly the same as the Essex type carriers of World War II and more of an ASW platform than an attack carrier. Although the Russians have indicated no plans to produce a significant number of these carriers, still five or six of them could be built for the cost of a single Nimitz class vessel. So the Russian comparison is brushed away, but there will be new arguments from the carrier lobby. Fuel consumption, brush-fire wars, naval presence—any credible excuse that will hold fast to budget dollars that might better be spent on more sophisticated underseas weapons or land-based aircraft with long-range patrol capabilities or improved ballistic missiles.

The carrier is not the only sacred cow in the U.S. defense arsenal; it is used only to illustrate the stakes of the military budget game played annually between the Pentagon and congressional committees. But while both sides toss around multibillion-dollar chips and bluff and raise the ante, it is the public who pays the bills and absorbs all the losses—and lately these reluctant backers are having trouble moving close enough to the action to even have a kibitzer's say in how their money is being spent.

29 The Wet Cold War: Fates and Fortunes

If we are to regard ourselves as a grown-up nation—and anything else will henceforth be mortally dangerous—then we must, as the biblical phrase goes, put away childish things; and among these childish things the first to go, in my opinion, should be self-idealization and the search for absolutes in world affairs: for absolute security, absolute amity, absolute harmony.

—GEORGE F. KENNAN

The Cold War is a unique conflict. There has never been a major war that has gone on for a longer period than the thirty-year struggle between the United States and the Soviet Union. But all wars have a beginning, a middle, and an end—even if the end is simply the beginning of a new war or a different kind of struggle.

The Cold War will end and something will come after it, even if at this juncture it is difficult to determine just what. Certainly not a warm peace or an ideological coming together of the two superpowers—but whatever it is, the development of the submarine and the movement of the nations of the world into the depths of the ocean will continue undisturbed. The sciences of ocean engineering, oceanography, and all of their related technologies and activities will progress along that scientific power curve that seems to apply to growth and expansion once a substantial interest is created by military applications or profit motive.

To see the end of the Cold War is to predict a conceptual change in the Russian and American political models; a new way of dealing with each other and with the other nations of the world, a new leadership, a redefined, competitive coexistence, a new era of Russian-American relations. This may be a long time in coming, and may not ever happen without some form of armed conflict. But that conflict will not come about simply because the two countries continue to arm. There seems to be worldwide fear that the two superpowers have now reached the limit of safety in the accumulation of weapons and that somehow they must back off or go to war. To save the peace, they must disarm—in conjunction with other countries or unilaterally. At the very least, they must acknowledge that some form of drastic arms control is necessary. But in reality arms do not continually stockpile, as the popular conception has it—countries do not obtain more and more arms until at some time there is an overweening pressure to use them. New systems replace old systems—the World War II fleet submarine that was a marvel of engineering excellence is now as obsolete as a World War I tank, and will also be consigned to the scrap heap and pass from the military scene. Weapons systems replace weapons systems in an endless sequence—and there seems to be very little prospect of a technological halt in their development, no matter what reductions or stabilizations are made in the weapon stockpiles.

The threat of thermonuclear war is not reduced by disassembling any number of hydrogen bombs, or decommissioning any number of ships or submarines, or discharging any number of soldiers or sailors. It is reduced by learning how to exercise the command and control function more effectively as more sophisticated and complex weapons come into being. In the absence of the deterrent systems that the United States and Soviet Russia depend upon, the world would have long since gone to war, in a devastating struggle which would have certainly eclipsed both world wars in horror and bloodshed. This has not happened because of technology; it will continue not to happen as long as the superpowers build weapons arsenals, extend military-oriented technology, and play a positive role in determining what the international political system of the world will be.

Now there is a new frontier opening up—in many ways more thrilling and challenging and as full of promise as the vastness of Russia's Siberia or the American West. The oceans of the world hold much more promise than outer space: they can be man's habitat, his source of an endless supply of food, of minerals, and of energy. Just as military power on land followed exploration and development of continents, so military power will follow exploration and exploitation of the oceans. And this is not bad—in fact it is probably a necessary corollary to the development of the oceans. So long as the United States and the Soviet Union can control the orderly entry of nations into the hydrospace of the world—so long as they can compete on near-equal terms and avoid a nuclear holocaust—then over the years this strategic interaction will maintain the peace. Although this may not be the equivalent of a warm and abiding atmosphere of cooperation and friendship—so long as it avoids Armageddon, it should be satisfactory.

Future generations will find wide ranges of opportunity for joint ventures and multinational efforts in developing the oceans of the world—in fact, the two superpowers could be mutually employed in assisting the emerging nations of the world to exploit their own ocean resources, and in doing so effect a nonideological truce. In such an atmosphere of even hostile cooperation, the two countries would come to a much closer accord, as other powers emerge and make their presence felt in the politics of the international environment. Thus, before we condemn the twilight struggle that is the present state of Soviet-U.S. relations let us examine the alternates and consider the long-range prospects of some other course of action. Things may be working out much better than we are led to believe.

Appendix A

Chronology of the War Under the Sea

415 B.C. Greek divers destroy booms at Syracuse.

333 B.C. Descent of Alexander the Great in a glass barrel.

196 A.D. Divers cut ship's cables, siege of Byzantium.

1203 Divers cut ship's cables, siege of Les Andelys, France.

1565 Turkish divers attack ship, siege of Malta.

1620 Dutchman Cornelius Van Dribbel builds first operational submarine boat with air-purification system.

1643 Russian 40-man cowhide submersible attacks Turkish ships, Black Sea.

1776 American David Bushnell invents hand-powered submarine *Turtle*. Attack on H.M.S. *Eagle* by Sgt. Ezra Lee in New York harbor during American Revolution.

1793 Divers cut ship's cables, siege of Mayenne, France.

1800 First practical hand-powered submarine built by Robert Fulton in France. Six-hour dive, Brest.

1815 *Mute*, 100-man submarine, built in New York by Robert Fulton.

1834 French submarine inventor Jean-Baptiste Petit lost with his submarine during a dive.

1850 Wilhelm Bauer builds sheet-iron submarine *Brandtaucher* with which he confronts Danish blockaders at Kiel.

1851 Bauer, Witt, and Thomsen make first submarine escape from *Brandtaucher* at Kiel, Germany.

1851 American inventor Lodner D. Phillips builds two 50-foot-long, hand-cranked submarines in which he dives up to ten hours in Lake Michigan.

1855 Bauer's submarine *Le Diable-Marin* makes record dives at Kronstadt, Russia.

1862 Spanish submarine *El Actineo,* with oxygen-regenerating breathing supply, dives 54 times up to five-hour submersions with 10 men.

1863 Frenchmen Simeon Borgeois and Charles-Marie Brun build first compressed-air-driven submarine 140-foot-long *Plongeur,* tested successfully to 20-foot depths.

1864 Confederate submarine *Hunley* attacks and sinks Union blockade ironclad U.S.S. *Housatonic* off Charleston, South Carolina; was herself destroyed.

1866 First automatic torpedo: invented by Robert Whitehead, England.

1872 *Intelligent Whale,* 26-foot submarine with air lock: invented by Oliver Halstead, U.S. Navy.

1878 American inventor John P. Holland builds the *Holland* I steam-powered submarine in Paterson, New Jersey.

1879 *La Pression Barométrique*—basic researches in altitude and pressure physiology in France by Paul Bert.

1879 52 one-man submarines with oxygen system, pedaled propeller, optical periscope, suction-cup time bomb built in Russia by Stephan Drzewieki.

1881 First practical electrically driven submarine, the *Goubet,* built by French inventor Boubet.

1884 Josiah Tuck's 30-foot, electric driven submarine *Peace Maker* with diver's lock tested successfully to 65 feet in New York.

1885 60-ton steam submarine, *Nordenfelt I* with steam reservoir for running submerged built by Garret and Nordenfelt.

1886 35-foot electric submarine *Porpoise* demonstrated in England by J. F. Waddingon.

1887 Lieut. Isaac L. Peral builds and demonstrates his 73-

foot electric submarine *Peral* on 35-foot dives in Cadiz, Spain.

1888 U.S. Navy competition for submarine design won by John P. Holland.

1890 *Gustaves Zede,* a 160-foot electric submarine designed by Ramazotti, built at Toulon, France.

1892 Italian submarine, 80-foot electric-powered *Pullino,* has three propellers.

1894 American inventor Simon Lake builds small wooden submarine with wheels. The *Argonaut Jr.,* included diver's air lock.

1900 First U.S. Navy submarine commissioned: the *Plunger,* by American submarine designer John P. Holland. Royal Navy submarine flotilla founded with 5 Holland-designed submarines built by Vickers.

1905 German U-boat flotilla founded with Krupp U–1, with torpedoes fired at a moving target in a demonstration. Berggraf performs echo-sound experiments in Norway.

1907 Submarine oxygen-regenerating escape lung adopted by Royal Navy. S. S. Hall and O. Rees.

1908 Frenchman Abbé Raoul builds wheeled "fishing submarine" with telephone, searchlight, mechanical claws; tested to 325 feet in Toulon, France.

1914 U–boat 9 sinks H.M.S. *Aboukir, Hogue,* and *Cressy.*

1915 Sinking of U.S. Submarine F–4 in Hawaii at 304 feet; helmet divers reach wreck. Raised by Comm. J. A. Furer. Deepest recovery of entire vessel. U-boat blockade of Britain. Sinking of *Lusitania.* German cargo submarine *Deutschland* crosses Atlantic.

1917 Germany declares unrestricted submarine warfare. U-boats sink 6 million tons of British shipping in one year. Russia orders 4,000-ton submarine, not completed. H.M. Submarine K–13 accidentally sunk off Garelochhead, Scotland; 46 crewmen saved by hauling bow to surface.

1918 Two giant M-class, aircraft-carrying submarines

launched in Britain, later lost in accidents.

World War I submarine war losses: Germany sinks 11,135,460 tons of Allied shipping, loses 178 submarines.

Miniature submarine called "underwater chariot" used by Italians Raffaele Paolucci and Raffaele Rossetti to sink battleship *Viribus Unitis* at Pola, Yugoslavia.

1925   Raising of U.S. Submarine S–51 by Edward Ellsberg and Ernest J. King.

1927   A. R. McCann, U.S. Navy, designs rescue bell for submarines.

1929   Founding of Experimental Diving Unit by U.S. Navy.

1930   U.S. North Pole Expedition in submarine *Nautilus* led by Sir Hubert Wilkins.

1931   Five escape from H.M. Submarine *Poseidon*, 125 feet down in China Sea, with Davis oxygen lungs.

1939   Sinking of U.S. Submarine *Squalus;* 35 crewmen escape from 240 feet in McCann bell.

First use of oxygen-helium for diving.

Sinking of H.M. Submarine *Thetis.*

1940   Midget submarines (one- and two-man enclosed types) developed in Japan.

1941   Underwater combat team with Lambertsen oxygen rebreathing lungs formed by U.S. Office of Strategic Services; directed by Christian J. Lambertsen.

British "underwater working parties" defend Gibraltar anchorage.

Five Japanese midget submarines assault Pearl Harbor, damage U.S.S. *Arizona.*

Italian frogmen led by Luigi de la Penne disable H.M.S. *Queen Elizabeth and Valiant* in Alexandria, Egypt.

First confirmed sinking by U.S. submarine. Japanese *Atsutusan Maru* sunk by U.S.S. *Swordfish.* Comm. C. C. Smith.

1942   Japanese midget subs attack Diego-Suarez, Madagascar;

sink tanker, damage H.M.S. *Ramillies*. Also attack Sydney harbor, Australia.

1943   *Kaitens*—Japanese suicide torpedo group—formed.

Twenty-four torpedo-plane carrying submarines launched by Japan.

British midget submarines commanded by B. C. G. Place and D. Cameron disabled German battleship *Tirpitz* at Kaafiord, Norway.

1944   British and Italian underwater demolition teams sink cruiser *Bolzano* in La Spezia, Italy.

Nazi underwater team attacks Nijmegen Bridge, Netherlands.

Eight Japanese one-man submarines attack U.S. Fleet anchorage, Ulithi Atoll. Tanker *Misissinewa* lost; all submarines sunk.

1945   Two largest submarines in history launched by Japan, designed to attack Panama Canal. Each carries 3 torpedo planes and displaces 3,500 tons.

British midget submarine XE–4 cuts telegraph cable, Saigon–Singapore and Saigon–Hong Kong.

Soviet submarines sink 2 Nazi troopships.

British midget submarine XE–3 sinks Japanese cruiser *Takako* in Singapore. Comm. Lt. Ian Fraser.

WORLD WAR TWO SUBMARINE WARFARE TOTALS

U.S.A. with 288 submarines sank 1,113 merchant ships with a loss of 52 submarines.

BRITAIN with 218 submarines sank 1,257 merchant ships with a loss of 76 submarines.

GERMANY with 1,072 submarines sank 2,606 merchant ships with a loss of 705 submarines.

JAPAN with 181 submarines sank 147 merchant ships with a loss of 130 submarines.

1946   U.S. Navy develops free-escape method for submarine.

1951   Echo-sounding of 35,847 feet in Philippine Trench made by H.M.S. *Challenger*.

1952   Keel laid for U.S. Navy atomic submarine *Nautilus,* at the Electric Boat Company. Construction directed by Captain Hyman Rickover.

1953   Bathyscaph *Trieste* with Auguste and Jacques Piccard dives to 10,400 feet in Ponza, Italy.

1955   United States launches first atomic submarine, *U.S. Nautilus.*

1957   Free-diving apparatus *Akvalang* produced in U.S.S.R.; national sea clubs founded.

1958   U.S. nuclear submarine *Nautilus* transits from Pacific to Atlantic under the polar ice cap via the North Pole. Comm. William R. Anderson.

U.S. nuclear submarine *Skate* surfaces in open water of polar ice cap, crosses North Pole from east to west. Comm. James F. Calvert.

1959   U.S. nuclear submarine *Skate* surfaces through ice at North Pole. Comm. James F. Calvert.

United States launches longest submarine ever constructed: the 447.5-foot-long nuclear submarine *Triton* with two nuclear reactors.

1960   Submerged circumnavigation of the globe by U.S. nuclear submarine *Triton.* Capt. Edward L. Beach.

Diving saucer dives 1,000 feet in Corsica with Albert Falco, Jacques Yves Cousteau.

Bathyscaph *Trieste,* U.S. Navy, dives 35,800 feet in Challenger Deep, Pacific, with Jacques Piccard, Don Walsh.

1961   U.S. Project Mohole obtains 601-foot-core from a depth of 11,700 feet off Guadaloupe Island, Mexico. Project organized by National Research Council–National Academy of Sciences.

1963   Nuclear submarine U.S.S. *Thresher* sinks in 8,400 feet, 220 miles off New England coast. Bathyscaph *Trieste* freighted from West Coast for search.

Deep Submergence Systems Review Groups formed by U.S. Navy: Admiral Stephan, Edward A. Link, Captain Henry Arnold.

1966   Commercial submarines *Alvin, Aluminaut,* and *Cubmarine* used in search for hydrogen bomb lost in aircraft collision near Palomares, Spain. Four H-bombs recovered with aid of CURV robot.

1968   U.S. nuclear submarine *Scorpion* sunk in 10,000 feet of water 100 miles south of Azores. Identified by remote deep-sea cameras.

1969   NR–I nuclear-powered ocean engineering and research vehicle delivered to U.S. Navy by General Dynamics Electric Boat. Designed for continental shelf exploration, operational to 2,000 feet.

1970   DSRV–1, U.S. Navy deep-submergence rescue vehicle completed, operational to 5,000 feet.

1971   DSRV–2 delivered to U.S. Navy.

Makaki deep-submergence research vehicle operated to 600 feet by U.S. Navy.

Trieste II (X–2) U.S. Navy bathyscaph designed for operational depths to 20,000 feet.

U.S. Navy *Finback* designed as mother sub for DSRV transportation to operational site.

U.S. Navy presents Underseas Long Range Missile System (ULMS) to Congress. Later designated Trident Program.

U.S. Navy commissions *L. Y. Spear,* first nuclear submarine tender.

French Navy submarine *Eurydice* lost during diving operations 35 miles east of Toulon. Sister ship to *Minerve,* lost in the Mediterranean in 1968.

Underwater Demolition Teams 11 and 12 in operation off Saigon blast five-mile-long channel between Van Co Dong and Van Co Tay rivers.

Deep Sea Research Ship *Mizar,* which located *Scorpion,* searches for French submarine *Eurydice.*

Soviet nuclear-attack submarine lost in the Atlantic 400 miles off Spanish coast.

Strategic Arms Limitation Talks (SALT) open in Vienna.

1972   U.S. Navy Mark I deep-dive system announced. Capable of protracted rescue and salvage operations to 1,000 feet, deployable in C–141 cargo planes.

General Dynamics Corporation proposes $3 billion fleet of 1,000-foot-long submarines to move Alaskan oil to the East Coast.

U.S. Navy Joint Surface Effect Ships Program Office studies feasibility of 100-knot, 5,000-ton Surface Effect Ship. Bell Aerospace launches 80-knot, 10-ton SES at New Orleans.

U.S. Navy successfully fires Poseidon MIRV missile. Nuclear submarine *James Madison* is first to carry missiles on patrol.

U.S. Navy hydrofoil *Tucumcari* operates in NATO exercises—demonstrates speed, maneuverability, and heavy-weather sea-keeping capability.

U.S. aerial intelligence detects construction of Communist China's first nuclear-powered submarine.

1973   U.S. Navy program reported successful in using porpoises to protect Cam Ranh Bay, Vietnam against enemy infiltrators.

Controversial navy Sanguine Project for giant ELF (Extremely Low Frequency) communications system involved in dispute between National Academy of Science and University of Wisconsin scientists.

U.S. Navy mines Haiphong and other North Vietnamese ports.

Treaty signed by United States and Soviet Union to prevent incidents at sea.

Soviet Union reports *Crab* remote-controlled robot exploring Mediterranean volcanoes at a depth of 4,000 feet.

1974   Navy announces first Trident submarine base would be built at Keyport, Washington on Puget Sound near Bangor.

China proposes that only an international body have power to directly exploit the resources of the sea bottom and that nuclear submarines be prohibited from entering international waters.

International Institute for Strategic Studies estimates Vietnam War cost United States over $108 billion, Soviet Union $1.66 billion, and China $670 million. Two of four scientists trapped in minisub 360 feet deep 20 miles off Key West, Florida, die from lack of oxygen. Sub and two survivors rescued.

1975   U.S. Navy announces suspension of research and development work on Sanguine Project.

Air Force contracts for three prototype satellites for naval research laboratory's NAVSTAR global positioning system.

1976   Soviet SONAR detection devices discovered on beaches in Iceland. String of 32 hydrophones 11 feet long and weighing more than one ton, a component of long-range passive-surveillance network.

General Dynamics Electric Boat Division designs Trident submarine. Contract placed for two submarines at cost of $1 billion each.

Navy's ELF communications system modified; name changed from Sanguine to Seafarer.

Howard Hughes marine mining vessel *Glomar Explorer* reported successful in attempt at raising Russian nuclear submarine sunk in 16,000 feet of water in the Pacific.

South Vietnamese forces capitulate. U.S. Navy evacuates Da Nang and Cam Ranh Bay.

Navy-CIA project Holystone described as a fifteen-year ongoing electronic surveillance of the Soviet Union's coastline by U.S. submarines.

1977   U.S. Navy ELF Project Seafarer canceled.

U.S. Navy *Tomahawk* cruise missile completed first underwater launch at naval underseas center, San Clemente Island.

SALT II preliminary negotiations discontinued in disagreement over deterrent policies.

Appendix B

United States Navy Ship and Submarine Classes

Fleet Ballistic Submarines (SSBN)—Nuclear

	Displacement (tons)	Length (feet)	Missile Tubes	Torpedo Tubes	Complement
Trident	18,700	560	24		150
Lafayette	8,250	425	16	4–21"	147
Ethan Allen	7,900	411	16	4–21"	139
George Washington	6,700	382	16	6–21"	140

Nuclear Attack Submarines (SSN)—Nuclear

	Displacement (tons)	Length (feet)	Torpedo Tubes	Weapons	Complement
Los Angeles	6,900	360	4–21"	SUBROC [1]	127
Gerald P. Lipscomb	6,480	265	4–21"	SUBROC	120
Narwahl	5,350	314	4–21"	SUBROC	120
Sturgeon	4,640	293	4–21"	SUBROC	120
Permit	4,300	279	4–21"	SUBROC	120
Tullibee	2,640	273	4–21"	A/S Torpedoes	87

1. SUBROC (Submarine Rocket). An ASW missile launched from submarine with nuclear warhead.

APPENDIX B (Cont.)

	Displacement (tons)	Length (feet)	Torpedo Tubes	Weapons	Complement
Skipjack	3,500	252	6–21″	A/S Torpedoes	112
Halibut	5,000	350	6–21″		120
Triton	6,670	448	6–21″		172
Skate	2,861	268	8–21″		108
Seawolf	4,280	338	6–21″		120
Nautilus	4,040	324	6–21″		120

Attack Submarines—Diesel Electric Drive (SS)

	Displacement (tons)	Length (feet)	Torpedo Tubes	Complement
Barbel	2,895	220	6–21″	79
Darter	2,388	269	8–21″	87
Sailfish	3,168	351	6–21″	87
Tang	2,700	287	8–21″	87

Special Purpose and Research—Diesel

Growler (SSG)	3,515	318	4–21″	84
Greyback (LPSS)	3,650	334	8–21″ Equipped to carry troops	87
Sealion (LPSS)	2,500	312	None. Equipped to carry troops	74
Dolphin (AGS)	930	152	Research	23
Albacore (AGSS)	1,850	211	None	52

ASW Aircraft Carriers (CVS)

	Displacement (tons)	Length (feet)	Aircraft	Complement
Hancock	32,800+ Air Group	895	45	1,615
Essex	33,000+ Air Group	820	45	1,615

Nuclear Powered Guided Missile Cruiser (CGN)

	Displacement (tons)	Length (feet)	Torpedo Mounts	ASW Weapons	Complement
Virginia	11,000	585	2	ASROC[1]	442
California	10,150	596	4	ASROC	540
Truxtun	9,200	564	4	ASROC, Helicopters	500
Bainbridge	8,580	550	2	ASROC	450

Guided Missile Cruisers (CG)

	Displacement (tons)	Length (feet)	Torpedo Mounts	ASW Weapons	Complement
Belknap	7,930	547	2	ASROC, LAMPS[2]	418
Leahy	7,800	533	2	ASROC	396

1. ASROC (Anti-Submarine Rocket). ASW missile launched from a surface ship. It can be either a homing torpedo or a nuclear-depth-charge warhead.
2. LAMPS (Light Airborne Multi-Purpose System). Sea-launched helicopter for ASW and missile-defense missions.

APPENDIX B (Cont.)

	Displacement (tons)	Length (feet)	Torpedo Mounts	ASW Weapons	Complement
Albany	17,500	664	2	ASROC, Helicopters	1,000
Long Beach	17,350	722	2	ASROC, Helicopters	1,060
Guided Missile Destroyers (DDG)					
Coontz	5,800	513	2	ASROC	377
Forrest Sherman	4,150	418	2	ASROC	335
Charles F. Adams	4,500	437	2	ASROC	354
Mitscher	5,200	493	2	ASROC	377
Destroyers (DD)					
Spruance	7,800	529	2	ASROC, LAMPS	250
Forrest Sherman	4,050	418	2	ASROC	292
Gearing	3,520	391	2	ASROC	274
Carpenter	3,410	391	2	ASROC, Helicopter	282
Guided Missile Frigates					
Brooke (FFG)	3,245	415	2	ASROC, LAMPS	241

	Displacement (tons)	Length (feet)	Torpedo Mounts	Weapons	Complement
Frigates (FF)					
Knox	4,100	438	4	ASROC, LAMPS	245
Garcia	3,400	415	2	ASROC, LAMPS	247
Bronstein	2,650	372	2	ASROC, Helicopter	220
Advanced ASW Ships					
Surface Effect Ship (SES)	2,000	240	Helicopter, Harpoon, Sea Sparrow		175
Guided Missile Frigate (FFG)	3,605	445	LAMPS—Torpedoes		176
Hydrofoil (PCH)	100	115	Missiles		13

Appendix C

Soviet Ship and Submarine Classes

	Displacement (tons)	Length (feet)	Torpedo Tubes	ASW Weapons	Complement
Antisubmarine Warfare Aircraft Carriers & Helicopter Cruisers					
Kiev	40,000	925		25 V/STOL, 25 Helicopters, 2 Missile launchers	1000
Moskva (HC)	17,000	645	2–21″	18 Helicopters, 3 Missile launchers	800
Fleet Ballistic Submarines (SSBN)—Nuclear					
Delta I	10,450	450	8–21″	12 SSN-8	120
Delta II	16,000	500	8–21″	16 SSN-8	120
Yankee	9,000	427	8–21″	16 SSN-6	120
Hotel	5,150	377	6–21″	3 SSN-5	90
			4–21″		
Ballistic Missile Submarines (SSB)—Diesel					
Golf	2,800	320	10–21″	2 SSN-4	86
Zulu	2,600	259	10–21″	3 SSN-5	85

	Displacement (tons)	Length (feet)	Torpedo Tubes	ASW Weapons	Complement
Cruise Missile Submarines (SSGN)—Nuclear					
Papa/Charlie	5,100	304	8–21"	8 SSN-7	100
Echo	5,600	391	6–21"	8 SSN-3	
			4–16"		
Cruise Missile Submarines—Diesel					
Juliet	3,600	285	4–16"	4 SSN-3	90
			6–21"		
Whisky-Long Bin	1,800	276	6–21"	4 SSN-3	60
Whisky-Twin Cylinder	1,600	249	6–21"	2 SSN-3	60
Fleet Submarines (SSN)—Nuclear					
Victor	5,100	285	8–21"		90
November	4,800	361	6–21"		88
Echo I	5,000	381	6–21"		92
			4–16"		
Patrol Submarines (SS)—Diesel					
Tango	2,500	300	6–21"		60
Bravo	2,800	230	6–21"		60

APPENDIX C (Cont.)

	Displacement (tons)	Length (feet)	Torpedo Tubes	Complement
Foxtrot	2,300	302	6–21"	70
Zulu IV	2,200	259	10–21"	70
Romeo	1,800	249	8–21"	60
Whisky	1,350	249	6–21"	60
Quebec	740	185	4–21"	42

Special Purpose Submarines—Diesel

	Displacement (tons)	Length (feet)	Torpedo Tubes	Complement
Whisky Canvas Bag (SSR)	1,350	249	6–21"	65

Cruisers (CLG)

	Displacement (tons)	Length (feet)	ASW Weapons	Complement
Kara	10,000	570	Helicopters, Missiles, Rockets, Depth Charges	800
Kresta II	8,000	520	Rockets, Depth Charges, 10–21" Torpedoes, Helicopters	500
Kresta I	8,000	510	Rockets, Depth Charges, 10–21" Torpedoes, Helicopters	400
Kynda	6,000	466	Rockets, Depth Charges, 6–21" Torpedoes, Helicopters	390

	Displacement (tons)	Length (feet)	ASW Weapons	Torpedo Mounts	Complement
Guided Missile Destroyers (DDG)					
Krivak	3,900	405	Rockets	8–21"	300
Kashin	4,500	471	Rockets	5–21"	350
Kildin	3,600	415	Rockets	4–21"	350
Kanin	4,700	457	Rockets, Helicopters	10–21"	350
Kotlin	3,600	415	Rockets	4–21"	285
Destroyers (DD)					
Skoryi	3,100	395	Depth Charges	10–21"	260
Frigates (FF)					
Mirka	1,100	270	Rockets	10–21"	100
Petya	1,150	270	Rockets	10–21"	100
Riga	1,600	299	Depth Charges	3–21"	150
Kola	1,900	315	Depth Charges	3–21"	190

Appendix D

United States and Soviet Submarine-Launched Missiles

Classification	Name	Length (feet)	Launch Weight (Pounds)	Range (Nautical Miles)	Warhead
USA					
SLBM	Polaris A-3	31	35,000(3)[1]	2,500	Thermonuclear (MIRV)[1]
SLBM	Poseidon C-3	34	65,000	2,500	Thermonuclear
SLBM	Trident I (C-4)	34	65,000	3,750	Thermonuclear
SLBM	Trident II	34	65,000	6,000	Thermonuclear
AAM	Sparrow	12	450	12	High Explosive
A/S	ASROC	15	1,000	5	MK 44 or 46 Torpedo or Nuclear D/C
A/S	SUBROC	21	4,000	30	Nuclear
ASM	Harpoon	15	1,397	60	High Explosive
USSR					
SLBM	SSN-4	37.5	—	300	Nuclear
SLBM	SSN-5	35	—	700	Nuclear
SLBM	SSN-6	42	—	1,300	Nuclear
SLBM	SSN-8	45	—	4,200	Nuclear
SSM	SSN-7	22	—	30	Nuclear
A/S	SSN-14	—	—	25	Nuclear
A/S	SSN-15	—	—	20	Nuclear

1. Multiple warhead.

Bibliography

Brou, Willy Charles. *Combat Beneath the Sea.* Translated from the French by Edward Fitzgerald. New York: Thomas Y. Crowell Company, 1957. 240 pp., plates.

Busch, Harald. *U-Boats at War: German Submarines in Action 1939–1945.* Translated by L. P. R. Wilson. London: Putnam & Co., Ltd., 1955. 176 pp., appendices.

Cousteau, Jacques-Yves. *Captain Cousteau's Underwater Treasury.* New York: Harper & Row, 1959. 415 pp.

Cowen, Robert C. *Frontiers of the Sea.* Illust. by Mary S. Cowen. New York: Bantam Books, 1960. 312 pages. Bibliography pp. 304–06.

Cross, Wilbur. *Challengers of the Deep: The Story of Submarines and the Exploits of the Men Who Build and Sail Them.* New York: Sloane, 1959. 258 pp., illust.

Ela, D. K. "Polaris Launching System," *Astronautics.* December 1958. Vol. 3, No. 12, pp. 40–41.

Farrago, Ladislas. *The Tenth Fleet.* New York: Ivan Obolensky, Inc., 1962. 366 pp. Bibliography pp. 341–50. Notes.

Hashimoto, Nochitsura. *Sunk: The Story of the Japanese Submarine Fleet, 1941–1945.* Translated by E. H. M. Colegrave, RN. Introduction by Edward L. Beach, USN. New York: Holt, 1954. 276 pp. Illust.

Heatter, Basil. *The Dim View.* New York: New American Library, 1948. 155 pp.

Hezlet, Arthur. *The Submarine and Sea Power.* London: Peter Davies, Ltd., 1967. 278 pp. Illust.

King, Ernest J. *United States Navy at War. Final Official Report to the Secretary of the Navy, Covering the Period March 1, 1945 to October 1, 1945.* Washington, D.C.: Government Printing Office, 1946. 305 pp. Illust.

Kuenne, Robert E. *The Attack Submarine: A Study in Strategy.* New Haven: Yale University Press, 1965. 215 pp.

Lewis, David D. *The Fight for the Sea: The Past, Present and Future of Submarine Warfare in the Atlantic.* Foreword by Jerauld Wright. Cleveland: World Publishing Co., 1961. 350 pp. Illust. Bibliography.

Link, Edwin A. and Gallery, Philip D. "Deep Submergence and the Navy," *Naval Review 1967.* Annapolis: U.S. Naval Institute, 1967.

Lockwood, Charles Andrews. *Down to the Sea in Subs: My Life in the U.S. Navy.* New York: W. W. Norton & Co., 1967. 276 pp. Illust.

Nimitz, Chester W., Adams, Henry Y. and Potter, E. B. *Triumph in the Atlantic: The Naval Struggle Against the Axis.* Englewood Cliffs, N.J.: Prentice-Hall, Inc., 1960. 188 pp. Charts. Index.

Nimitz, Chester W., Adams, Henry H. and Potter, E. B. *Triumph in the Pacific: The Navy's Struggle Against Japan.* Englewood Cliffs, N.J.: Prentice-Hall, Inc., 1963. 186 pp. Charts. Index.

Piccard, Jacques and Dietz, R. S. *Seven Miles Down: The Story of the Bathyscaphe* Trieste. New York: G. P. Putnam's Sons, 1961. 249 pp. Plates.

Roscoe, Theodore. *United States Submarine Operations in World War Two.* Illust. by Fred Freeman. Annapolis: U.S. Naval Institute, 1949. 577 pp. Plates. Maps.

Sokolovskii, Vasilii Danilovich. *Soviet Military Strategy.* Annotated and translated by H. S. Dinerstein, L. Goure, and T. W. Wolfe of RAND. Englewood Cliffs, N.J.: Prentice-Hall, Inc., 1963. 544 pp.

Bibliography of Western military books published in translation in the Soviet Union on pp. 530–33.

Soule, Gardner. *The Ocean Adventure.* New York: Appleton-Century-Crofts, 1966. 278 pp. Illust. Bibliography.

Stafford, Edward Perry. *The Far and the Deep.* New York: G. P. Putnam's Sons, 1967. 284 pp. Illust.

Stambler, Irwin. *The Battle for Inner Space: Undersea Warfare and Weapons.* New York: St. Martin's Press, 1962. 259 pp. Illust.

Uhlig, Frank, Jr. (ed.) *Naval Review 1962–1977.* Annapolis: U.S. Naval Institute. Annual Summary Issue.

Index